IMBIBING VALUE EDUCATION : VARIOUS PERSPECTIVES

IMBIBING VALUE EDUCATION
Various Perspectives

Editors
Rameshwari Pandya
Anuradha Mathu

Publications

KALPAZ PUBLICATIONS
DELHI-110052

Imbibing Value Education : Various Perspectives

(*Education*)

Rs. 690

ISBN: 81-7835-213-3

Published in 2004 in India by
Kalpaz Publications
C-30, Satyawati Nagar
Delhi-110052
E-mail : kalpaz@hotmail.com

Laser Typesetting at: Sharma Graphic, New Delhi
Printed at: Mehra Offset Press, Delhi

Content

PART II—VALUE FOR WOMEN'S EMPOWERMENT

PART III—HEALTH

PART IV—HUMAN RIGHTS

PART V—VALUES FOR SAVING THE ENVIRONMENT

Preface

The Department of Home Science Extension and Communication, Faculty of Home Science, M.S. University of Baroda organized a two-day National Seminar on "Value Education: A Challenge for the Millennium for Home Science Extension" during 15th–18th January 2002. There were about 50 delegates from all over India who comprised of Educationists; Dean, Faculty of Home Science; University and College Teachers.

There ware about 45 paper presentations on the following sub-themes:

- Values for Home Science Extension
- Values for Saving the Environment
- Values for Women's Empowerment and Human Rights
- Values for Women's Health
- Training needs for Value Education amongst Home Science students.

This book is the culmination and outcome of the Seminar. The papers have been reviewed, edited and modified by the authors after presentation in the Seminar.

This book is mainly published with the intention of delivering value-based education to Home Scientists especially specializing in the area of Home Science Extension.

Values may be regarded as important ratings which people attach to things, conditions and circumstanes. They may also be regarded as goals, objectives to which people orient their thinking, action and feelings. Value education may thus be explained as experience, state, ideal or thing-exiting or conceived ideally. which is faboured or desired.

Educational institutions constitute the biggest organized sector for imparting various kinds of values amongst the growing youth. In fact, it is rightly pointed out by many educators that the development of values and attitudes begins at birth and is fed from many sources.

Thoughtful people in all walks of life are greatly disturbed by a progressive erosion of values and the resultant pollution of public life. The fact that this crisis of values is as pervasive in schools, college and universities, amongst teachers as well as students as in other walks of life, is seen as highly dangerous development. Learning from past experience, it is expected that a coherent and an operationally viable value-system would be inclucated through educational process, based upon rational and scientific and moral approach to life.

It is not only the teachers in charge of moral instruction who are responsible for building character. Every teacher, whatever be the subject he or she teachers, must necessarily accept their responsibility.

The college assembly, the curricular and co-curricular activities, the celebration of festivals of all religions, work-experience, team games and sports, subject clubs, social service programmes, all these can help in inculcating the values of cooperation and mutual regard, honesty and integrity, discipline and social responsibility. These values have a special significance in Indian society today, when young men and women are passing through a crisis of character.

The present system of education, needs to be focusing on giving value education in the true sense to make students stronger to face the world. Some of the desirable values that were identified by the Home Scientists may actually contribute to personal, social and professional development viz. Gender equality, Familism, Dignity of labour, Vocationalism and Collectivism.

We live in a society where all interactions and experiences account for learning situations. These situations may lead to the development of certain characteristics and values. Broadly, these aspects could be either related to institution or personal or even familial. So, it is here that we have to give value education which encompasses all these aspects and leads to desirable and meaningful results.

This seminar provided an opportunity to get an insight into

various issues like why values, which values are necessary and how to develop values.

Further, our Chief Minister Shri Narendra Modi in his message for the Seminar said,

Our ancient learning and educational system has been built up on the VALUES; but under the alien rule, we nearly lost our educational and social identity, and ultimate result was a fragmented society. The post-independence era also witnessed the same scenario, for a very long time. However, prudence prevailed, and the people started to realize the forgotten 'VALUES'.

Education should be always VALUE based, and it is with this concept in mind, our forefathers had evaluated educational institutes as ''VIDYA-MANDIRS'', and naturally, ''MANDIRS'' lead to bringing peace, harmony, integrity, and devotion.

The National SEMINAR on the Value Education will go a long way to make efforts to restore, the faded glory of our educational culture.

Thus, it is here that our role as educationists comes in by way of designing strategies that could be implemented by educational institutions—schools, colleges and universities. Further, it becomes our responsibility as educationists, teachers, programme planners to make concerted efforts towards bringing about positive changes with regards to healthy and transformational changes in our educational practices which will go a long way in bringing about changes in educational systems.

This book will give direction for inculcating values in various focused areas. It will also assist as well as guide students, teachers, educationists and researchers for planning and conducting value based education in their educational institutions. Thus, this book is just a humble beginning for the magnanimous task!

Rameshwari Pandya
Anuradha Mathu

List of Contributors

1.	Role of Family in Value Education	***Sarjoo Patel,*** Ph.D. Scholar and ***Dr. Maneesha Shukul,*** Reader, Department of Home Management, Faculty of Home Science, M.S. University of Baroda, Vododara.
2.	Emerging Needs of Value Education in the Traditional Universities Home Science Curriculum	***Ulka Shinde*** and ***Rajkumar Kamble,*** Department of Home Science, Rajaram Government College, Kolhapur, (MS).
3.	Work Values of Male and Female College Teachers	***Santosh Tikoo,*** Arya College, Panipat - Haryana.
4.	Need to Incorporate Value Education in Home Science Curriculum	***Sarika Sharma*** and ***Preeti Shah,*** Department of Home Science Extension and Communication, Faculty of Home Science, The M.S. University of Baroda, Vadodara.
5.	Value Education - As a Part of Course Curriculum in Home Science Extension and Communication.	***Awa Trivedi*** and ***Priyanka Pandey,*** Department of Home Science Extension and Communication, Faculty of Home Science, The M.S. University of Baroda, Vadodara.
6.	Projection of Marital and Related Aspects in Media and its Perception by Young University Students	***Amiteshwar Ratra,*** Ph.D Scholar and ***Praveen Kaur,*** Professor, Department of Human Development and Family Studies, I.C. College of Home Science CCS HAU, Hisar.

	Title	Authors
7.	A Study on Selected desirable Values of undergraduate Students of Home Science in the State of Gujarat	***Susan Jacob,*** Asistant Professor, ASPEE College of Home Science, Gujarat Agri, University, Sardar Krushinagar and ***Anupama Shah,*** Former Dean, Faculty of Home Science, The M.S. University of Baroda, Vadodara.
8.	A Study to Identify the Desirable Values Needed for Home Science Students	***Susan Jacob,*** Asistant Professor, ASPEE College of Home Science, Gujarat Agri, University, Sardar Krushinagar and ***Anupama Singh,*** Former Dean, Faculty of Home Science, M.S. University, Baroda.
9.	Wise Buying Values: A Tool for Family's Economic Health	***Neerja Jaiswal and Ami Shah,*** Department of Home Management, Faculty of Home Science. The M.S. University of Baroda, Vadodara.
10.	Innovate Ways of Developing Excellence in Character	***Geeta Sikdar,*** Counsellor, Navrachana School, Sama Road, Baroda. Gujarat.
11.	Value Education : A Challenge for the Millennium for Home Science Extension	***S.D. Deshpande,*** Prof. and Principal, ***S.D. Majumdar, P.V. Deshpande,*** Professors, ***A.W. Vinchurkar,*** Librarian, Shri Shivaji Agriculture College, Amravati. Maharashtra.
12.	Perception and Value Orientation of Undergraduate Girl Students regarding Women Empowement	***Malaya M. Bora,*** Sr. Lecturer, Department of Home Science, Handique Girl's College GU, Panbazar, Guwahati, Assam and ***Kamala Kanta Saharia,*** Asso. Prof. Department of Extension Education, College of Veterinary Science, AAU Khanapara, Guwahati, Assam
13.	Opinions of Rural Home-Makers regarding women empowerment programmes in Ludhiana District	***Gill, J.K. Sureinderjit Kaur, Dhillon,*** M.K. College of Home Science, P.A.U. Ludhiana, Punjab.

14. Empowerment of women and Environmental degradation : In today's changing human values era	*Amiteshwar Ratra,* Ph.D. Scholar, Department of Human Development and Family Studies, I.C. College of Home Science, CCS HAU, Hisar *Shivani Bala,* Assistant Professor-cum-Junior Scientist, Department of Family Resource Management, College of Home Science, RAU, Pusa, Samestipur, Bihar and *Neeti Sharma,* Speical Educator, Sadhu Vaswani International School for Girls, R.K. Puram, New Delhi.
15. Women and Work Values	*Viyayanthimala Kodali,* Home Science Department SBRG Women's College, Berhampur, Orissa.
16. Value Education - Empowering the Status of Women	*S. Parvathi,* Associate professor, Home Science Extension and *C. Karthikeyan,* Assitant Professor, Agricultural Extension and Rural Sociology, Tamil Nadu Agricultural University, Coimbatore.
17. Women Empowerment through Education	*Bakhale Rupa, Kalra Nishi and Suri Geetubala,* M.Sc. Students, Department of Home Science Extension and Communication, Faculty of Home Science, The M.S. University of Baroda, Vadodara.
18. NGO's and Women Empowerment	*Mona A. Mehta* and *Asha V. Dass,* Dept. of Home Management, Faculty of Home Science, The M.S. University of Baroda, Vadodara.
19. Empowerment of Rural Women in Agriculture	*P.R. Kanani, P.D. Verma* and *V.J. Savaliya.* College of Agriculture, G. A.U. Junagadh, Gujarat.

20. Gender Equality for Adolescents : A Pedagogic Value	***Sangeeta Chaudhary,*** Lecturer and ***Bhamini Mehta,*** Ph.D. Student , Department of HDFS, Faculty of Home Science, The M.S. University of Baroda, Vadodara
21. Financial Empowerment of Hill Women through their active participation in Food Processing Units of Nainital, district Uttranchal, India	***Meeta Agarwal*** and ***Promila Sharma,*** Dept . fo family Resource Management, G.B. Pant University, Uttaranchal
22. Discrimination of Girl Child	***Anita P. Patel,*** Lecturer Shri R. P. Arts and Commerce College, Khambat, Gujarat.
23. SHG as a Strategy for Empowerment of Women	***K.C. Leelavathy,*** Pofessor, Avinashilingam University, Coimbatore.
24. Factors responsible for the living conditions of urban elderly women of Punjab.	***P. Sandhu,*** Asst. prof., ***R. Bakhshi,*** Prof. ***and M. K. Sidhu,*** Asso. Prof., Dept. of Family Resource Management, Punjab Agricultural University; Ludhiana.
25. School Health Education-Today's Concern	***Sonia Thakur*** Research Scholar, Dept. of Home Management, The Faculty of Home Science, M.S. University of Baroda and ***Monika Sharma,*** Research Scholar, CASE, Dept. of Education, Faculty of Education and Psychology, The M.S. University Baroda, Vadodara.
26. Nutritional Education to Eradicate Malnutrition among the Rural Children	***K.N. Balapurkar, M.V. Bonde, Ch. Balamani; V.R. Bonde, V.B. Sutar,*** Krishi Vigyan Kendra, College of Agriculture, Dhule, Maharashtra.
27. Child rearing practices with special emphasis on health and dietary habits of children	***Ila Jogi,*** Head, Department of Home Science, Mahila Mahavidyalaya, Karad, Maharashtra.

28. A Study on Health Awareness in Women of Chak, Kamed and Surasa Village (M.P.)	***Asst. Prof. Madhu Gautam and Asst. Prof. Preeti Gupta,*** Government Kalidas Girls College, Ujjain, Madhya Pradesh.
29. Self Concept of Orphan Adolescents in Delhi	***Neeti Sharma,*** Special educator, Sadhu Vaswani International School for Girls, New Delhi, India and ***Priyanka Aeri,*** Lecturer, Department of Child Development, Guru Nanak Girls College, Kurukshetra University, Kurukshetra.
30. Misuse of Human Rights and Our Changing Values	***Neeti Sharma,*** Special educator, Sadhu Vaswani International School for Girls, New Delhi, ***Amiteshwar Ratra,*** Ph.D Scholar, Department of Human Development and Family Studies Management, College of Home Science CCS Haryana Agricultural University, Hisar and ***Shivani Bala,*** Assistant Professor- cum- Junior Scientist, Department of F.R.M; College of Home Science, R.A.U. Pusa, Samastipur, Bihar.
31. My Views about Human Rights	***Arya Gupta,*** Department of Home Science Extension and Communication. Faculty of Home Science, The M.S. University of Baroda, Vadodara.
32. Violation of Women Rights in Induatries : A Need for Value Education	***Reema chaurasia,*** Ph.D. Scholar and ***Maneesha Shukul,*** Reader, Home Management Dept., The M.S. University of Baroda, Vadodara.
33. Impact of Environmental Degradation on Human Health	***Shivani Bala,*** Assistant Professor- cum- Junior Scientist, Department of F.R.M., College of Home Science, R.A.U., Pusa Samastipur, Bihar, India,

Part–I
Training Needs for Value Education Amongst Home Science Students

1
Role of Family in Value Education

Sarjoo Patel and Dr. Maneesha Shukul

Introduction

Today, what confronts us all is an enormous and unprecedented opportunity to develop the human resources of this nation to a broader and fuller degree than ever our most optimistic forebeare dreamt of. The challenge presented by this opportunity points at rather than supplants the cardinal role of education. That role is to develop human beings of high character, of courageous health and independent mind, who can transmit and enrich our society's intellectual, cultural and spiritual heritage who can advance mankind's eternal quest for truth and beauty and who can leave the world a better place than they found it. Only by pursuing these paramount goals of education can we ensure a free society and a sane and peaceful world in which all individuals may live in greater dignity and achieve greater fulfilment. (Rao, 1961).

First and foremost, it is in the interest of individuals and societies to expand and improve the education of children and youth in order to meet their basic learning needs better. Education is one of the important values which the family possess. (Henry, 1961). The family has major responsibility for fostering values among the children. The family is not only the best conveyer of values but is the producer of values.

In order to achieve real education, children should learn certain values at the very initial stage of their learning process, i.e., at the pre-primary and primary level. Value education should be introduced at the pre-primary and primary stages because the children of today are the adults of tomorrow and whatever they are taught as young students, is what will mould them for later life. The education which is such an important phase of life is certainly influenced by the values that the parents hold about education. If the values are positive it will greatly influence their views and opinion about education. Also it is seen that if views of the parents regarding education are positive and they rank education high among the values held by them they will motivatc and encourage their children to study well. It is essential to find out the value held by the parents so that their values can be influenced through nonformal education.

Objective

To find out the position of education in value hierarchy held by parents.

Methodology

Descriptive research design was used for the study. Interview schedule was used as an instrument for gathering data. The instrument contained a list of values which the respondents had to rank. The sample of the study consisted of 120 respondents (mother of children studying in two schools of Baroda city). List of the children studying in 5th and 6th standard was collected from two schools and from each class 15 boys and 15 girls were selected through systematic random sampling technique. The parents of these children were contacted and interviewed.

Major Findings

A list of values were provided to the homemaker, and she was asked to identify according to her the most important five values in order of importance. The main purpose behind this was to trace out the position of education in particular family.

Based on the percentage of respondents who considered certain values as important, a list in descending order was made. It was observed that on the whole in the boy child's family the first place was given to health, then to work, education, leisure and knowledge.Thus, place of education is third among other values in boy child's family. It shows that among the first five important values education holds a place.

Further a look into the girl child's family values reveal that the work is given the most importance followed by health, comfort, education and convenience. Here the education holds the fourth position. So it can be said that there exist a difference in the importance of values among boy and girl child's parents. Only 45 per cent of the respondents valued education.

References

1. Henry, D.D. (1961) "What priority for Education" cited in.

2. Rao, D.B. "Encyclopaedia of Education for All" cited in.

3. "Challenges in School Education in 2000," Abstract, Faculty of Education and Psychology, M.S. University of Baroda.

4. De Vanathan, R. 'Valuing the values' *University News*, Association of Indian Universities, Tara Art Press, New Delhi, 1999.

5. Herris, M.C. *Value Leadership*, Prentice Hall of India, New Delhi, 2000.

6. Joseph, K.S. Helping Children move towards self Actualization. New Frontiers in Education. Vol. XXVII, No. 2, 1997.

2

Emerging Need of Value Education in the Traditional Universities of Home Science Curriculum

Ulka Shinde and Rajkumar Kamble

The aim of Home Science education is to provide intellectual, cultural, moral, aesthetic, vocational, utilitarian, econmomic and social values not only to the individuals but to the society as a whole. The study of Home Science has also initiated and directed a burning desire to achieve higher standard of living and the will to give better humanity. The knowledge of home science provides an opportunity to many professions.

The value of Home Science education is having a high quality level, if it is implemented at a proper level. Certain values of Home Science education can be classified as:

Academic Value

Education plays an important role in all round development of an individual. Home Science education imparts knowledge, skills and attitudes that enable each member of society to develop fully his or her capacities to lead a rewarding life. Applied or fundamental knowledge of this science also helps to liberate women from inequality within and outside the home and helps to develop awareness and readiness to accept different life style.

The field of education develops better self concept, self-identity and helps in taking active participation in decision making. Home Science education helps to get employment in academic and training institute and in research organisation such as DBT and ICMR. It also gives opportunity to do research in different areas with the sponsorships of UNICEF and other voluntary agencies and UGC.

Economic Value

Home Science education has helped many women not only to become economically self reliant but also proficient in managing their homes efficiently and economically by planning and controlling the budget of their homes. It also fosters independence in girls and prepares individuals to meet challenges. It not only develops or improves the status of an individual in a family or in a community at large but it also develops consumer consciousness for better economy, and utilizes scarce resources for achieving national goals by participating in governmental and non-governmental projects such as ICDS. CRECHE and other Child Development projects.

Social Value

Home Science education is not only confined to strengthening of home and family life but it also helps to serve the society in different ways. It develops capabilities to face, understand and solve the problems in contributing to hospitals and industries with their expertise in areas such as therapeutic nutrition, nutrition counselling, industrial catering, food processing, textiles and interior decoration.

Political Value

Home scientists are the policy makers of the nation, who frame policies and give them to the Government for implementation such as family and child welfare programmes, women's studies, population education, care of aged, etc.

Emotional Value

This education helps the women to keep them busy in leisure time activities, which helps in maintaining the mental health of the individual. Sometimes women live under extreme insecure conditions, prone to violence and theft. Thus, education becomes an asset to the family and society.

Traditional Value

In this world of globalisation Home Scientists are best equipped in empowering women because of their traditional sound training. This education makes one self perfect by proper scientific training and practice. This education helps us to preserve the centuries old unique cultural values alongwith accepting the safe and useful modern trends.

Biological Value

This education also contributes in maintaining the health status of vulnerable group. Home Science education plays a major role in bringing quality life and health status of both rural and urban poor through extension work and activities on nutrition education.

Environmental Value

Home Science education brings a successful environment in the family and work place because it helps to understand the importance of the ways and means of achieving healthy home environment and also helps to control population and reduce pollution by adopting hygienic practices.

Technological Value

This education enhances in creating technical knowledge and creative thinking. It also helps to adopt easily technological skills and its utilisation in their respective fields, i.e., food technology, health and nutrition technology, fashion technology and textile technology.

Hence, the knowledge basket of Home Science is of great value to women at large, their community and the nation because it is the women who rock the cradle that rules the world.

Moreover, the Home Science education in the twin areas like traditional and agricultural institutions, and universities are observed to be not similar in nature, particularly the traditional colleges, who run Home Science Department under the region of western Konkan Maharashtra, where the value of this education is the emerging. need to improve their quality and strengthen their linkages. For assessment of the factors which are responsible for the value of this education, this study has been undertaken. For the evaluation of value of home science education in this region, 10 colleges who run Home Science departments were selected. Kolhapur, Sangli, Satara, Jaysingpur, Gadhinglaj, Ichalkaranji, Slampur, Palus, Karad and Kagal were the areas selected for this study. The value education of home science was assessed with the help of observation of infrastructure, examining their syllabus feedback and its utility and opinions of 500 graduate students. The observations, opinions and the information was compiled systematically.

In this study different lacunae were strongly observed which are found responsible to the quality and value education of home science.

1. Non uniform syllabus as compared to other universities syllabus.
2. There is no provision for internship. Hence these students do not get opportunity in the professional world.
3. Minimum utilisation of technology, lack of implementation of this knowledge due to less technological approach, the students fail to get jobs.
4. Lack of infrastructural support such as laboratory and library facility.
5. Gender inequality based and women centred.
6. No provision in coordination with administration and civil services exams.
7. Marginal level of net-working at intra and, inter universities in the state and other state universities.
8. Majority of syllabus is covered by lecture and demonstration, and practical method only.

Hence for the improvement in the quality of home science education in the traditional colleges and for better identity, opportunity and status symbol of this education in the advanced technological era, the following recommendations were suggested.

1. Home Science syllabus should be modified to include some additional aspects such as management skills, advertising, accountancy to help the students to meet the ever increasing challenges of life.
2. Technological and professional approach should be given to the students.
3. Research is very essential for which Government should take initiative in strengthening the infrastructural facilities by giving enough funds.
4. Home Science subject should be included in civil services exams, which will help them to serve the country as an administrator.
5. Gender bias should be eliminated.
6. Net working needed at grass root level. Linkages with other

institutes, intra-home science and inter department and their institutional linkage with industry, Government and national agencies need to be established for academic, research and generating more employment opportunity.

7. Innovative methods of teaching should be adopted.
8. Horizontal education should be given to the students. For that emphasis should be given on one particular subject which make then expert in that particular field which will be beneficial in getting the job in the specific area.

References

1. Basanti, Sharma. A Critical evaluation of High School Home Science Curriculum and its Teaching in the schools of Lucknow. M.Sc. dissertation, Lucknow University, Lucknow, 1960.

2. Dewey, John. *Theory of valuation*, Chicago. The University of Chicago Press. 1933.

3. Fraenkel, J.R. *Analysing value conflict in values, concepts and Techniques*. Washington D.C. National Education Association, 1976.

4. *Human Values–The Tagorean Panorama*, New Delhi : New Age International Ltd., 1996.

5. Kohlberg, Lawrence. The Cognitive Developmental Approach to Moral Education. In values, concepts and Techniques, Washington, D.C. National Education Association, 1976.

6. Kothari, D.S. *Education and Values in School Education in India, Present Status and Future needs* : Malhotra, Parikh, B.S. Mishra C.H.K. (eds) NCERT, New Delhi, 1986.

7. *Management by Values–Towards Cultural Congruence*, New Delhi, Oxford University Press, 1991.

8. Saroja Krishnaswamy and Meera Rao Women's Perspective in Home Science. *University News*. Vol. 36, No. 26, Jan 29, 1998.

9. Venkataiah, N. Value Education–An overview in value Education, New Delhi, APH Publishing Corporation, 1998.

3

Work Values of Male and Female College Teachers

Dr. Santosh Tikoo

Introduction

Work is essential not only for satisfying a man's economic wants but also his social and psychological wants. A work is so central to human life that it is truly impossible to conceive life at the human level without work.The concept of work implies that someone is supposed to do a job, to be held accountable for what is done or not done. Work may be mental or it may be physical or it may involve both at the same time. Work is an effort we put to do something. It is the activity in which man engages to earn money, the activity that occupies much of his daily time, the activity that utilizes his abilities or skills in some social or economic enterprises. Work is the social act around which each of us organises much of our daily working experience and hopefully establishes a meaningful and rewarding life routinc.

The word value had been derived from the Latin word "value" meaning valiant or valor which means strong and vigorous. Work values are the aspects of work or motivation factors in the work that inspire a man to choose or adhere to a particular job. Work values are defined as qualities which are extrinsic to as well as those which are intrinsic in work and which are outcome of work. Men are expected to come to terms with requirements and the conditions for work. If work is as high valued in our society as it appears to be, it is necessary to study the relationship of man to his work and to study his /her attitude towards work. It is within this context that the study was undertaken to study the demographic and socio-economic characteristics of the respondents; to determine the work values held by the respondents; to rank order the assessed values in terms of the most dominant and less dominant work values held by the respondents. Few hypotheses were also formulated and these were: (i) There would be an association between experience of the respondents and the work values of economic returns and intellectual stimulation, (ii) There would be an association between age and work values of prestige, independence and achievement, (iii) There would be an association between sex of the respondents and work values of aesthetic creativity and altruism.

Methodology

The present research is an exploratory study attempting to identify the work values of college teachers. Work values are the aspects of work or motivating factors in the work which inspire a man to choose or adhere to a particular job. These are the satisfactions which men and women seek in the work and the satisfactions which may be outcome of work. The following work values (Super,1970) are chosen for the present study:

Altruism	:	This work value enables one to contribute to the welfare of others.
Aesthetic	:	This permits one to make beautiful things.
Creativity	:	It is value associated with work which permits one to invent new things or develop new ideas.
Intellectual Stimulation	:	A value which provides opportunity for independent thinking.
Achievement	:	A value which gives one a feeling of accomplishment in doing a job well.
Independence	:	A value which permits one to work in his own way as fast or as slowly as he wishes.
Prestige	:	A value which gives one standing in the eyes of others.
Management	:	This permits one to plan and layout work for others to do.
Economic Returns	:	This represents a type of value in work which pays well and enables one to have things one wants.
Security	:	It provides one with the certainty of having a permanent job.

Surroundings : A value associated with work which is carried out under pleasant conditions.

Supervisory Relations : A value in work which is carried out under a supervisor who is fair and with whom he can get along.

Associates : This value brings one into contact with fellow workers whom he likes.

Way of Life : This permits one to live the kind of life he chooses and to be the type of person he wishes to be.

Variety : This provides an opportunity to do different types of jobs.

Data was gathered with the help of questionnaire. The questionnaire consisted of two main sections: Part I included a set of questions, utilized to elicit the background characteristics of the respondents. The second part included the statements relating to work values. In order to test the validity of the statements prepared, a list of 70 statements was submitted to a panel of 5 judges consisting of experts from those fields relevant to present study. The judges were instructed to check each statement for its relevance and clarity. The statements which more than 80 per cent of the judges proclaimed as being clear and relevant were retained. The tool consisting of 65 statements was administered to 30 non-sample college teachers. The answers were sought in terms of strongly agree, agree, uncertain, disagree and strongly disagree. The reliability of the scale constructed was also calculated by split-half technique. The reliability coefficient calculated was 0.70. The sample comprised of 60 college teachers (30 male and 30 female) from three different colleges of Panipat (Haryana). The college teachers were teaching art subjects, commerce and science subjects. The data were coded, tabulated, scored and analyzed in terms of frequencies and percentage. Chi-square test was used for testing the hypothesis predicted for the study.

Results and Discussion

An examination of the data indicatd that the age range of the respondents varied from 25 to 50 years. About 37 per cent of the respondents fell in the category of 25-30 years.

Forty-five per cent of the respondents were postgraduate, 37 per cent were M.Phil and 18 per cent were holding Ph.D. degree. 60 per cent of the respondents were teaching art subjects, 22 per cent were teaching science subjects and 18 per cent were teaching commerce subjects.

Forty-two per cent of the respondents were in teaching profession from 5 to 20 years and 58 per cent were from 20 to 30 years. This shows that majority were experienced teachers.

It was found that mean scores for the value of altruism obtained by male teachers were 120 whereas, these were 126 in case of female teachers. For the work value of aesthetic the mean scores obtained by male teachers were 120.66, whereas in case of females were 125.63. The mean scores for the male teachers for the work value of creativity were 116.33, whereas these were 131.33 in case of female teachers. The scores of female teachers were more as compared to male teachers for work value of creativity. For the work value of intellectual stimulation, there is not much difference between the mean scores of male and female teachers. For the work value of achievement, female teachers scored 122.66 scores and male 124. The mean scores for the male and female respondents for the work value of independence were same, i.e., 123.

There was not much difference between the mean scores of male and female teachers for the value of prestige. For the work value of management, both the male and female teachers placed equal value. The teachers want to do well organised and well planned work as it will save their time and energy and will make them more efficient.

The mean scores for the work value of economic returns in case of male teachers were 132.22 and in case of female were 131. The scores gained by both type of teachers (male and female) were approximately same for the value of security. The surroundings of the work place was considered equally important by both the type of teachers. For the value of supervisory relations, male teachers obtained 123 and female 125. For the value of associates, male teachers obtained 122 mean scores, whereas female obtained 120 mean scores. The mean scores of the respondents for the value of way of life and variety in work were almost same.

Rank Ordering of Assessed Values on the Basis of Mean Scores

Work values assessed from the respondents were ranked according to the mean scores in order to find the most dominant and less dominant work values, Data showed that work value of economic returns got the maximum scores, i.e., 263.33 mean scores. The value of security got the less mean scores, i.e., 241.33 as compared to other work values. The work values of creativity, independence, altruism, aesthetic variety, achievement, associates and way of life had the same mean scores in pairs. So these two values of equal mean scores were given one rank order, i.e., 6, 7, 8, 9 simultaneously.

A significant association was found between experience of teachers and work values of economic returns and intellectual stimulation. A significant association was also found between age of teachers and work values of prestige, independence and achievement. A significant association was also found between sex of teacher and work values of aesthetic creativity and altruism.

Conclusions

On the basis of the findings, following conclusions were drawn:

1. The work value of economic return was given more importance as compared to all other values.
2. More experienced teachers were of the view that job should give the maximum economic returns and should also be mentally challenging.
3. Older teachers were more interested in prestige and independence of the job, whereas younger teachers liked the work which enabled them to go ahead with the plans and the work in which they got the feeling of having done a good day's work. Female teachers were more interested in work in which they need artistic and creative ability. Female teachers also liked the work in which they could help other persons and which gave them a chance to be of service to others.

References

1. Fried man, E.A. and R.J. Havinghrust (1974). *The Meaning of Work and Retirement*. Chicago University, Chicago.

2. Super, D.E. (1962): 'Structure of Values in Relation to Status Achievement, Interest and Adjustment.' *Journal of Applied Psychology*, Vol. 46, pp. 234.

3. Wair, P. and Wall, T. (1975). *Work and Well being*. Penguin Press, New York.

4. Anita Devi. A study of role structure of working women in teaching profession. Ph.D. Thesis. Barelly College, Barelly, U.P.

5. Carfagna, Rosemarie. Creating gender equality in the college classroom : An inclusive core curriculum. *College Board Rev*. 172, 8-13, 1994.

6. Dutta, Anuradha. The meaning of education of equality. *University News*, XXXI (51) pp. 7, Dec. 21, 1992.

7. Kang, Bhavdeep. A dent in 'Male Stream' academics. *The Telegraph* 5.5.94.

8. Latifa Beegam, N.H. An analytical study of factors related to Job Satisfaction among college teachers. Ph.D thesis. University of Kerala, Thiruvananthapuram.

9. Om Prakash, Challenge before College Teachers. *University News*, Vol. XXXII. No. 25, pp. 4-5 June 20,1994.

10. Rao, K.S. Work Values of men and women secondary school teachers. *Experiments in Education* XVII (6) pp. 159. June, 1990.

11. Rohde, J.E. On closing the gender gap. Increasing the value of women in India. *The Indian Journal of Pediatrics*. 58 (3) p. 295, May 1991.

4

Need to Incorporate Value Education in Home Science Curriculum

Sarika Sharma and Preeti Shah

Introduction

Our human society has always laid importance on values and attitudes of individual. If a society is to have an efficient and effective functioning, it must incorporate a strong value base. Today, in a continuous changing condition, values are left far behind in the race with time for finding solutions to problems and achieve success in life. Thus, today we see the gross erosion of values of individuals to keep pace with society in order to fulfill one's desire to be at the top. In the present scenario if we look into exactly what are values, it has become a difficult task all together. So let us try to rediscover and discuss few aspects of values. As per various scholars, values are as below:

According to G.M. Inlow—1922

"Values are the determiner in a man that influence his choice in life and thus decides his behaviour and action".

According to Hall and Lindzey—1966

"Value is a very important factor in the motivation of the person's behaviour."

Ostrender and Dethy—1968

"Values as something, i.e., chosen from alternatives, is acted upon and enhances creative integration and development of human personality."

International Encyclopedia of Social Science—1968

"Values are a set of principles whereby a conduct is directed and regulated as guide for individual or social groups."

Bhusan, Anand and Ahuja—1987

"Values are standards that are to a large extent derived, learned and internalised from society and its institution and that drastic changes in the circumstances of an institution provide an impetus for changes in self concept and values."

Karim—1991

"Values are any experience, state or ideal thing—existing or conceived ideally, which is favoured or desired provided that the experience, state, ideal or thing is justified endswise as well as meanswise."

Prahallada—1994

"When education builds up true values in the life of students it has equipped the ship of students with radars and compass to sail clear on the stormy sea of life."

Introduction to Home Science

The beginning of Home Science at colleges and universities was made in 1932 by Lady Irwin College at Delhi. Then in 1938 and onwards, Madras University accepted home science at the degree level and Home Science thus arrived in another part of India.

The well known and pioneering home science colleges of Madras are the Queen Mary's college and the Women's Christian college, which appeared on the Indian horizon in 1942. The Agricultural Institute of Allahabad had also started a home science diploma course in 1935 and it became university level department in 1945. Thus, Delhi, Madras and Allahabad were the pioneering home science institutions in the pre-independence era of 1930's and 1940's.

Baroda became a significant nucleus of Home Science in 1950, when the first Faculty of Home Science was established by Ms. Hansaben Mehta, the first Vice Chancellor of the M.S. University of Baroda, who created this Faculty with a well-planned objective of preparing good home makers and professional home scientists. To date, Baroda has supplied Home Science teachers and Home Science extension workers to many schools, colleges and agencies all over the country.

In the post-independence period, Baroda (Gujarat) was the most important landmark. Not only was the Faculty of Home Science able to offer five specialisations at the B.Sc. (Home) degree level, within only the first eight years of establishment, but by 1980 it offered B.Sc., M.Sc. and Ph.D degrees in all five specializations.

The other outstanding home science colleges which have developed since 1950 are the ones within the traditional universities at Coimbatore (Tamil Nadu), Ludhiana (Punjab), Bombay (Maharashtra), New Delhi, Udaipur (Rajasthan), Tirupathi (Andhra Pradesh).

Then in the mid 1960's and 1970's another landmark was made when the Agricultural Universities were established in most of the states. Home being an important unit of production and consumption in an agrarian country like ours, the need of teaching home science was recognised in most of the agricultural universities where home science colleges were opened within the initial years. Thus, home science colleges also had great physical resources at their command, e.g., spacious building, many teaching, technical and managerial posts, large contingencies, and resources for home science extension and research.

The Philosophy of Home Science

The Philosophy of home is the first concern of the home scientist. The philosophy of home science is linked with the philosophy of home. Home stands for the material and emotional well being and security of its residents and, therefore, the science of home concerns itself with all the knowledge which could contribute towards the fulfillment of these objectives. Some home scientists consider strengthening of the family life as a major component of the philosophy of home science. But, to use the direct approach, the philosophy of Home Science is strengthening of family life for the purpose of development and gratification of human beings.

The Philosophy of Home Science can be Expressed Comprehensively in terms of following Principles

1. The education in home science centres around the individual.
2. Home Science contributes to the personal and professional

development of the individual. The knowledge in Home Science is primarily derived from the physical, biological and social sciences and applied to Home Science in order to achieve personal and professional growth of the individual.

3. The personal and professional development of the individual contributes to the satisfactions within home and family.
4. The objectives, methods and contents of home science are determined through consideration of roles of women in family and in profession. The roles mean the function women perform in the family, community, and on job, alongwith corresponding needs, qualification and problems.
5. The basic principles and objectives of home science are subject to change in the social, professional and other related contexts with the changing roles of women and families.
6. It is necessary to extend the knowledge of Home Science outside the college to provide benefit to women, men and children, who do not have an access to formal education in home science.
7. Home Science requires fundamental and applied research for development of knowledge.

Broad Objectives of Home Science

1. To educate the individual for family living.
2. To manage the use of resources so that the values and goals of the individual, the family and the society may be attained.
3. To develop a wholesome personality.
4. To help students to develop a sense of beauty in every phase of daily living.
5. To establish values which give meaning to personal, family and community living.
6. To unify knowledge from related sciences and arts in order to widen the horizons of home science.
7. To interpret home science to students and public in the light of the larger purpose of education and of basic social needs.
8. To prepare students for employment in home science and related fields.
9. To achieve good quality of life with emphasis on personal and family living.

As we all know, education is a process of development from birth to death. Man becomes a full human being through education. The system of education is meant to achieve the social, economic, political, cultural and spiritual goals. The educative process is aimed at developing individual personality, and to preserve and improve, the society. Education, hence, as a system becomes a potent instrument for achievement of society's goals.

Swami Vivekananda defines education as the manifestation of the perfection already in man. According to him, the teacher should be able "to transfer his soul into the soul of every student, see through the students' eyes and hear through their mind".

Values, can after all, be learned / (caught) not 'taught'. For example, when a boy wants to learn to ride a cycle, what he has to do is to undergo training in the technique of riding. Elaborate lectures on 'how to ride a cycle' would never put him on the saddle and help him move. Values, similarly, are not imparted through "Professors of Charity, Readers in Probity (Honesty) or Lecturers in Patience". They could be inculcated by examples, training and self-training. Values are neither skills nor proficiencies to be developed on the same lines that we normally do for skill, proficiency development etc., in the learners. What then is to be done regarding 'values'? How if at all, can 'values' be brought into the process of learning and academic curriculum?

Conclusion

In general, the curriculum should aim at the development of the individual in an irreversible sort. There should be no 'room' for one returning to the 'basic elements' after acquiring higher values and development through education. Mere physical changes (of acquiring some skills) will not help the learner as well as the society in the long run. The sequential process of education and development should ultimately bring forth a flourished human being who will be continuously inspired by values of making the 'good quality of life' possible and abundant in the society. The real value orientation in education will be to make the learner feel that the quality of work that he is going to do in future is not to be determined by what others expect, but what he expects from himself.

Imparting Essential Values to the Students Of Home Science Through the Curriculum

(1) The foremost values in any student are moral values like:

- Punctuality
- Respect
- Obedience
- Hard work
- Capability
- Cooperation
- Sincerity
- Honesty
- Empathy
- Responsibility
- Patience
- Self confidence

Objective

To inculcate moral values required in Home Science Students.

Learning Experience

- Discussion
- Talk
- Seminar
- Field work
- Educational Trips
- Community projects

(2) Feeling of Equality

Objective

Learning Experience

To impart the sense of equality in the Students.

- Discussion
- Talk
- Seminar
- Workshop
- Exhibition
- Field work

(3) Respecting and Appreciating the inter-departmental functioning in Home Science

Objective

To inculcate respect and appreciation required in Home Science Students.

Learning Experience

- Discussion
- Talk
- Lecture
- Workshop
- Encouraging Extra curricular activities
- Celebrating various days together

(4) Feeling of Cooperation in Students with respect to their course curriculum

Objective

To inculcate feeling of cooperation required in Home Science students.

Learning Experience

- Discussion
- Talk

- Making students aware of the advantage of Home Science Education through of media of involvement

(5) Increasing sense of responsibility for career

Objective

To inculcate sense of responsibility in Home Science students.

Learning Experience

- Seminar
- Elocution
- Symposiums
- Career Counseling
- Panel Discussions
- Aptitude Tests

References

1. Chandra, A. Introduction to Home Science, Metropolitan New Delhi, 1994.

2. Eurectt, W. Hall. What is value. Routledge and Kegan Paul Pvt. Ltd. Broadway House London, 1952.

3. Gujaral, S. Pandit, S. Ogale, N. Universities and Colleges of Home Science Education in India. Published by the Home Science Association of India, 1991.

4. Palliwala, S. Interest in creative activities among Home Science Students. *Report* Department of Education and Extension, M.S. University, Baroda, 1982.

5. Parlikar, K. What is Home Science, Jay Mudra Publisher, Baroda, 1999.

6. Pattison and Chhaya, Annodated Bibliography of Research related to Home Science in India. Faculty of Home Science, M.S. University, Baroda, 1967.

7. Reddy and Parameswar, Factors influencing the value patterns of college students. *Educational Review*, 23 July-Dec. 1983.

8. Snyder B.R. The Hidden Curriculum, New York Knopf, 1971.

5

Value Education—As A Part of Course Curriculum in Home Science Extension and Communication

Awa Trivedi and Priyanka Pandey

Introduction

"Gurur Brahma Gurur Vishnu Gurur Devo Maheshwara, Gurur Sakshat Parah Brahma Tasmay Shri Guruve Namah."

Even today many schools and colleges settings are seen or heard reciting the same *shlok* every morning in order to greet their *gurus*. The matter of concern is that, whether students really perceive their Gurus as Brahma, Vishnu or Deve in the present days context ?

Gone are the days, when there was Gurukul system, the identities of a teacher were nothing less than a God. We still narrate the story of *Eklavya* to our younger generations telling them that, "*Eklavya* Ne To Guru Dronacharya Ko Guru Dakshina Me Apana Angutha De Diya Tha." Can we think of such Eklavyas in today's scenario ?

Education was not a joke in those days. Those who had to study, had to sacrifice their luxurious lives. Arguments with teachers had no space in the lives of students. There wasn't any commercialisation in terms of fees, or money. The student and teacher both used to be identified by each other's performances.

Those were the days when teaching and learning process proved its real meaning. Here it becomes important to know the role of teaching. Teaching cultivates selfless love to produce prosperous communities and peaceful nations and moulds the rising generation into self-confident and self-reliant citizens.

Education is an effective instrument in the hands of nation to prepare its people to meet the challenges of time through development of attitude. Values and capacities of both, knowledge and skill and teacher being the pivot the educational process can play a significant role in shaping the future of a nation.

Education can never be complete unless it equips the individual for meeting the real challenges of life, prepares him for his moral responsibilities as adult and helps him in achieving full growth. The real aim of education according to Gandhiji should be 'the development of integrated man by drawing out the best in him.'

However, during the last few years, instead of helping the students to develop meaning and purpose of life, educational institutions have given more emphasis only on achieving higher percentage of marks in schools and colleges keeping the development of the human being aside.

All these changes are due to a number of causes and at the same time leading to unpleasant consequences. Today commercialisation has created its place everywhere. Owing to such things, the feeling of belongingness, devotedness, dedication, loyalty, honesty have lost their significance. However, nowadays, competition, which is considered to be the backbone of growth has given rise to dishonesty, jealousy, hatred, etc. which in turn gives birth to a society facing dearth of values.

What are Values?

The term value has been defined in various ways.

According to G.M. Inlow (1922), "Values are the determiners in man that influence his choice in life and thus decide his behaviour and action.

Henry (1963) defines value as something that we consider well such as "love, kindness, quietness, contentment, fun, honesty, decency, relaxation, simplicity".

Raths, Harmin and Simon (1966) say that "out of experience may come certain general guides to behaviour. These guides, which tend to give direction to life, may be called values."

Rogers (1969) says, "Valuing is the tendency of a person to show preference."

In short, values are defined as reasonably permanent identification of the individual with ideal, or moraly desired, human actions. Spranger considers them as deeper layers of human personality, character and action developed in interaction between inherited structure and environmental situations.

There are various categories of values such as traditional values, cultural values, political values, social values, moral values, professional values, and so on.

All these categories are although quite distinct, but still they are linked with each other. A student studying in a college not only needs to carry professional values but also moral, social and cultural values. The Ministry of Education and Culture on value oriented teacher training, suggested that values can best be taught through the instrumentality of a number of subjects rather than through introducing any special subject like moral education or value education.

An indispensable condition of the moral and spiritual development is secured only when the learner is given ample opportunities to exercise his free will.

It is being increasingly recognised that there are, for different categories of learners, different cognitive styles and different ways of learning. Some students have better aesthetic appeal, others learn through manual work, still others learn through intellectual contemplation. An ideal system of education should provide to each learner that method which suits his learning needs and cognitive style. This is more valid in the area of value education than cognitive component of education.

We have discussed a lot about general students and values. It is time now to concentrate on our own field, i.e., need for value education for the students of Home Science Extension. For knowing this, we first need to brush our knowledge regarding the field of extension.

What is Extension?

According to Ensminger (1957) extension is education and that its purpose is to change attitudes and practices of the people with whom the work is done.

Leagans (1961) conceptualised extension education as an applied science consisting of content derived from research, accumulated field experiences and relevant principles drawn from the behavioural sciences synthesized with useful technology into a body of philosophy, principles, content and methods focused on the problems of out-of-school education for adults and youth.

The National Commission on Agriculture (1976) refers to extension as an informal out-of-school education and services for the members of the farm family and other directly or indirectly engaged in farm production.

According to Dahama and Bhatnagar (1987) extension education is a behavioural science following a continuous, persuasive and discriminating educational process. It aims at affecting the behavioural components of people in a desirable direction, through convecting, communication and diffusion, by its proven methods, principles and philosophies resulting in learning involvement of both client and change agent systems.

Bhatnagar and Desai (1987) gave a simple definition of extension. According to them extension is to bring the desirable changes in the behaviour knowledge, skills, attitude, understanding, goals and confidence of the people through mutual learning.

Need for Extension

The need for extension arises out of the fact that the condition of the rural people in general, and the farm people in particular, has got to be improved. There is a gap between what is the actual situation and what ought to be the desirable situation. This gap has to be narrowed down mainly by the application of science and technology in their enterprises and bringing appropriate changes in their behaviour.

According to Supe (1987) the researchers neither have the time nor are they equipped for the job of persuading the villagers to adopt scientific methods, and to ascertain from them the rural problems. Similarly, it is difficult for all the farmers to visit the research stations and obtain first hand information. Thus, there is need for an agency to interpret the findings of the research to the farmers and to carry the problems of the farmers to research for solution. This gap is filled by the extension agency. Therefore, UGC made it mandatory that extension alongwith teaching and research should be incorporated in the course curriculum in every university.

Objectives of Extension

Objectives are expression of the ends towards which our efforts are directed. The fundamental objective of extension is to develop the rural people economically, socially and culturally by means of education. More specifically, the general objectives of extension are:

1. To assist people to discover and analyze their problems and identify their felt needs.
2. To develop leadership among people and help them in organising groups to solve their problems.
3. To disseminate research information of economic and practical importance in a way people would be able to understand and use.
4. To assist people in mobilising and utilising the resources which they have and which they need from outside.
5. To collect and transmit feedback information for solving management problems.

Criteria for Effective Extension Teaching

(i) Extension teaching requires specific and clearly defined teaching objectives. Teaching must be clearly conceived and specifically defined.

There must be clear cut conception about the end product, i.e., what is going to be achieved. In deciding on the objectives of teaching, the following aspects are to be considered—

(a) People to be taught
(b) Behavioural changes to be developed in people,
(c) Content or subject matter to bring the desired change in behaviour, and
(d) The life situation in which the action is going to take place.

(ii) Extension teaching requires a suitable learning situation. The learning situation consists of the following five interrelated elements—Instructor (extension worker), Learners (farmers, farm women, rural youth, etc). Subject matter (say, social forestry), Teaching materials (seeds, plants, audio-visual aids, etc) and Physical facilities (suitable facilities for conducting demonstrations, training, etc.)

(iii) Extension teaching requires effective communication. Communication involves the transfer of knowledge from a source to one or more receivers. Extension teaching, to be effective, must take into consideration proper functioning of the elements of communication—communicator, message, channel, treatment and audience. Effective communication can motivate people to act.

(iv) Extension teaching requires both content and method. Content means what to teach, the subject matter. Method means how to teach, the delivery system. The content should be relevant to the audience.

(v) Extension teaching must be looked upon as an intentional process. Extension teaching should be properly planned and designed on the basis of relevant data on the situation and available research. There is no scope for trial and error or haphazard thinking and action in extension teaching.

(vi) Extension teaching must result in effective learning. The meaning of the topic which is taught should be understood and internalised by the learners. This usually requires a combination of teaching methods and aids relevant to a particular situation. An effective learning experience is one which results in a maximum number of desirable changes in the behaviour of the learners.

(vii) Extension teaching must accomplish certain kinds of educational changes in relation to the subject matter taught. Desirable changes in the knowledge, skill, attitude, understanding, goal, action and confidence of the people are to be achieved in relation to the topic being taught.

(viii) Extension teaching requires careful evaluation of results to find out if teaching has been able to attain the objectives set forth, i.e., whether desirable changes in behaviour of the people have taken place and these have to be assessed or evaluated. Steps are to be taken to meet the deficiencies identified in the process.

And for teaching effectively the teacher has to have certain qualities which will help her/him in inculcating values in students.

Qualities of a Teacher

- Deep understanding of teaching and learning.
- Committed to the success for all students.
- Knows how to evaluate and able to give frank powerful feedback.

- Engages in continuous dialogue about what good teaching looks like.
- Provides permissive atmosphere.
- Makes quick decisions.
- Uses Brain storming technique.
- Has her goals clear with a vision.
- Inspires trust and confidence.
- Makes others feel capable.
- Highly energetic and goal oriented.
- Smiles, what may come.
- Expresses her emotions and feelings frequently.
- Makes everybody feel that he/she is important.
- Helps people to look beyond self-interest and also understand the need for change.
- Reflects critically on what has been done.

Criteria for Effective Learning

The basic purpose of education is to transform human activity to more productive and effective purposes. Learning involves acquisition of knowledge, skill, attitude, etc, retention to stop reversion; and transfer to use it in real life situations. Learning, to be effective should have the following characteristics:

(i) Learning should be purposeful. The learning must make sense and be useful to the learners. Objectives must be clear and meaningful to the learners. What is to be learnt must be important to, and wanted by, a relatively large number of participants in the group, and must be attainable:

(a) Through the educational process,

(b) Within the time limitations of the extension worker and the participants,

(c) Within the physical and economic resources of the participants.

(d) Within the social condition and learning ability of the participants.

(ii) Learning should involve appropriate activity by the learners that engages a maximum number of senses. Messages reach the human mind through five senses, namely, seeing, hearing, feeling, tasting and smelling. In extension, most of the messages to be learnt reach the mind through seeing, hearing and doing. Learning should be experience centred, i.e., farmers should primarily learn by doing, in addition to seeing and hearing.

(iii) Learning must be challenging and satisfying. Abilities acquired through learning should help the farmer to solve their problems, to overcome the difficulties and gradually lead to a more satisfying life.

(iv) Learning-must result in functional understanding. Mere acquisition of knowledge is not enough, it must be understood and applied in real life situation. One must first see the form of the whole, then its parts, then the distinct function of each part, then the relationship of the parts to each other, and finally, the relationship of each part of the whole. Ultimately, the learner must see the role of the whole idea in the total context of which it is a part and is expected to perform a role.

Course Curriculum

I. *Objective*

To inculcate moral values required in the field of extension, among the students.

Moral Values

Honesty	Friendly	Humble	Courageous
Sincere	Self-confident	Polite	Selfless
Genuine	Open-minded	Loyal	

Learning Experience

1. Seminar
2. Debate and Discussions

II. *Objective*

To inculcate education values required in the field of extension among the students.

Educational Values

— Acquainted with the nature of problems and cultural background.

— Thorough knowledge of the subjects.

— Firmly determined to achieve his/her goal.

— Resourceful—to satisfy the village needs by obtaining assistance of various NGO's.
— Act as guide.
— Searching new ideas and techniques, approach the subject matter specialist, uptodate ideas.
— Perfectionist.
— Vision to frame future plans and programmes.
— Well acquainted with ways and means of teaching account to new methods and AV Aids.
— Hardworking and enthusiastic.

Learning Experience

— React upon situations.
— Working in collaboration with NGO's for a specific number of days.
— Orientation to Government offices and schemes.
— Orientation to the correct procedure to be followed while implementing and programming.
— Seminars on Extension at National Level, State Level, with NGO's and GO's.
— Promotion of action projects.

III. ***Objective***

— Adjustability in village circumstances.
— Prompt and able to influence the villagers in a positive way.
— Sympathetic to and sharing the joys and sorrows of the people.
— Hold the ideal of simple living and high thinking.
— Effective Communicator.
— Encourage the growth of leadership ability
— Promote the sense of community, feeling.
— Good attentive listener
— Good negotiator
— Persuasive
— Inspiring and motivating
— Team builder

Learning Experience

— Reacts to situations.
— Experience of working with different groups and its presentation.

— Gaining first hand experience by assisting the seniors.
— Collection of articles informing about different festivals being celebrated and their significance.

References

1. Chaubey, B.K. A handbook of education extension. Jyoti Prakashan, Allahabad, 1978.

2. Devadas, R.T. "Teaching of Home Science in India" *The Educational Quarterly,* Ministry of Education. GOI. Vol. 13. No. 50, 1961.

3. Home Science Association of India. Home Science Colleges and Universities in India. Ministry of Education. New Delhi, 1958.

4. Hanson, J. and Ginsberg, A. Gaining ground values and high school success. *American Educational Research Journal.* **25** (3).

5. Komal Singh. A comparative study of value of different occupational groups. Ph.D. Thesis Rohilkhand, K.G.K. College Moradabad, U.P., 1990.

6. Kellam, R.B. Home Economics graduates perception and Job satisfaction. Diss. Abst. International 49(1). July 1988, 48-A. Thesis (Ph.D)-Oklahama State University, 1987.

7. Kluckhe and Strodbeak. *Variation in value orientation.* Row Peterson and Company Publishers, New York, 1980.

8. Supe, S.V. Introduction to Extension Education Oxford and IBH Publishing Co. New Delhi, 1982.

6

Projection of Marital and Related Aspects in Media and its Perception by Young University Students

Amiteshwar Ratra, and Praveen Kaur

The researcher analyzed various articles coverage in popular magazines, taking five volumes of each, selected randomly, the maganizes were published in recent past (1999-2000). The researcher analyzed two popularly read newspapers, The *Tribune* and The *Hindustan Times*, for a period of two months December 2000 and January, 2001 regarding their coverage of marital and its related aspects. Information was also collected about the popular channels and serials related to marital relations. An interview schedule was prepared to know the opinion of the respondents regarding role of magazines, TV. serials and movies in marital relations.

Analysis

Review of Popularly read Magazines.

Table 1. Magazine contents of marital and its related aspects

Magazines	*Husband*	*Extra Wife*	*Pre-martial marital*	*Pre-marital Love*	*In-laws Sex*	*Beautif–ication*
Grihshobha	7	1	3	0	3	30
Femina	2	0	6	2	0	34
Women's Era	8	1	15	2	1	16
Cosmopo-litan	11	3	5	5	0	23
Sarita	4	1	1	0	2	12

Review of popularly read newspapers

The Tribune and *The Hindustan Times* were reviewed for the months of December, 2000 and January, 2001.

Table 2. Newspaper Contents of Marital and its Related Aspects

Theme	*No. of Articles*
Husband wife	6
Extra-marital relations	1
Pre-marital sex	2
Pre-marital love	1
In-law relationship	2
Beautification	12

Main themes of popularly watched TV serials

The popularly watched soap operas identified as related to husband wife, pre-marital, extra-marital, in-laws and parent child relationships are given in Table 3.

Table 3. List of Serials

Nazdekiyan	Amanat
Kyunki Saas Bhi Kabhi Bahu Thi	Ek Mahal Ho Sapno Ka
Rishtey	Gharwali Uparwali
Hum Sab Ek Hain	Kanyadaan
Siski	Thodi Si Bewafai
Tu Tu Main Main	Mehndi
Heena	Kora Kagaz
Saaya	Saans
Ghar Ek Mandir	Family No. 1

Adolescents opinion about media preference and its role.

Table 4. Preference of Maganizes

	Magazine	Often	Occasionally	Never
(a)	*Femina*	34	12	4
(b)	*Grihshobha*	7	15	28
(c)	*Eve's Weekly*	4	15	31
(d)	*Sarita*	27	6	17
(e)	*Women's Era*	32	16	2
(f)	*Manorama*	14	14	22
(g)	*Cosmopolitan*	28	13	9

Table 5. Preference of Article Themes (Multiple Choice)

	Theme	Yes
(a)	Law	23
(b)	Adoption	19
(c)	Sex and molestation	48
(d)	Working women problems	50
(e)	Marital conflict	47
(f)	Problems in opposite sex friendship	50
(g)	Maraital adjustment	43
(h)	Query columns	39

Tables 6. Role of Magazines in Problem Solving

	Relationship	Yes	No
(a)	Martial relations	23	27
(b)	In-laws relations	33	17
(c)	Understanding of children	30	20
(d)	Understanding of own self	28	22
(e)	Parent child relations (adolescents)	31	19
(f)	Opposite sex friendship	26	24
(g)	Encouragement to go against parents wishes	0	50

Table 7. General theme of movies these days

Theme	*Very often*	*Often*	*Partly*
(a) Love triangles	41	9	0
(b) Premarital relations	16	34	9
(c) Extramarital relations	12	30	8
(d) Youth is ignoring parents view points in opposite sex friendship	10	34	6
(e) Family conflicts and their healthy solution	38	12	0
(f) Anti-social behaviour	7	38	5
(g) Parent-child ties getting strong	11	26	13
(h) Brother-sister ties getting strong	5	17	28
(i) Traditional family ideology	8	29	13
(j) Rebellious youth	21	23	6
(k) Love marriages	47	3	0
(l) Inter-caste marriages	13	20	17
(m) Women's struggle against suppression	7	8	35
(n) Family violence	14	19	17

Table 8. Type of Songs/dances these days

Types	*Yes*	*No.*
(a) Exotices	43	7
(b) Erotic	46	4
(c) Classical based	10	40
(d) Simple meaningful	12	38
(e) Religious/Spiritual	3	47

Table 9. Linking of types of songs/dances

Types	*Yes*	*No.*
(a) Exotic	23	27
(b) Erotic	17	33
(c) Classical based	4	46
(d) Simple meaningful	38	12
(e) Religious/Spiritual	6	44

Table 10. Effect of movies on family relations

Effect	*Subject*
(a) Positively	23
(b) Negatively	27

Table 11. Benefits of Portrayal of Marital Family Relations on the Society

Age-group	*Yes*	*No.*
(a) Children	0	50
(b) Youngsters	45	5
(c) Adults	0	50

Femina, Women's Era, Cosmopolitan and *Sarita* were popularly read magazines by the respondents while *Grihshobha, Eve's Weekly, Manorama* are less popular (Table 4).

It is clear that respondents read articles related to working women, sex and friendship followed by molestation, marital conflict and martial adjustment, query columns, law and adoption at the last (Table 5).

It is clear that readers have opined that magazines at large helped respondents in solving problems aroused in various relations like in-laws relationship, understanding of children, parent-child relations, understanding of own-self, opposite sex friendship (Table 6). None of the respondent viewed magazines as providing encouragement to go against parent-child relations, understanding of own-self, opposite sex friendship (Table 6). None of the respondent viewed magazines as providing encouragement to go against parent's wishes.

It was love triangle, love marriages, family conflicts and their healthy solutions, which were the most popular themes of movies these days as reported by the respondents (Table 7). While movies on women's struggle against suppression were rarely made.

It was seen that most of the respondents felt that songs/ dances these days were erotic, exotic and rarely were classical based, simple meaningful or religious (Table 8). Also, most of the respondents liked simple meaningful songs/dances, followed by exotic and erotic, while few liked classical based and religious songs/dances (Table 9).

The respondents regarding the effect of movies on family relations was divided 46 per cent reported positive and 54 per cent as negative as it was leading to increase of people's expectations (Table 10).

It is evident that almost all the respondents did not find much benefit of portrayal of marital relations in the current serials on the society because every family situation varies (Table 11). Family oriented TV serial might have a positive effect on youngsters and negative effect on children and adults according to the respondents.

Conclusion

In summary, the following would appear to be the central findings from the above discussions:

- Media is a crucial shaper of teenagers' values and attitudes.
- Television presents attitudes and values, which may differ from those of family and peers and information in quantities far greater than what is available regarding sexual life.
- There is substantial observation that TV models account for social models through which young people identify themselves.
- Media serves as a source of social learning about adult relationships marriage and its related aspects.
- Television has a major influence on teenagers about sexuality and responsibility. It may now be more important influence than school, parents or even peers. The problem is that television is putting out an unbalanced view about sex, which is causing more problems for teenagers and society.
- Magazines constitute part of the media stories that shape both society's sense of culture and our sense of self in culture.
- There is more emphasis on beautification both in our magazines and newspapers. Earlier beautification had more coverage for women but now it is covering men also.
- Husband wife relations articles are closely followed by premarital relations articles in popularly read magazines by the respondents. This is true for the newspaper also.
- In our soap operas, a lot of emphasis is on pre-marital relations, husband wife relations, in-laws relations and parent child relations.
- The most popular magazines read by subjects of the present study is *Femina* and *Women's Era*.
- Popularly read articles by the respondents are working

women problem, marital conflict, marital adjustment and opposite sex friendship.

- Respondents felt that magazines helped to solve problems in opposite sex friendships, in-laws, marital partners and parent-adolescent understanding.
- According to the respondents, general themes of movies these days revolve around love marriages, love triangles and family conflicts and their healthy solutions.
- More than half of the respondents felt that movies had negative effect on family relations as it raised expectations in the viewers.
- Most of the respondents felt that portrayal of marital and family relations benefits only the youngsters as it pre-warns them about problems they can face due to their illicit relationships.

Suggestions

There is virtually not much coverage about ill effects of casual sex like sexually transmitted diseases, AIDS (Acquired Immunity Deficiency Syndrome) in mass India. There are not may reflections regarding disruptions brought about in one's marital and family relations due to casual sexual behaviour. If young people take media messages to heart, they will continue to enact a vision in which men are the citizens of the world and women are the citizens of the world of the men. Therefore, following are some of the suggestions, which may imbibe proper values in youngsters through media:

- Television should also take up the responsibility for teaching values are, thereby, move from being part of the problem to be part of the remedy.
- Parental mediation is necessary for children and youngster's television viewing. For children these days watch media content is considered more appropriate for older viewers. Parents may regulate their viewing through rules, prohibitions and discussions. Parents should eavesdrop children and youngsters television viewing.
- Such studies in India are only a few, as reported in journals, so there is a need to conduct such studies at large scale.
- Some non-governmental organisations should take up screening and rating of TV programmes as per the needs of the society.

- Older siblings, grandparents should also co-view programmes with youngsters and discussions regarding programme be held.
- Proper measures should be adopted by both schools and parents to educate children regarding adversaries of casual relationships.
- Magazines and newspapers should also emphasize about various problems related to marital and family problems caused due to unrealistic expectations aroused by media among the partners.
- Personal guidance and counselling should be provided to adolescents so that they can find appropriate solutions to their problems instead of going to mass media for the same.
- There is need to bring a change in the social consciousness of the audience or viewers, so, as to change the programmes viewed. As what is not purchased is not sold, therefore, not produced.

References

1. Akhileshwari, R. *Male chuvinist Media,* Vidura, Jan-Feb. pp. 25-27, 1998.

2. Bathia, Sonia. *Women Democracy and the Media,* Sage Publication, New Delhi, 1998.

3. Banerjee, C. Women in Media. A mirror of our aspiration. *Mainstream.* April 9, pp. 23-25, 1988.

4. Desai, N. and Krishnaraj, M. (eds). *Women and Society in India.* New Delhi. Ajanta Publications, 1987.

5. Gohosh, S.K. *Women in a Changing Society,* New Delhi, Ashish Publishing House, 1984.

6. Govt. of India, Towards Equality-Report of the Committee on the status of women, New Delhi, Govt. of India, Ministry of Education and Social Welfare, 1974.

7. Joshi, I. *Women Dimension on Television (Policy, Personnel and Programme)* Concept Publishing Company, New Delhi, 1991.

8. Mahajan, K. *Television and Women's Development,* New Delhi Classical Publishing Co., 1993.

9. Subramanayan, V. Mirror Image : Media and the Women's Question. Centre for Education and Documentation. Bombay, 1986.

7

A Study on Selected Desirable Values of Undergraduate Students of Home Science in the State of Gujarat

Susan Jacob and Anupama Shah

Values may be regarded as important ratings which people attach to things, conditions and circumstances. They may also be regarded as goals, objects to which people orient their thinking actions and feelings. The present study was to find out the level of selected desirable values of undergraduate students of home science. Some of the desirable values that were identified by the Home Scientists may actually contribute to personal, social and professional development of women. They are gender equality, feminism, dignity of labour, vocationalism and collectivism.

The sample consisted of 600 final year students of under graduation from fifteen colleges offering Home Science programmes under 10 different universities in Gujarat. The tools for research consisted of a questionnaire, checklist, standardized scale, rating scale and situational test. The investigator personally collected data. The data was analyzed with the help of computer SPSS-I C + Program. The various statistical measures used included ANOVA 1st t-test and product moment correlation. The major findings of the study were as follows.

At least fifty per cent or more of the Home Science Programmes:

- were under arts college
- were established since five to fifteen years only
- were in cities
- had Gujarati medium

- had General course of study rather than specialisation for under graduation
- admitted students irrespective of their streams of study in 12th standard
- had number of students ranging from 26-50 in final year
- had teaching staff members in the designation of lecturer or its equivalent, with postgraduation and less experience.

At least fifty or more per cent of the respondent's personal and familial background showed that they:

- were Hindus
- belonged to middle socio-economic status group, with their monthly income ranging between Rs. 2001to Rs. 10,000/ father's education ranged from 12th standard to professional head of the family had semiskilled occupation and had two wheelers in the family and moderate level of vocational aspirations.
- had moderate level of family climate
- the level of selected values were moderate overall and among the different universities
- among the values, gender equality had the highest and collectivism had the lowest intensity indices
- the Gujarat Vidyapith, the Maharaja Sayajjirao University and Saurashtra University were found to be the leading Universities in terms of overall levels of values. While Gujarat Agricultural University, Sardar Patel University and South Gujarat University were having the low levels.
- the overall level of values differed significantly according to different universities at 0.05 and 0.01 level significantly on the whole the above mentioned three leading universities had significantly higher level of values when compared with other universities.

  The correlation among and between the different values was significant and positive.
- wherever the significant differences were found, the respondents from residential universities,well established colleges, Gujarati medium, general programme of study, the Home Science Colleges with less teaching staff but high qualification and experience had significantly higher levels of values than their counterparts (Table 1)

Table 1. Showing Significant Differences in the Level of Values According to the Personal and Familial Variables

Personal and Familial variables		*VALUES*				
		Gender equality	*Familism*	*Dignity of labour*	*Vocation-alism*	*Collect-ivism*
•Academic achievement	Low	-	-	-	-	-
	High	✓	✓	✓	✓	✓
•Mother's education	Low	-	✓	-	-	-
	High	✓	-	-	-	-
• SES	Low	-	-	-	-	-
	High	✓	-	-	-	-
•Vocational aspiration	Low	-	-	-	-	-
	High	✓	-	-	✓	-
•Family climate	Low	-	-	-	-	-
	High	✓	✓	✓	✓	✓

✓ Mark denotes significantly higher level of values than their counterparts.

- Wherever the significant differences were found the respondents with high academic achievement, high family climate, high vocational aspiration, higher level of mothers education and high SES were found to have higher level of values than the respondents with low level of these personal and familial variables (Table 2).

Table 2. Showing Significant Differences in the Level of Values According to the Institutional Variables

Institutional variables		*VALUES*				
		Gender equality	*Familism*	*Dignity of labour*	*Vocation -alism*	*Collect ivism*
• College	Arts	-	-	-	✓	✓
	Home Science	✓	-	-	-	-
• Type of University	Affiliated	-	-	-	-	-
	Residential	✓	-	-	-	✓
• Location of the college	City	✓	✓	-	-	-
	Town	-	-	-	-	-
• Number of years since	5-25 years	-	-	-	-	-
	Above 25 years	✓	✓	-	-	-
• Medium of instruction	English	✓	✓	-	-	-
	Gujarati	-	-	-	-	✓
• Programme of study	General	-	-	✓	✓	✓
	Specialisz-ation	✓	-	-	-	-
• Number of teaching staff	Less	-	-	✓	✓	✓
	More	✓	-	-	-	-

(Contd.)

• Educational qualification of teaching staff members	Less	-	-	-	-	✓
	High	✓	✓	-	-	-
• Experience of Teaching staff members	Less	-	-	-	-	✓
	More	✓	✓	-	✓	-

✓ Mark denotes significantly higher level of values than their counterparts.

The Gujarat Vidyapith and the Maharaja Sayajirao University being high on overall levels of values can act as role models for developing other Home Science colleges. The Home Science colleges identified as having lower level of values must improve the conditions for promoting themselves.

The study showed that the residential type of University, science oriented courses, Gujarati medium, well-established colleges, qualified and experienced teachers are the contributing institutional factors for promoting values. Close inter-linkages with leading Home Science Colleges will help to have better ideas of development. The Home Science Association of India or the University Grants Commission (UGC) Panel of Home Science must accredit the Home Science Colleges. This will help to set-up common goals and constant monitoring of the developmental process, which may give a professional status to the programme and hence attract the serious students who are really interested in this field.

The education of the girls, the raised standard of socio-economic conditions, mother's education and family climate are of importance as that they are conducive factors for developing desired values. Families must be made gender sensitive so that they provide conducive environment for the achievement of the highest level of values to their daughters. It will help them to accept the challenges posed by an even more egalitarian society.

References

1. Bharti, T. Towards a new direction in women's education. *University News* XXXII (5) Jan. 1994.

2. Kar, N.N. Value education. A philosophical study. Thesis (Ph.D.), M.S. University, Baroda, 1985.

3. Malti, M. Value orientation of rural woman. *Maharashtra Journal of Extension Education*. 8th October, 1989.

4. Prahallada, N.N. Contemporary significance of value education. *University News*. XII (7): 1994.

5. Rose, K. *Where women are leaders. The SEWA movement in India*, New Delhi, Vistar Publications, 1992.

6. Lakshmi, V. A Study of Values of College Students in relation to their mother's educational level. *Asian Journal of Psychology and Education*, 29 (3-4) 1996.

7. Kumari, P. Relationship of creativity with intelligence and value patterns of adolescents M.Ed Dissertation, M.S. University Baroda, 1975.

8. Herris, M.C. *Value Leadership*, Prentice Hall of India, New Delhi, 2000.

9. Veenkataiah, N. *Value Education–An Overview in Value Education*, New Delhi, APH Publishing Corporation, 1998.

8

A Study to Identify the Desirable Values Needed for Home Science Students

Dr. Susan Jacob and Prof. Anupama Shah

The worldwide resurgence of interest in value education has been explained as the natural response of the modern industrialized societies to the serious erosion of values in all aspects of life and the crisis of values experienced in modern times. The sweeping political, economic and social changes have overtaken human civilization during the past few centuries and these have been largely responsible for the predicament of the modern man. There are also other factors like personal greed, meanness, selfishness, indifferences to others, interests and laziness, that have brought about large scale corruption in almost all spheres of life personal and public, economic and political, moral and religious (Prahallada, 1994).

Whatever be the cause of present value crisis, there is no gainsaying the fact that the weakening of values in our social life is creating serious social and ethical conflict. It is this changing context—the declining standard in personal and public life on the one hand the national ideological commitment to the value of democracy, socialism, secularism and modernisation on the other hand—that constituted the driving force behind the recommendation stressing the need of values.

According to Singh (1994),

"The issue of selection of values probably goes beyond secularism and subjectivity. The core group's values are really about improving the self. The values in the national policy on the other hand, see the individual in the social context. The two are different: improvement of self does not necessarily include sensitivity to social issues. The two could even be incompatible. The striving for social justice and gender equality is often at the cost of stability and peace."

We have come a long way, but we are now in the process of changing and the way to go is still very far. We need to be more strong and more specific to eliminate the factors which impede women's development, of course just saying is not enough, but women have to have the background where new values and lifestyles will be accepted too.

As the wind of change is blowing on women's role ethics in the home and outside, it is time to change the age old values of womanlihood and swift over to the values needed for modern life. The women are striving to gain equal status with men in all their activities. Hence, they should have the values suitable for taking up courageously, willingly and competently the new roles.

Hence, a study was planned to identify the desirable values needed for the students of home science. An extensive reading in search of the values was done and a number of them were listed down keeping their contribution to women's personal, social and professional development for coping up with the rapidly changing society. A checklist for identifying the desirable values needed for home science students were made. Senior home scientists who were having many years of experience in teaching, research and extension activities of various reputed home science institutes in India were contacted, either personally or through home science teachers at the time of conferences (XXth Biennial Conference of Home Science Association of India at Avinashlingam, Deemed University, Coimbatore in December 1993 and 18th Indian Science Congress at Jaipur, January, 1994) or through post. A total number of 51 checklists as in Table 1 were returned and the data were computed. Intensity indices were calculated and are specified as in the given Table 2.

Table 1. List of Experts for Selecting Values

Sr. No.	*Name of Institutions selected*	*Number of Experts from Different Departments*					*Total*
		C.D./ HDFS	*C.T.*	*E.E.*	*F.N.*	*H.M.*	
1.	Avinashlingam Institute of Home Science		Not specified				10
2.	Indian Science Congress meeting at Jaipur		Not specified				6
3.	S.N.D.T. Women's University, Mumbai	2	2	2	2	2	10
4.	Faculty of Home Science, M.S. University, Baroda	2	2	2	2	2	10
5.	Institute of Home Economics, Delhi	1	1	1	1	1	5
6.	Punjab Agricultural University, Ludhiana	2	2	2	2	2	10
	Total						51

Table 2. List of Desired Values according to the Decreasing Intensity Indices Selected by Senior Home Scientists

Sr. No.	*Values*	*Intensity Indices*
1.	Dignity of Labour	2.80
2.	Feminism	2.78
3.	Collectivism	2.72
4.	Gender equality	2.64
5.	Vocationalism	2.62

Dignity of Labour

The dictionary meaning of the word is worthiness of doing physical or manual work.

It can be defined as person's own attitude towards doing physical work. No work is mean or low but how one performs it makes it mean or noble.

However, the educated men and women find it difficult to do physical work because of its low dignity. They feel that doing physical work reduces their status in society. In this present situation, if we ignore to value the dignity of labour, it will affect the development of our country. The health status, sanitation, cleanliness within and outside the home, institutions and offices will be affected. This will lead to degradation in the strength of the citizens and hence weakness in our economy and nation.

In the days of modern technology the work in the homes has simplified and this has affected the physical fitness of the individuals. We have welcomed many diseases due to lack of exercise. In order to overcome this situation the dignity of labour must be encouraged to keep fit and healthy.

Women, being the future mothers to inculcate the values in the younger generation should know the importance of dignity of labour. If she values it, she can make changes in the attitudes and behaviour of younger generation and thus the future of the country will be saved.

Familism

Family is the smallest unit of democracy or dictatorship, exploitation or sharing, friendship or sharing. At the same time it is the place to which individual members look to derive physical comfort and social satisfaction. It warrants protection and support to its members. It provides a safety net in terms of financial, material and social security, which is essential to the growth of its members. It remains a vital means of preserving and transmitting cultural values. From the knowledge of the family we can read the character of a whole culture and civilization. The family circle is the clearing home for the raw materials and design of our human nature. The family does educate, train, motivate and support its individual members, thereby investing their future growth and acting on a vital resource for development.

Goethe (1994) sees that, the family, like the rest of society, has undergone a process of wholesale, transformative change. In this process, the family has been both the purveyor and the recipient of change: sometimes acting as its agent or, alternatively, being transformed by external force. In some cases the process has been adaptive, in others, destructive, threatening the survival of the family. One of the severe changes in the family is in the structure. The families are becoming smaller and individuals often feel less responsible for family relationships, unequal relationship, exploitation and abuse result in slow personal development and initiative. Today the family relationship is more voluntary, more conscious. Men and women have become more conscious of their personal insecurity of mood and character, outside the attachments of soul string and character forming love.

According to UNICEF Report (1994), in India, disturbed families suffering from the economic pangs of rapid modernisation can herald a whole generation of emotionally unstable citizens, many of whom may take to crime or other anti-social behaviours.

The women play a number of roles in the family, as a mother, as a sister, as a wife, as a grandmother, all of them are enmeshed in the current family system. There is a need to assess the status, role, contribution of a woman towards strengthening the bonding in the family.

Collectivism

The Self-Employed Women's Association (SEWA) defines collectivism as a continual process of distilling issues and building unity around them, raising the consciousness of the concerned, society and government, pressing for policy change and enforcing the policy so that women get their rights.

The collectivism means the humanistic concepts oriented towards the development of human resources and which seek to establish participatory attitudes, open relationship, primary to improve conditions and enhance opportunity rather than to make or change social policy. In another way, it may be defined as the process which enhanced human values like giving an opportunity to a meaningful contribution to the organisation.

Women are better fighters of day to day problems which force them and they are concerned about the emerging future. There is not just one goal which is fought for. The only way to bring change is to organise and organise some more. In numbers remain the voice and strength. If women stand together in sufficient number, then their voices do shake the balance and change things in their favour up to the national and international policies.

In recent years, various development programmes for women have been implemented. Women however have not been able to take complete advantage of them, particularly the poor and the illiterate women. It is important to realize that until the beneficiaries are well organised and well equipped to make use of the programmes they will never be effective.

According to Rose (1992) until women have extensive exposure to new ideas and technologies, their desire and ability to assume responsibility are big constraints in their success. The time is now ripe for women to come together, pool their resources and stand up on their own strength and free themselves from all the disabilities they suffer. With a multipronged approach to meet women's issues and solve their problems to bring about their total development, interest in women's education is now focused on improving their living conditions. In this context sustained development of family and society as integral units appears to be the dire need of the hour.

The women from all levels of society should join together to plan. The strength of any group is in its membership which generates the understanding and ideas. If India wants to pull itself forward, it will be accomplished through giving the women access to resources, decision making, planning and implementing of their own programme.

Gender Equality

According to Sharma (1992), equality is another acclaimed value of society. A society which grants to its members the right to equality, is by all means more developed than the one which does not do so. The right to equality means assurance of non-discrimination, based on ethnic, gender, religious or regional consideration.

In the case of gender equality, the right of women to have equality with men means equality in matters of movement, access to occupations, equal pay, equal share in property and so on. It is not just the availability of such rights in principle but the changes of their exercise in practice which is the critical measure of the rights to freedom and equality. Equality of women is necessary not merely for social justice but also as a basic condition of the social, economic and political development of the nation. The awareness on gender equality is recognised as vital to abolish the sexual discrimination in society.

Previously developing a woman specific component of national development was never thought of. However, this task was first performed by the Report of the Committee on Status of Women in India (1974). The report towards equality laid the right emphasis on equality of sexes as a major value to be inculcated through the educational process. Thus the Committee on the status of women noted that from early childhood boys and girls were indoctrinated to accept gender inequality and observed that the only institution which could reduce the effect of this kind of traditional socialisation process was the education system. In Committee's view, if education is to promote equality for women, it must make a deliberate planned and sustained effort so that the new value of equality of the sexes can replace the traditional value of inequality. The educational system today has not even attempted to undertake this responsibility.

We live in a time and society where equal access to education and employment has become a critical factor to provide for themselves and their families with dignity and confidence. We live in a society in which the contributions and activities of all people are not valued equally. There are challenges for each one of us. These challenges include dealing with gender biased attitudes, stereotypes, myths and behaviour.

Vocationalism

Vocationalism can be defined as a general activity centering around subsistence or it may be the activities undertaken by an individual for his/her economic productive activity. Such participation may be physical or mental in nature (Sundaram, 1984).

Men are traditionally socialised to assume the responsibility of supporting the family financially through investment of their human capital in the economy and receiving the financial remunerations. Women were considered to depend on them. But the scenario is changing due to social and other phenomena. Women have started working and attaining positions in the various sectors.

Management expert Tarneja in a Seminar on "emerging opportunities and challenges for women in nineties," New Delhi, 1993, said that the employment of women should be seen as development of human resources and not from a sexist point of view. More opportunities should be created for women.

Women as a vital constituent of the human resource of the country can contribute effectively, only when opportunities and freedom to use their potential is extended and their participation in the economic sector, for development and societal progress is realized. Economic necessities and leisure time released by science and technology have given the chance to an increasing number of women to seek wage earning activities and jobs outside the home. According to Nehru, "Freedom depends on economic conditions even more than political and if a woman is not economically free and self-earning, she will have to depend on and dependents are never free."

References

1. Goethe, O.R. *Marriage and family*. The Crow-well Collier Publishing Co., 1994, p. 270.

2. Prahallada, N.N. Contemporary significance of value education. *University News* XXXII (7): 1994, p.12.

3. Rose, K. *Where women are leaders. The SEWA movement in India*, New Delhi. Vistar Publications, 1992, p. 330.

4. Sharma, S. and Ganesh, K. A ear for women's chitchat. *The Economic Times*, (Mumbai, 15th Jan, 1992).

5. Singh, K. The issue of values in education. *The Times of India* (Ahmedabad) 30th March, 1994.

6. Sundaram and Dutt. *Indian Economy*, New Delhi, S. Chand and Co. Pvt. Ltd., 1984, p. 217.

7. Argyris, C. Teaching smart people how to learn. *Harvard Business Review* 69 (3) 99-101, 1991.

8. De Vanathan, R. Valuing the values, *University News*. Association of Indian University, Tara Art Press, New Delhi, 1999.

9. Biswal, A. "Value Orientation in Teacher Education" in Venkataiah, N (ed) *Value Education*. New Delhi, APH Publishing Corporation, 1998.

9

Wise Buying Values: A Tool for Family's Economic Health

Neerja Jaiswal and Ami Shah

Values permeate all aspects of human thought and action; they are strategic in the family system's inter-relationship with its environment. They provide the underlying meanings that indicate what is desirable and has worth to an individual, giving continuity to all decisions and actions of an individual.

Money as a non-human resource plays a crucial role in family's living. It is one of the vital and scarce resources, which is always in great demand to meet number of family goals. Thus, its wise utilisation is of utmost importance and need to be carefully planned, so that optimum results may be achieved in most economic way. Consumers must develop values for money and thrift to get maximisation of their money's worth. An attempt has been made in the present paper to educate about the values and practices one should adopt and take care while spending their money wisely.

Ample literature is available on advertisement, salesmanship, and marketing, filled with numerous ways and means for successful selling. There are professional sellers in the market, but there is comparatively very limited literature on buymanship, particularly for consumers. Generally books on purchasing, invariably, concentrate on industrial purchasing or merchandise useful for industrial buyers and merchants.

Better buymanship substitutes rational or intelligent action for emotional consumer action in the market. An alert and informed consumer is his/her own best friend and needs no consumer advocates or world savers to protect him/her. He/

She needs no protection from big, and business, which is incidentally the producer of largest variety bad best quality of goods and services in the world. Better buymanship is insurance against high-pressure salesmanship advertising and high-powered sales promotion. Better buymanship is the counterpart of equal and balanced contest in the market. The principles of "Wise Buying" are enumerated as follows:

1. A Plan for Spending

Very few people earn so much money that they can buy all they want without considering whether they have enough money to pay for all their purchases. Therefore, a spending plan is necessary. A spending plan is a guide for spending and saving. It is also called a budget. The plan helps a person to decide how much to spend and how much to save for a given period of time. When the actual spending is broken down into months and weeks, it should be checked with the spending plan to be sure that over spending is not taking place. The spending plan may have to be changed to take care of unforeseen problems as they arise.

It is advisable to plan one's needs in advance, particularly the more expensive items, to take full advantage of regular sale.

2. Purchase at Proper Time

One should make a list of items to be based on a family's needs and requirements before going to the market. Prices of certain goods are subject to seasonal variables. For example, cereals like wheat, rice, etc. are cheaper immediately after harvest as compared to other times of the year. Such items should be bought at such time when the prices are at their lowest. Tax structures on consumer goods are usually revised in the month of February/March every year during declaration of annual budget of various Governments. Though it is not possible for everyone to predict the proposed changes in the tax structure, but a well read, informed and prudent person can fairly guess the likely changes that may affect the prices of the commodities and accordingly he/she may plan to buy such goods. Even for daily shopping, appropriate time should be chosen for the right selection of perishable items like fruits and vegetables. Usually the prices are lower in the late evenings, when vendors are in a hurry to windup their stalls and before that intends to empty certain commodities for various reasons.

During periods of generally high prices, wise consumers avoid buying anything they do not really need. Wise consumers save their money and wait until prices are lowered. Of course, families have to eat regularly; purchases of food cannot be put off until prices fall. However, one can watch prices and buy the kinds of foods that are currently been sold at the most attractive prices.

3. Shop around before the Purchase

Shopping around before actual buying can save easily 20 per cent of one's income. It is desirable to have price comparsion study of the product in several stores. Consumer who shops around comparing quantity, quality and price get definite reduction in their purchase bill. One can save easily on all monthly purchases through shopping around. A careful shopper does this with interest.

Consumer should compare values and shop around. It is not advisable to spend more time and energy in shopping around to save Rs. 3/- on purchase of Rs. 50/-. One should select stores accordingly for certain kinds of merchandise and services and thus minimize shopping around.

The practice of shopping around will yield savings in the purchase of all types of consumer goods from automobiles to apparel. Those persons, who habitually buy at one store, form the basis, on what merchants call goodwill, which the larger store values more than the small time retailers in general. Goodwill is the probability that patrons will continue to make all of their purchases at the same store. Consumers who shop around, comparing quantity, quality and price form the basis for real competition.

It leads to the conclusion that one who wishes to be an intelligent buyer cannot restrict himself/herself to any one type of store or to any individual firm. The consumer who wishes to get the most for his money will take advantage of those price variations by making his purchases in those places where merchandise prices are lowest, and proper care is being taken for quality.

4. Always shop in person

Personal shopping alone makes possible an intelligent

buying. One may use the telephone to secure comparative price information, but it is not usually wise to use it to place orders. Still less desirable is the practice of sending children to stores alone although it is a good practice to allow them to accompany adult buyers so as to learn proper buying procedures.

5. Get the right information

The consumer should get required information from the manufactuers/shopkeepers about the commodity, as incomplete and vague information given in advertisements do not help the consumers in making proper decisions. These days there are eye-catching advertisements in newspapers, magazines and television, etc., which are more luring than informative. The purpose behind all such advertisements is fund raising rather than the guidance to the consumers. Manufacturers claim that their own products are purer, healthier and cheaper with better results than others. Claims are also made in superlatives quite often.

Hence, it is advisable to read labels carefully to see that they state definitely what the article is and what it will do. Watch for deceiving containers, such as boxes and bottles having false bottom. Many such containers, which appear large, contain little.

Consumer should insist on a definite answer from sales people and not an evasive one. One should refuse to buy articles, which do not show the name and address of the maker. Such articles are usually "seconds" or "defective ", and makers fear to be known.

Consumer should have adequate and up-to-date information. One can collect from consumer journals and newletters, from informative labels and advertisements and from other buying guides published in newspapers and general magazines.

6. Do not be an impulsive buyer

A consumer should also not buy impulsively. At certain moments while shopping a particular product appeals to his psychological instincts and he buys it, though product is not of urgent need, which exceed one's budget. Thus, a person should be a rational consumer and not an impulsive buyer. One should overcome impulsive buying habit and should not be influenced by customs, fashions, invitations, advertisements and other selling methods.

Consumer should keep in mind the amount needed and should not buy just to get a better price, more than one can use. Average consumer buys on impulse on at least 50 per cent occasions. The sellers exploit the buyer's tendency to purchase impulsively. One should be aware of impulse purchase traps.

7. Always buy in bulk

People who buy in smaller quantities usually pay more than those who buy in larger quantities. Besides buying in larger quantities, it is often possible to buy more units at a reduced price, for example, one unit might be sold for Rs. 10/-, two for Rs. 18/-and three even for Rs. 25/-. But buying more than needed or a larger size than can be used without waste is not economical.

While buying normal supplies, careful buyer can buy in bulk and secure special price concessions in bulk purchase. Buy staples in bulk quantities and in larger sizes. Be sure that such goods will not deteriorate, or one may lose more than one gain.

Pool your buying, "Pooled" buying is increasing in our country. Several families can often make pool purchase and save money. Retailers and wholesalers can afford to sell more cheaply to groups than to individuals because their cost of doing business with groups is lower.

8. Be sure of quality, price, economy, value and quantity

The goods to be purchased should also be judged according to the right quality in relation to its use. While buying, one should identify the quality standardization marks like "ISI" on electric appliances, cooking utensils, and stoves, etc. "Agmark" on agricultural products like ghee, vegetable oil and "FPO" on preserved items like jam, jelly, pickles, squashes and juices, etc.

There are two extremes of thinking in regard to prices. One is that the highest priced item are the best. The other is that the lowest priced items are the best bargain. Neither viewpoint is correct. The price of an item must be related to its quality, quantity and its economy, and how it satisfies one's need and wants.

It is not true that one gets what one pays for. There is no correlation between price and quality. Seller wants consumers to believe that higher price means higher quality. Many things determines quality for different people in different way. For some people, beauty is what they want, for others long wearing economy is sought, still others want special features and facilities/conveniences such as a timer on a stove, zoom facility in cameras and TVs, full functional remotes in gadgets, etc.

What is quality? It may be many things to many people. In general it is a combination to design, colors workmanship, beauty, wearing quality, and economy. The best bargain may be the product that is the best buy for the money. Besides these one must also survey the market and then only should go in or purchasing the products at the right price after assuring the right quality of the product. Intelligent buying thus calls for preliminary information gathering. Check the quantity. Do not be fooled by the size of the package. Label points out net weight, measured or count. Find out whether the package is full or semi-empty.

9. Do not be taken in by sales techniques

A consumer who believes in the reliability of the shopkeepers can be easily cheated. A consumer should remember that a salesman uses all psychological means to impress the consumer to sell his products. He might go on praising his goods being durable, economical or suits buyer and so forth. So the consumer should always be aware of all such tactics played by the salesman and should buy the items only after identifying its genuineness and proper need.

Watch for lures and traps, deceptive labels, etc. Advertising is used to lure innocent consumers. The low priced advertised items may not be shown in the sales counters and the salesman may urge one to see more expensive item and persuade one to buy it. Buymanship helps one to guard against such deceptive and fraudulent sales methods.

10. Ensure Services

Price may not be the most important consideration in buying even when buying the well-reputed branded product. When buying mechanical or electrical equipment as well as many other products the main consideration should be given to obtain a product that will operate without trouble. However, when trouble occurs one must be sure that one gets good repair service. Thus, it is advisable to buy reputed and popular goods and service which have enough and accessible service centers.

11. Avail special sales and bargain

All retail stores have special sales during which price are lower than at any other time. Some sales include standard items that are kept in stock regularly. Other sales are clearance sales to clear out old stock of old styles, models or items at the end of the season. Some are sales of special goods brought in for the sale. In almost every community most stores follow a specific identifiable pattern yearly. For example out of season sales of merchandise leftover at the close of a season like Sweaters Sale in the month of April, School uniform sale in the month of August, anniversary sale as a special event to stimulate business. One should take advantage of such sales.

One should bargain for lower prices and other concessions or services. This is possible even under our price system. In retail trade, retailer would not allow himself to remain undersold. He is prepared to meet competitor's prices. Careful buyer must compel him to give price reduction directly or indirectly. For example, free home delivery or free installation. If one is to learn the art of buymanship, one must learn to bargain. There are several ways in which price reductions may be obtained.

(a) Reduction in the price : This is not as difficult to secure, as many buyers believe. By using exactly the same competitive weapons that businessmen use when they buy, price concessions may be secured. Normally the buyer should not hesitate in using these tactics for the seller will not cut his price to a point too low to cover his cost.

(b) Securing on indirect price reduction : It refers to an attempt to prevail on the seller to include certain extra items or services not usually included in the price list. For example, the buyer of an automboile may secure some extra equipment while the purchase of a household appliance may secure free installation.

(c) A shrewd buyer will attempt to secure an open discount from the retail price. The extent to which retail prices are marked up over wholesale prices may be studied. In many cases it is quite possible to secure through employer, professional, family or friendly connection a discount to a reasonable extent.

12. Adopt cash and carry system

Consumer should always adopt cash and carry system. Pay cash and avoid instalment buying unless the pleasure one gains compensates for the increase in the cost of the article. Credit costs more money. Cash purchases are economical and free from future worries. As far as possible daily necessities should be bought on cash at competitive prices. One should avoid the store, which advertises that it sells on credit at the same price as for cash. Such terms are unsound business and unfair to cash customers.

13. Check Bills

Most of the homemakers show poor "buymanship" because she is careless in checking the bills properly. Such practices should be avoided.

One should check prices and totals on the bills. There may be clerical errors in calculations and totals. One should also keep records and receipts of purchases. This will help one to protest and get quick redressal against their complaints.

No matter what reputation a store may have for integrity, it is important always to check additions and change. Even though there is no intent to defraud buyers, mistakes may occur, particularly in those cases where products are weighed on non-computing scales.

When one buys large quantity it is always more important to check additions even though an adding machine be used. The wise buyer simply must discard any sense of embarrassment at what so many people regard as pinchpenny policies.

14. Check guarantee and warrantee

All guarantees should be put in writing. Do not accept oral promises. Check who is giving the guarantee, the manufacturer or the seller ? The person giving the guarantee is bound to repair the defects. Check how the guarantee will work. Will the whole product be replaced, repairs made to the damaged parts only, or refunds made for useless parts? Are repairing charges included? Lifetime guarantees should be clarified as to whether it is attached with the product's lifetime or buyer's lifetime.

Conclusion

Thus, conclusions can be drawn that if the consumer's value

economy and saving of their money by adopting the practices of wise buying, undoubtedly it will help them to meet more number of their family goals by employing the saved economic resource ultimately resulting in a healthier and happier family living.

References

1. Betila, P. (1971) : Consumer Education. Malasia : The Selengor Consumer Association.

2. Bloom, N.P. (1994) : Misuse of New Technologies, Information in Advertising. Journal of Marketing Research. 59 (3) p. 157.

3. Bymers, G. (1992) : Seller Buyer Communication. Jouranl of Home Economics. 64 (2) p. 59.

4. Cooper, J. (1986) : Consumer Education Topics in Home Economics. London Oxford University Press.

5. Dawar, N. (1994) : Consumer Use of Brand Name, Price Physical Appearance as Signals of Product Quality Journal of Marketing Research. 58 (2) p. 124.

6. D' Souza, M. (1990) : The Indian Consumers : A Sleeping giant awakes. The Independent Oct. 3, p. 10.

7. Eleanora, A. (1987) : Consumer Education Knowledge, Attitude of Experience of Selected groups in Trinidad and Tobago. Dissertation Abstracts International. 47 (11) p. 1145.

8. Giorden, M. (1980) : Consumer Education–A Handbook for Teachers. Methuen and Co. Ltd. pp. 46-65.

10
Innovative Ways of Developing Excellence in Character

Geeta Sikdar, Counsellor

Introduction

Value education is the fine art of moulding the consciousness of children towards nobler and finer living. Any quality that a society needs becomes a value for it. Children should not only develop universal values such as love, courage and faith but also socially relevant values such as self-reliance, civic consciousness, environment awareness, tolerance, etc.

Today we expect perfection from our children in all spheres of life. But with increasing academic pressure, extra curricular activities and media involvement change in social life style, one is left with little time to inculcate the basic values in time. The result is the erosion of human values like truth, cooperation right conduct, peace, love, non-violence, respect for parents, elders and authority. etc. Which is leading to the decay of moral and social fabric of societies at a speed never witnessed in the history of civilization. The negative influence of the media like newspaper, films, T.V., Internet and videos is a reality. The need of the hour is to do some introspection and implement means and methods to combat the menace of these external forces.

The problem of teaching human value is as easy to understand, as it is difficult to teach. Let us accept the fact that most of the times we see the mistakes of others and turn a blind eye to our own. This is not due to modernisation or technological development but due to our own pride, ambition and self-righteousness.

At this juncture, I am tempted to share a poem written by "Miplred Howland", which goes as follows:

How shall we teach
A child to reach
Beyond himself and touch the stars
We who have stooped so much?
How shall we tell a child to dwell with honour,
Live and die for truth
We who have lived a lie?
How shall we say
To him the way of life is through the gate of Love
We who have learned to hate?
How shall we dare
To teach him prayer
And turn him towards the way of faith
We who no longer pray?

The Need

Now we accept that the ultimate disease of our time is valuelessness. In the adult's world newspapers are full of reports of bride burning, homicides, kidnapping, demand for ransom, corruption and what not? Classroom teachers face problems of disobedience, lack of respect for others and their bodies, abusive demeaning language, inability to make responsible choices, low self-esteem, self-confidence and self-motivation. One can even observe the inability to work through challenges personal interpersonal and academic. We the adults of today, during our childhood had in our home environment, subconscious purveyors of everyday human values in the form of mother, grandparents, uncles and aunts who either lived under one roof or were neighbours. They conveyed various values through songs, stories, and parables, etc. To what extent and intensity were we exposed to values that are totally foreign to our own culture and upbringing? Today the scenario is different. Our future adults, the children of today, do not seem to have the advantage of strong family culture. The traditional teachers of human values are no more accessible to our children as working mothers seek their fulfillment in life outside the house environment. Also young couples with children find it more convenient and fashionable to live away from their parents and in-laws making only occasional visits to fulfill their familial obligations. Local maids, day care centres, neighbours (if they oblige) thus becomes the substitute purveyors of family love and human values for good part of the daily life of modern children. Moreover, one cannot ignore the fact that TV, VCR and computers have a frightening control over our lives. The hours children spend in front of these machines have tremendous influence on the tender minds. Would we allow any couple to come into our home, make passionate love in our living room in front of our children? Our minds shudder at the very thought yet it is happening everyday in our living rooms through the medium of TV and VCP. The adults watch with interest, the children with awe at this obviously modern behaviour pattern. Every possible deviation of human character is portrayed. Children rebelling against parents, husbands being unfaithful to wives and vice-versa, pre-teenage romances, hitting, lying, disrespect, violence and bitterness in relationship, etc. Since the young mind of the children observe everything like a sponge, the visual projection on the TV screen, by the much loved and admired actors seems to them as the normal accepted behaviour. It is here that we as parents and teachers should realize the need for effective moral value based development of our children.

The Method

Human nature being diverse and attention or interest span of children being short and fast changing it becomes essential to design a wide variety of programmes and methods. Children are very good observers and excellent listeners. The communication we do with them, the words we use need to be carefully monitored. The school and home together should shoulder the responsibility of inculcating character-building values. The following methods can be integrated while teaching in classroom and can also be used in homely environment.

Story Telling

Teachers/Parents should read and then say in their own words with social expressions and body language to obtain the desired effect. Another engaging technique of story telling is the art of pantomime as you tell the story, invite a group of children to silently act out the roles and drama.

Quizzes and Questionnaires

Quizzes and Questionnaires meant to encourage thoughtful and honest answers, rather than what might be considered the right answers. Building trust between teacher and student is a must here.

Group Discussions

These help to give everyone the opportunity to express their opinion. Class can be divided into small groups with an appointed leader who has the topic to be discussed. A reporter can note down the points and later share with the whole class.

Play Writing

Suggest a theme for a play and divide the class into small groups. Let children plan an improvisation for ten minutes and perform their ideas without any script. This can lead to a play being scripted by one or two members of the group, including the suggestion given by those in the audience.

Play Reading

This can be very effective if the cast sits in front of the class and each character stands when on stage and sits when off. No action need to be done but a narrator should be appointed to read the main stage directions.

Conscious Cueing

In cueing the child tries to relate actual experiences, challenges and conflicts the child is currently facing. For example.

Ask: "Today if someone teases you and calls you names what will you choose to do ?

— Tease him and hurt him back ?

— Cry and tell others to go away ?

— Stay calm inside and pretend you don't even hear his words ?

Self -Assessment

Self-assessment inducing questions about a specific challenging experience the child is facing helps her develop two vital social emotional skills.

— Awareness and identification of feelings and emotions.

— Awareness and identification of behavioural and attitudinal choices.

The self-assessment questions can be open ended or with alternatives. For example,

When Ram teased you and called you names, how did you feel ?

When you teased the boy who teased you and hit him, how do you think he was feeling ?

OR

A boy at school snatched your ball away, how did you feel ?

Did you cry ?

Did you yell back at him and hit him ?

Did you run and tell your teacher ?

Film Shows

Some good films can be shown after which questionnaires should be given to the students to answer and discuss the film. It is sometimes helpful before the film to give certain points for the students to look for, without divulging the story.

Chart Displays/Bulletin Displays

Prepare a class display of cuttings and pictures to illustrate the theme. For example. "The world as it is". Have a map of the world and mark on it the places concerned with the cuttings and pictures. It helps the students if they are continually aware of what is happening in the world.

Acknowledgement

When the child has made sincere effort or progress in expressing the targeted quality, acknowledging and affirming feedback from a valued parent or a family member or teacher it is vital to the process of nurturing the new, positive behaviour trait. Thus, the more you 'catch' the child doing or attempting to do what is right-acknowledge it—for example. I saw you sharing things with your friend or I am happy that you are practicing to control your language.

Easy Writing

Relevant topics related to social values can be given according to age.

Collection of Pictures and Material

This can be done from newspapers and magazines to make a display of certain topics.

Art Work

Art work related to various themes/values.

Displays of Various Value

This can be on various things, themes and can be displayed

in the classroom or school corridor.

Conclusion

The growing concern over the erosion of essential values and an increasing cynicism in society has brought to focus the need for readjustment in the curriculum in order to make education a forceful tool for the cultivation of social and moral values.

The values we teach our children are their best protection from the influences of peer pressure and the temptation of culture. With their own values clearly defined, our children can make their own decisions. Today the question is not only how to raise children in a difficult world and what to teach them but how to balance the priority of children with the priorities of work and personal needs of parents in modern times.

Begin today, for a better tomorrow and save this planet from degradation and destruction. Creating unity in the world beings with a change in individual consciousness. Inner focus and introspection of self will be the beginning because ultimately it is the morality of the man that makes him or breaks him.

References

1. Dewey, J. *Theory of Moral Life*. Rinchart and Winston, New York, 1990.

2. Dhar Benulas. Moral values and intersubjectivity : A Phenomonological understanding. NBV.

3. Donaldson, G.A.A. & Marnik, G.E. *Becoming better leaders*, Sage, New Delhi, 1995.

4. Downey, C.J. Frase. L.E. & Peters J.J. *The Quality Education Challenge*, Coricuium Press. Colifornia.

5. Mishra, C.H.K. We are what we learn. *Journal of Value Education*. NCERT, 2000.

6. Ministry of Education and Youth Services. Education and National Development : Report of Education Commission. New Delhi, NCERT, 1977.

7. Rajput, J.S. Teachers in Search of New Perspectives, *University News*. 35 (30) pp. 1-5, 1999.

8. Sunita Chugh. Classroom Processes : Need for change. *New Frontiers in Education*. Vol. XXXII (1) pp. 33-37, 2001.

11

Value Education : A Challenge for the Millennium for Home Science Extension

S.D. Deshpande, S.D. Mujumdar, P.V. Deshpande and A.W. Vinchurkar

Introduction

Before switching over to the relevant structure of the proposed text, the writers of this paper do like to emphasize the referendum that education does not mean teaching people to know, what they do not know, but it means teaching them how to behave. The term 'behaviour' in turn gives birth to what is called as behavioural attitude which tends to exceedingly establish the relationship between learning and doing. The value education obviously constructs the long lasting bridge to abridge the invisible gap between the very objectives of education, i.e. learning and doing. The purpovise noble objective of Home Science Extension Education does not cause any deviation from any inherent and intrinsic ideology of moral values associated with philosophy of education to generate inquietitude.

The concept of 'Extension Education' states, "Extension education means the activities concerned with the training of the farmers and home makers and other groups serving agriculture in improved agricultural practices and marketing the various phases of scientific technology, related to agriculture and agricultural production and marketing. It includes the work which may be done throughghs, demonstrations and other methods for teaching improved agricultural practices and training of workers required for the conduct of these educational activities."[1] At the outset, the said concept of Extension Education depicts the considerations of different segments of agriculture prominently. However, this concept of Extension Education should not be treated in absolute consideration of agriculture, for agriculture is the fabric of various cultures, linked with human civilisation from an ancient age, and therefore, 'Home Science Extension' can not be isolated from the very concept of 'Extension Education', defined earlier. What is therefore, urgently required is to inculcate identified moral values, while we cope with instructional programme of 'Home Science Extension' for it is the felt need of new millennium.

It is with a particular sense of gratification that almost all Universities in India have been bringing subtle changes in the instructional programmes by introducing value based ideology, so as to make them more effective, more sound and virtually moral based to finally turn their physiognomy affectionate and self reliant in recognition. Our entire network of educational system since the recent past has been undergoing a radical change in such as way that every academic discipline is expected to bear the fruits of productive enterprise. In this context, 'Home Science Extension has to play a vital role with a view to ameliorating the situation as it is, the impediments coming in a way of creative walk over to reach the purposive propositions, viz. gender equality, familism, dignity of labour, vocationalism and collectivism, etc., which noble characteristic factors are taking cognizance of for the deliberations to be exchanged in the proposed seminar. The faculty writers of this paper, accordingly, have attempted to express orderly in unanimity the practical views to make a furious assault on painful agony on academic and social evils to pursue quality pursuits, required for renaissance in the field under question to cope with so called challenges of millennium.

Gender Equality

Equality constitutes the base of social justice. It envisages specific rights, like natural rights to all sections of community irrespective of religion, race, sex, creed, caste and colour. The struggle to establish equality has to be continued because there exists the perpetual inequality. "Apparently like fundamental rights, in general, equality belongs to those concepts that resist standardisation, while remaining open to a range of interpretations." Barker observes, "equality after all is a derivative value. It is derived from the supreme value of development of personality in each-alike and equality, but each along its different line and of its own separate notion." His principle of equality asserts that, "equality is the beginning, not the end."[2]

In the social context, equality refers to certain treatments and opportunities. The critical follow up of the concept of equality in modern age to be diagnosed on the basis of traditional criterion of equalitarianism. Felix E. Oppenhiem mentions six segments relative to practical approach of equality. These are "impartiality, equal shares to all, equal shares to the equal, proportional equality," unequal corresponding to relevant differences and to each according to his desert"[3]

Besides gender inequality, the precedence of inequality emerging out of uneven and unimpressive economic growth is widely experienced amongst distressed classes of human society. Further, despite women population in India subscribes substantial share to gross national output, their economic and social status in the harmonic society has been for years together jeopardized due to several limitations like fragility, marginality and inaccessibility which exist due to their massive illiteracy in general and considerable untouchability to professional academy in particular, prevalent specially because of frivolous policy affairs. The panacea to eradicate such evil of inequality is not other than the follow up of the appropriate technology.

Appropriate technology is not a uthopian concept, because it deals with practical reality. Appropriateness in technology is expected to generate fructiferous confidence during its implementation by the technocrats on one hand, and it be readily treated acceptable and not the tedious on the other by the users. "Any technology strategy therefore, should concentrate on preserving the rural bio-diversity by preventing it from plunder, and any technology prescription should in principle be pro-poor, pro-nature, pro-employment."[4]

"In other words, technology should be need based, self-reliant, poor-oriented, people-centred, employment generating, ecofriendly and culture specific."[5] John F. Kennedy said, "if a free society can not save the many who are poor, it can not save the rich." Mahatma Gandhi, an uncompromising votary of rural India wanted India to adopt its own path of development in keeping with her own realities and cultures, preventing people from parting from their creative lifestyle and noble customary belongings. This would certainly help to aim at our moto the right should learn to live simply, so that poor may simply live."

The development oriented research achievements and results of welfare exercises brought forward by faculties, attached to every academic discipline without any exception to Home Science must reach to the doors of deprived millions in demos to serve their lot with a view to brining them in a state of equality. The value education in the domain of Home Science Extension should therefore, focus an attention at culture preservation, ecofriendship, employment generation, while choosing an appropriate technology to cope with an attitude of creation of gender equality irrespective of races, caste, creed and religion. Under present circumstances, Home Science Extension Technology has a wide scope for promoting sustainable development which invariably requires ethical shift in favour of the poor and the nature.

Familism

Ever explosive rather than sporadic use of population despite family planning measures, both mandatory and voluntary in vogue, since the recent past has been taxing our limited land resources beyond imagination. Further, agricultural production being subjected to the law of diminishing return, coupled with high degree of risk and uncertainty, the food crises in India in years to come is bound to touch the sky height, if we fail to exhort and preach the importance of the reasonable biological standard of living, attainable out of an adoption of the comprehensive family welfare programme having prominence of family planning in it.

The faculty members, especially belonging to biological and social sciences should necessarily launch intensive instructional programme for apprising the inhabitants of the areas concerned about the delineation of benefit of sizable family living. The family welfare programme can yield healthy fruits of success, if women's participation is effectively sought in it. It is therefore, imperative on the part of Home Science Extension Workers to treat "Ideal Familism" as the nucleus in the dissemination of various innovative undertakings through Extension Education Cell, meant for females to vehemently fight fallacious fanaticism, hither-to directly or indirectly found instrumental in the victimisation of women and relegating them to subordinate position even in this era of feminism.

Mahatma Gandhi's social reforms could be well recogsised for his untiring attempts, he made in bringing about significant change in the then orthodox and traditional attitude towards women, responsible for their physical and social exploitation. Mahatma Gandhi said "I do not need to be a girl to be wild over man's atrocities towards woman...,I am uncompromising in the matter of woman's right."[6] Gopal Krishna Gokhale "disliked seclusion of women and was deeply interested in the promotion and spread of their education. The women were more religious minded and combination of ignorance with religion made them the willing victims of customs, unjust and hurtful in the highest degree and also the most formidable because they become the most effective opponents of all attempts at change or innovation."[7]

Since the better half of ourselves being women, it is apparently needed that all academicians concerned with doing something concrete to deliver good for them without much dilly-dally ought to dedicate themselves to search out evils paralyzing women's improvement and progress, and then they need to suggest ameliorative measures not only to improve their social and economic lot but make them free from all sorts of emancipation also for bringing them? In the mainstream of civilisation to be experienced through ideal familism.

Dignity of Labour

Alike specific economic ideas in his mind, Mahatma Gandhi had certain peculiar reservations in regard to social considerations, on the strength of which, he dreamt of creating of homogenous social society to preserve communal harmony irrespective of individualistic wealth variations. Gandhian ideology covering this noble thought, 'work is worship' indicates that his same philosophical considerations were greatly influenced by the principle of Ruskin and Tolstoy. This factual confirmation could be made from the assertion of Mahatma Gandhi himself, as he articulately quoted under the caption, 'Magic Spell of Book' in the 18th chapter of the fourth part of his Biography that he critically appraised the thoughts of Ruskin in his book, *Unto-this-last*. He further agreed that he desired to apply these principles for they being of practical importance in real life as they cope with

(i) Individual welfare is hidden in community welfare.
(ii) All works are of similar status and value.
(iii) Dignity of labour is to be monitored by physical devotion.

Gandhiji had firm faith in the dignity of labour. Physical labour to him was a man's dignity, his sacred duty and obligation. Gandhiji therefore, regards the demand for more leisure as dangerous and unnatural. Gandhian economic principle gives stress in the change in the standard of value. He emphasized the importance of moral and human values, as against the value of money and material wealth for he argued that life is more important than money. In his own style Bernard Shaw says, "the best definition of hell is a perpetual holiday."[8]

Vocationalism

Particularly, during post independence period, Educational Commissions and Committees, from time to time, appointed by Both Central and some State Governments, specifically recommended the introduction of vocational stream of education with a view to pruning unwanted youth crowd, knocking the doors of general higher education. This ideology of this Vocationalism had the legacy in the conceptual framework, associated with the movement of Buniyadi Talim, Gramodyog and Mulodyog, launched for rural reconstruction by Mahatma Gandhi and Acharya Vinoba Bhave. The ideology of Vocationalism, although indwelled tenacious tenet of self sufficiency, suffered a flippant decadence, for it was not implemented in letter and spirit.

Various factors which have been noticed detrimental in effective implementations of vocational education during last two decades can not be short listed. The present position in respect of original concept of Vocatioanlisation is not that congenial, but it is disarray, creating dreary trend amongst academicians. The reason behind this helm of affairs is that new constraints have very conveniently occupied their reservations to devastate this noble project of vocationalisation, meant for the uplift of academically and financially rested stationary class of proletarians group or rabble rousers section of the learning community. The detrimental factors, preventing vocational education to day are too many and of varied nature. The prime movers out of them dominating the scenario under proposition are: excessive growth of urbanisation due to massive exodus of rural population on urban fringe, decary of cottage industries, goodby given to dexterity of Indian historic heritage, universal acceptance of market globalisation, generated outs of unlimited liberalisation, imperfect rather than mythy perfect competition in both factor and product markets, and lastly the foreign culture, acceptance of which is meant to taste its piquancy non stopped. All these mishaps have defaced the physiognomy of our gentle living in Indian Civic Society. This disastrous appearance has taken such an ugly form that our integrated and amatory home system has been fragmented in to delirious housing. At the behest of the search of solace, the disgruntled youths have been entrapped by touchy tendencies, onerous character, scrappy living, burglary, bellicosity and obscenity, etc.

We have therefore, to dedicate ourselves within and outside the four walls of our educational institutions to preach energetic youth community, presently standing on devious way, the secular temper of mind, scientific method, secular religion and moral, dignity and equality of man, assimilation of races and culture, and lastly the social unity and brotherhood of mankind. All academicians including Home Science Extension Faculties therefore, have not to emulate with traditional system of education, but their task should be such that educational appeasements, characterized by mastermindness, noble behaviour and self sufficiency through self reliance to be cropped up through massive expansion of vocational education are accelerated. It should be emphasized that top of all values, the 'job Value' occupies the significant and super position. Vocationalism therefore has no substitute in existing state, for mere reason that Vocationalism is capable of providing substratum for minimizing involuntary unemployment, prevalent in Indian job market.

In this context, we do like to state that giving trade education through vocationalisation has become a time need which can be very well compiled by concerned faculties without any exception to Home Science's faculties. To stress the value of the 'Vocationalism', we prefer to quote Talmad (Hebrew) who says,

"He who does not teach his son a trade, virtually teaches him to steal."

Collectivism

The principle of collectivism is invariably important and needs to be critically followed for common community welfare, for it relates to proper distribution of assets and property attached to private sector. "Property is a social fact which alongwith other social facts must submit to the laws of progress. Accordingly, it may be extended, curtailed or regulated in various ways at different times."[9]

With a view to causing social justice and affording every one equal chance, economic prosperity and all round development, it is necessary to properly regulate the laws of inheritance. The communal property would be distributed to deserving producers who would use it for the maximum social benefit. The collectivism, overall requires special optimistic treatment so that it would rebuild a new type of social organisation in which all economic activities shall be controlled and directed by competent authorized hand. This type of administration for the use of property in question is necessary as elimination of the parasites who live on the toils of others is mandatory.

Approach to follow up of effective collectivism can be had through constant preaching by Extension Workers to local leaders directly and to masses through voluntary and social organisations, which have been serving to the cause of uplift of distressed community. Home Science Extension workers best by virtue of their approach can do their network with masses in general and women's organisations in particular. The remarkable, success in this respect can be had with due consideration of the fact, man as he is and on this very logical aspect, customs, habits, work for pleasure and power, love of family and neighbours and such other ideal variables should be taken as means for operative part to generate effective collectivism as desired with its relative value.

Conclusion

Restoration of value education is really a challenge for the millennium for Home Science Extension, but it can be accepted if identified prime variable factors viz. gender equality, familism, dignity of labour, vocationalism and collectivism and subsequently segments of worthy life viz. health, environment, human rights, empowerment of women and specific values for home science students are treated on utilitarian grounds by concerned faculties and extension education officials through adoption of following measures.

(i) Adoption of appropriate technology compatible and based on specific cultural and economic conditions.
(ii) Means to be adopted for the purpose should be readily accessible to identified beneficiaries.
(iii) Ecological and environmental factors should be taken properly cognizance of.
(iv) Critical attention be paid to gender equality.
(v) Every innovative technique to be applied should be cost and energy reducing and must be labour intensive and capital minimizing.

In short, since modern information and communication technology provides uncommon opportunities for developing effective extension system, the existing extension staff is to be properly trained. However, retraining and redeployment and not retrenchment should be the pathway for development of impressive and effective extension system to reach the targets under proposition.

References

1. Maharashtra Agricultural University Act No. XLI of 1983—pp. 10378 (Item 'G').

2. "Social Legislations and Status of Hindu Women." Shailly Sahai, p. 14.

3. *Ibid*, p. 15.

4. "Defining Technology for Rural Development for the 21st Century." Dr. D.K. Giri Kurukshetra, p. 3.

5. "Defining Technology for Rural Development for the 21st Century." p. 3 Dr. D.K. Giri, Kurukshetra, October, 2001.

6. "Mahatma Gandhi: A Social Technocrat" ha. Su. Rengarajan. Kurukshetra Jan. 1999 p. 10. "Social Legislation and Status of Hindu Women"—Shailly Sahai, pp. 22.

7. "Gandhi's Economic Ideas", pp. 440 A History of Economic Thought K.P. Bhatnagar and Satish Bahadur.

8. St. Simon and the St. Sinonians History of Economic Thought, pp. 187. K.P. Bhatnagar and Satish Bahadur.

9. Budilal, R.A. Sethee Rao, M.K. Manju. Value orientation of farmers and their knowledge level and adoption behaviour. *Indian Psychological Review* 32, 15-25, 1987.

10. Chakraborthy, S.K. *Management by Values*, Oxford : Oxford Publishing. Co., 1991.

11. Singh, S.K. Farmers values in relation to commercialization on farms. Doctoral dissertation in Agricultural Extension, New Delhi, I.A.R.I, 1996.

12. Sinha, D. *Indian Values in transitions: A motivational analysis.* Associated Publishing House. 1977.

13. Peters, R.S. *Authority, Responsibility and Education*, London, Allen and Unwin, 1990.

14. Mckernan. J. *Curriculum Action Research*, London. Kogan Payal Ltd., 1991.

15. Nagpal, S. Humanistic Approach to Teacher Education. *University News* 35 (47) pp. 6-9, 1998.

Part II
Value for Women's Empowerment

12

Perception and Value Orientation of Undergraduate Girl Students Regarding Women Empowerment

Dr. Malaya M. Bora and Kamala Kanta Saharia

Introduction

In spite of social liberalisation, historically associated facts of honouring women in different fields of life and livelihood, mythological features depicting women as the goddess of power, wealth and knowledge, etc. highlighted stories on women every now and then, the constitutional safeguards and legal rights, women in our country in general and the society of the North Eastern Region in particular have been the victims of deprivation, depression, discrimination and dogmatism. No doubt that they are in different situations and not exactly comparable to other parts of the country by any standards, because the social systems, position of women in the society and their roles differ a lot. One simple example in support of the statement can be the fact that according to the 2001 census of Government of India, the sex ratio in the states of the region has not declined during the last one decade. Whereas, in the North Western states of the country, it has gone down from 95 to 93.7 per every 100 males. The single most important reason for such a happening is believed to be the result of foeticidal effect. Nevertheless, keeping aside the day to day status of women in the various societies of the country, the women in the North East are also handicapped by unequal access to political, social and economic affluence. They, most often than not, do not get any chance to participate in the process of planning, decision making, intellectual sharing of issues and facts, implementation of various planned processes and activities/evaluation and progressive adaptation to new ideas, thoughts and happenings.

The contribution of women to the family and to the society is viewed as secondary and in the pedestals of procreator, caretaker, facilitator and additional. They are yet to be brought handsomely to the atmosphere of political systems, literary world, network of social transformation and forceful entity of change agents. An environment is yet to be created in our surrounding where women can fully realize the rights and express their potentials. Under the backdrop of such a situation, it is important to know how the educated females (girls) feel about the concept of women empowerment and what thoughts they really harbour for the overall change of the situation for betterment. Keeping these guidelines in mind, a study on the perception of value orientation of undergraduate girl students regarding women empowerment was studied with the following objectives.

1. To know about the background information and social psychological make up of the girl students studying in the undergraduate classes, which are likely to influence their knowledge about women empowerment.
2. To identify the persons who influence them in upcoming and decision making process.
3. To map the perception and value orientation of the girl students relating to the concept of women empowerment.
4. To enumerate the suggestions put forward by the girl students to enhance, ensure or guarantee women empowerment in the society.

Methodology

A predominantly descriptive methodology was used for this study. The respondents of the study were the undergraduate girl students from Handique Girls' College of Guwahati, the oldest women college in the state and the students belong to different states of the North Eastern Region coming from different strata of the society. Their backgrounds are varied, social situations are far ranging and life habits are different. A pre-tested, reliable and valid interview schedule was prepared and placed before the respondents for data collection. The test-retest method was used in a nearby girls' college in the same city of Guwahati. The reliability coefficient was found to be 90 percent. Content Validity method was applied and in accordance with the Nunnally (1967)'s guidelines representative method of item selection and sensitive method of test construction were followed. The variables included in the interview schedule were (a) being hosteller or day- scholar, (b) from science or arts stream, (c) year of study, (d) education of parents, (e) occupation of parents, (f) annual income of the family, (g) total number of family members, (h) position of the family in the order of the children, (i) frequency of family get together, (j) social participation of the respondent, (k) most influential person to the respondent, (l) perception of the respondent on women empowerment, (m) value orientation of the respondents on women empowerment and finally, (n) the suggestions favourable to women empowerment. Fifty each students from science and arts streams were randomly selected and asked to give their responses on a structured schedule constituted of objective and open-ended questions. The respondents, both hostelers and day-scholars were to put their opinions instantly in presence of the investigator (the author). The collected data were transformed to objective data and they were put to different statistical tests like percentage, mean, standard deviation, 't' test, correlation and regression. Depending on the outcome of the statistical analyses, the results were placed in tabular forms and the important results were highlighted in accordance with their spontaneity of findings.

Results and Discussion

Social-personal and psychological background: Growth of personality and development of perception about various aspects of life are not the single day events. They are gradual and incremental. People because of their primary and secondary kinds of socialisation, which they receive in their homes and working places respectively, play a big role in building a person fit to the society. Therefore, the socio-personal background and the kind of social exposures the girl students get in their lives are believed to have some impact on their overall view to different burning issues in the world today, including the subject of women empowerment. The data obtained with regard to the socio-personal background and social participation of the subjects have been presented in the Table 1. While looking into the standards

Table 1. Socio- Personal Background and Social Exposure of the Girl Students

Serial No.	*Traits*	*Science Mean*	*SD*	*Arts Mean*	*SD*	*'t' value*
1.	Education (X_3)	4.04	1.05	3.48	0.91	2.85**
2.	Occupation of parents (X_4)	2.14	0.86	2.2	1.06	0.31
3.	Income of Family (X_5)	204140	74272	166940	100453	2.11*
4.	Family size (X_6)	4.92	1.26	5.42	1.53	1.79
5.	Position of the respondent in the family (X_7)	2.56	1.23	3.28	1.61	3.01**
6.	Family get together (X_8)	3.18	1.10	3.28	1.09	0.46
7.	Social Participation (X_9)	11.06	3.35	9.14	2.84	3.09**
8.	Influence of individuals (X_{10})	8.13	1.16	7.67	1.64	1.62
9.	Perception on women empowerment (X_{11})	21.02	8.03	22.1	5.2	0.79
10.	Value orientation (X_{12})	24.14	7.58	23.58	6.22	0.40

* $P< 0.05$
**$P<0.01$

of parental education of the girl students of Handique Girls' College, it was seen that all the parents were well educated. On an average, that is—barring a few, almost all of them were degree holders. However, in case of parental education of the science stream students, score was found to be higher than the parental education of the students of arts stream. That is while the average education level of the parents of science stream students was found to be more than post graduate (i.e., including some doctorate degree holders) in case of the parents of the arts stream student's the average education level was from degree to post graduate levels. Although the basic reason for such a difference is not known, it might be due to the fact that the better educated parents could guide their children in a better way and as a result of that, their children might have excelled in the qualifying examinations and got a berth in the science stream. When the scores were put to 't' test, it was found that there was a highly significant difference between the parental education of students of science and arts streams.

Similarly, the average yearly family income in case of the students of the science stream was found to be higher than that of the arts stream students.There was not much difference among the students of science and arts streams as far as occupation of the parents, family size of the students, frequency of family get together, degree of influence of different individuals on the students, perception of students regarding women empowerment and value orientation of the students on women empowerment were concerned. They could not show any significant mean difference as well. One feature to be marked here was the fact that there was a large variation among the income of the families of the students of the arts stream. This could be due to several reasons as students from different parts of the North East studying in the college and one of the major reasons being the fact that the parents of the students of the arts stream depended on business for their livelihood. When the data were put to 't' test, it again revealed that there was a significant difference between the mean values of income of the families of science and arts stream students. Highly significant mean difference between the science and the arts stream students also got revealed with regard to position of the respondent in the order of family members and social participation of the students. The interesting fact was that while the students of the arts stream on an average had a later position in the family (because of having more number of family members, though not to a significant level), the science stream students revealed more average frequency of social participation. It might be due to several reasons like the occupation of the parents, better education of parents and requirement of science students to get exposed to different scientific affairs of life.

Influential Persons of the Students

"The kind of family in which the children grow up affects their development by determining the kind of relationship they have with different family member. Not all members of the family exert equal influence on children. How much influence a family member exerts depends largely upon the emotional relationship that exists between that child and the family members", said Hurlock (1987). Assuming that depending upon the influence of different family members on the respondents their outlook to issues like women empowerment will be different, the study also encompassed the identification of most influential person to them.

The respondents were asked to place their response in an order of percentage of influence that they received from various persons around them including family members, relatives and friends. It could be seen from Table 2 that in case of girl students

Table 2. Frequency Distribution of Different Individuals Influencing the Respondents

Individuals	*Raw frequency Science*	*Arts*	*Average perceived percentage of influences Science*	*Arts*	*Rank*
(a) Grandfather	7	17	16	28	VIII
(b) Grandmother	12	14	24	29	VI
(c) Father	48	47	75	73	II
(d) Mother	47	49	78	82	I
(e) Brothers	32	24	40	32	III
(f) Sisters	26	20	37	32	IV
(g) Friends	25	15	35	22	V
(h) Relatives	15	7	23	15	IX
(i) Teachers	20	11	32	21	VII
(j) Any other	6	13	17	22	X

the science and arts streams, mothers were found to be the most influential person in their growth of personality followed by the fathers. While in case of science stream students, the frequency of fathers becoming more intense, it was interesting to note that their impact was less as far as the percentage of influence were concerned. Again, brothers were found to have more influence on the respondents in comparison to the sisters. In a way, friends (fifth ranked) and grandmothers (sixty ranked) excelling over teachers was a matter to be looked critically. While teachers standing above the grandfather, relatives and other persons in their influence on the students was a healthy sign, the reasons for teachers getting less rank might be due to the reasons like stereotyped educational system where they have little chance to exchange views except completing the courses, influence of different teachers in a single day, subjects of teaching at times getting obsolete considering the present day requirements and so on. The crucial finding of influential person of the girl students being the mother was of great importance looking into the subject of the study. It revealed the necessity of getting the parents in general and the mothers in particular educated to be aware of the issues like women empowerment in detail before teaching the girl students about the same.

Perception and Value Orientation of Girl Students on Women Empowerment

People living in similar situation, growing up in the same community and getting exposed to the same environment, because of their respective varying mental make up and some associated factors have different perceptions on the socially relevant matters. That is the reason why so much of hue and cry is made over issues of contemporary worth. An attempt, therefore, was made to study the perception of the girl students studying in the degree courses about the subject of women empowerment.

The students were asked to put their rank in order of their preference from high to low in a descending manner on nine perceptual variations relating to women empowerment. The Obtained ranks have been presented in the Table 3. A quick glimpse on the table revealed that neither all the girl students felt alike on the different perceptual components on women empowerment nor they responded on all of them. However, both in science and arts streams, the girl students perceived women empowerment to be "a social forum to fight against exploitation of women" in their highest order of ranking. Further, the intensity of such ranking was much more in number in case of the students of the arts stream. Fifty per cent of the total respondents gave their first rank in this perceptual component. This finding brings several hidden things into mind. As understood, women in the North-Eastern states of the country are much liberated, free from many social taboos and not the victims of many social crimes including dowry deaths. But their feeling that women empowerment to be a fight against exploitation meant that some degree of deprivation, Suppression or taking advantage of women were still there in the society, which were to be found out. The

Table 3. Frequency Distribution of Respondents and Their Rank Orders on Perception Regarding Women Empowerment.

Areas of perception	*Science (n=50) Rank orders*									*Total response*	*Arts (n=50) Ranks orders*									*TR*	*GTR*	*Rank*
	1	2	3	4	5	6	7	8	9		1	2	3	4	5	6	7	8	9			
(a) A slogan	-	-	6	1	1	4	7	8	7	34	1	1	4	4	3	14	9	6	2	44	78	IX
(b) A campaign	2	6	1	8	3	8	6	9	2	45	-	2	2	5	9	6	14	5	2	45	90	VI
(c) A need	11	6	9	3	3	6	6	3	-	47	10	6	2	6	6	5	3	5	2	45	92	IV
(d) A propaganda	3	5	3	6	6	11	8	1	1	44	-	2	1	5	13	8	5	7	5	46	90	VI
(e) A movement	1	5	6	7	19	6	3	-	1	48	5	6	3	15	9	4	2	1	1	46	94	III
(f) A social forum to fight against exploitation of women	19	7	8	2	5	4	1	1	1	48	25	8	5	5	2	2	1	-	1	49	97	I
(g) A useless activity	1	1	2	4	7	8	4	1	15	43	1	1	3	1	1	2	3	11	20	43	86	VIII
(h) A way out to gender equality	16	4	7	3	5	2	2	6	1	46	15	7	7	5	5	2	2	4	2	49	95	II
(i) Any process of alleviating the status of women	6	13	6	5	-	1	6	4	1	42	2	13	12	3	2	3	4	5	2	46	88	VII

finding was in accordance with the opinion of Sudha Rani and Surendra (2001). Similarly, their second rank was or the component of " a way out to gender equality" which surely indicated that women were not treated equally in the society. In both science and arts streams, the students behaved similarly on this component and the response was interesting to note that going by the maximum number of responses, women empowerment was perceived as "a movement" in the third rank, but third highest number of students ranked women empowerment as "a need". Going by a holistic approach, it could be stated that the realistion of the students was clear from the point of view that it was a burning issue and as such a proper redress was urgently needed. The healthy finding was that maximum students never felt that women empowerment was either a " useless activity" or "a slogan". It meant that the students did not take the issue of women empowerment lightly and in their ranking of perception, it got revealed that they felt women empowerment as a serious concern.

Similar approach was adopted to study the value orientation of the girl students on the issue of women empowerment. The students were asked to rank their opinion from higher to lower in order of their preference in a descending manner on eight areas of value orientation of women empowerment. The resultant ranking pattern has been presented in Table 4.It could be easily seen in the table that the response pattern of the students varied a lot and except one area, i.e., "self respect and equal opportunities in work conditions" in no other area, the respondents came out so emphatically. As high as 68 per cent in the science stream and 50 per cent in the arts stream, the students favoured the area as their first prefercence. It was a hard reality that the women in this part of the country in their work conditions never get the equal standing in all possible endeavours . Many social forces and ethos work against them and their working conditions. This finding was similar to the observation, "women not only deserve respect but also equal opportunities for realizing their potential in society" by Sinha (2000).

Relational Analysis among Different Correlates of Women Empowerment

In an attempt to examine if there is any relationship among

Table 4. Frequency Distribution of Respondents and Their Rank Orders on Value Orientation on Women Empowerment

Areas of perception	Science (n=50) Rank orders								Total response	Arts (n=50) Rank orders								TR	GTR	Rank
	1	2	3	4	5	6	7	8		1	2	3	4	5	6	7	8			
(a) Self respect and equal opportunities in work conditions	34	3	6	2	2	-	-	2	49	25	8	7	2	4	1	-	3	50	99	I
(b) Right to political voice	-	6	4	10	7	4	3	10	44	2	1	2	9	10	3	10	12	49	93	V
(c) Right to property and assest	4	7	9	7	6	6	10	1	46	2	6	3	5	7	6	8	-	37	83	VIII
(d) Freeness from male domination	3	12	8	7	6	4	5	2	47	10	8	8	4	6	3	4	6	49	96	III
(e) Access to law and justice	2	4	8	6	11	8	4	1	44	3	3	3	7	8	12	9	2	47	91	VI
(f) Elimination of social inhibitions and taboo against women	1	7	3	5	5	9	10	5	45	1	4	4	12	5	9	13	1	49	94	IV
g. Partnership in decision making process	2	2	12	9	8	5	4	4	46	2	11	14	6	5	5	2	5	50	96	III
h. Status of self reliance	1	5	3	3	3	13	6	8	42	5	7	9	6	-	7	1	6	41	83	XII

the different variables undertaken for study as influencing factors of women empowerment, the objective values of the different correlates were put to a relational test. The coefficient of correlation (r value) obtained from the analysis have been presented in Table 5. It could be seen from the table that few expected areas showed positively significant (P <0.05) relationship with each other. For example, day-scholars and having frequent family get together and respondents having higher number of their order of placement when there were more family members. More relevant findings from the inter-correlation analysis were that there existed positive and significant relationship (P<0.05) between students studying from their home and the occupation of the parents, better the occupation—higher was the family's monthly income; higher the income of the family—more was the social participation of the student, higher the value of the respondent in the family position—better was the perception about women empowerment. Similarly, two variables showed highly significant (P<0.01) and positive correlation with other correlates. First, higher the education of the parents—better was the occupation and higher was the income of the family. Secondly, higher the perception about women empowerment, better was the value orientation of the respondents. Both the later findings had far reaching implications. Because, when people find that better education is linked with better job and better income, there will be an effort to excel in life to ensure bright and secured future. Looking into the trends in the society that girls and women are gradually coming up in different walks of life quite emphatically, such a result is believed to be encouraging so that they get much more encouragement for better pursuits in life. Further perception and value orientation getting associated with more intensity revealed the very truth inherent in the subject of women empowerment. Persons with better horizon of understanding can only have better appreciation of facts and as such, the finding was quite encouraging in the sense that young girls should be made more exposed to various matters relating to women empowerment.

Suggestive Measures to Ensure Women Empowerment

At the end of the interview schedule the students were asked to give their suggestions so as to ensure, enhance or guarantee

Table 5. Inter Correlation Among Different Variables Relating to Women Empowerment

	X_2	X_3	X_4	X_5	X_6	X_7	X_8	X_9	X_{10}	X_{11}	X_{12}
X_1	0.075	0.043	0.219*	0.013	0.038	0.033	0.219*	0.107	0.079	0.085	0.051
X_2		0.152	0.085	-0.024	-0.028	0.085	0.157	-0.164	-0.162	-0.141	0.114
X_3			0.382**	0.374**	-0.112	-0.015	-0.050	0.090	0.008	0.096	0.076
X_4				0.203*	-0.095	0.028	-0.028	-0.083	0.130	-0.050	-0.004
X_5					-0.042	0.028	-0.064	0.223*	-0.016	0.181	0.101
X_6						0.650*	0.060	-0.183	-0.091	0.030	-0.183
X_7							-0.068	-0.149	0.143	0.041	-0.122
X_8								0.034	-0.082	0.232*	0.051
X_9									0.068	0.151	0.149
X_{10}										0.088	-0.057
X_{11}											0.296**

* P 0.05
* P 0.01

women empowerment in our society. It was in a way, not a very healthy sign that as many as seven respondents refrained from suggesting any measure's. As there was no order to be maintained in responding to the question and no restriction was given over the maximum suggestions they could write, many eye opening suggestions from the upcoming generation were expected. Nevertheless, the students showed their maturity by practically visualizing the issue and responded in nine major categories. While responding in their own way, they looked like varying a lot initially. But while similar responses were clubbed, only nine major areas were identified. The obtained data have been presented in the Table 6. For the reasons best known to the students from the arts stream, it was noticed that they were not coming up with much number of options of suggestions in comparison to the students from the science stream. In almost all the suggestions finally obtained, their frequency was much lower. Going by the serious concern of Government of India, the maximum number of girl's students also came out with the opinion that "education for women" is the best measure for women empowerment. As high as more than half of the total students made up their mind in favour of education. This finding gets the support from the opinion of Amartya Sen (2001), the Nobel Laureate, who recently expressed his opinion in a similar manner. Vijayapriya (2001) also gave similar opinion. The secondly placed maximum number of frequency was on "equal opportunity in decision making, public speaking and self respect." This findings again has the relevance with the existing social systems in the country in general and the states of the region in particular where women have not been able to get their share of attention with regard to decision making, public speaking and self respect. These findings were in accordance with the finding of Khemchand (1995), Gupta (2001) and Vijayapriya (2001). Economic independence and for that formation of some kind of a forum is of paramount importance to obtain justice in the society by any section. The girl students were right to identify "forming self-help groups for economic independence and income generating programmes" in the third place. This finding revealed two facets at the same time—economic reason is one of the major factors for discrepancy against women on one hand and many opportunities are coming up under the new format of

Table 6. Suggestive Measures to Ensure Women Empowerment

Sr. No	Measures	Frequency Science	Arts	Total	Rank
1.	Forming self-help groups for independence and income generating programmes	24 (48.00)	16 (32.00)	40 (40.00)	III
2.	Forming Mahila Samittee/Union/ Club/Organisation	10 (20.00)	3 (6.00)	13 (13.00)	VI
3.	Special court to deal with women related problems	6 (12.00)	2 (4.00)	8 (8.00)	VIII
4.	Motivation of women entrepreneurship, vocational training	13 (26.00)	5 (10.00)	18 (18.00)	V
5.	Education for women	36 (72.00)	22 (44.00)	58 (58.00)	I
6.	Equal opportunity in decision making public speaking and self-respect	25 (50.00)	17 (34.00)	42 (42.00)	II
7.	Protection of women from domestic violence	3 (6.00)	8 (16.00)	11 (11.00)	VII
8.	Equal rights in family, job opportunities and proper decision of work	23 (46.00)	10 (20.00)	36 (36.00)	IV
9.	Free from male domination in family and society	2 (4.00)	4 (8.00)	6 (6.00)	IX

Figures in parentheses indicate percentages.

rural development programmes and the respondents were aware of it on the other. This finding got support from Suguna (2001). All other findings were with minimum number of support. Interestingly, no respondent had said anything about reservation but they spoke about the right, which was a good sign and had tremendous value to be appreciated.

References

1. Azim, S. (2001). Gender empowerment—where does India stand? *Journal of Social Welfare*, Vol. 48, No. 2, May 2001, p. 9.

2. Gupta, K.N. (2001). Women's empowerment and protection of their rights. *Journal of Social Welfare*, Vol. 47, No. 12, March 2001, p. 22.

3. Hurlock, E.B. (1987). *Child Development*. Sixth Edition. McGraw Hill International Editions.

4. Khemchand, M.S. (1995). Beijing and Beyond. *Mainstream*, August 26, p. 28.

5. Nunnally, J.C. (1967). *Psychometric Theory*. McGraw Hill Book Co., New York, pp. 494-495.

6. Sen, Amartya (2001). Women's empowerment linked to education. *The Assam Tribune*, 15th November 2001. p. 5.

7. Sinha, M. (2000). Samaj Kalyan Chetna Parv-1999. The Twelfth Step. *Journal of Social Welfare*, Vol. 46, No. 10 January 2000.

8. Sudha Rani and Surendra, G. (2001). Continuing Education—A vehicle for Community Development. *Journal of Social Welfare*, Vol. 48, No. 4, July 2001 p. 17.

9. Suguna, B. (2001). Planning for Economic Empowerment of Women. *Journal of Social Welfare*. Vol. 48, No. 5, August 2001, p. 31.

10. Vijayapriya S. (2001). Attitudes of youth towards status of women. *Journal of Social Welfare*, Vol. 48. No. 3, June 2001, p. 8.

13

Opinions of Rural Home-Makers Regarding Women Empowerment Programmes in Ludhiana District

Gill, J.K. Sureinderjit Kaur, Dhillon, M.K.

The process of women empowerment is multidimensional. It enables women to realize their full potential, empowers them in all spheres of life. Women's empowerment, in fact, begins with the awareness about their rights and capabilities. So women's awareness about development is basic to her empowerment.

Women play a pivotal role for the overall development of the family, but still denied equal status. In order to give equal opportunities, improve their overall status, to remove various gender biases, the Government of India had declared year 2001 as women empowerment year and had launched many useful programmes for awakening women, who in turn could think of raising standard of living of their families.

Government had chalked out impressive programmes and enacted many laws to empower women. But how far these are effective and being implemented could only decide the success of such programmes. Keeping all this in view, present study is being intended with the following specific objectives:

1. To know the utilization of women empowerment programmes by rural home-makers.
2. To know the opinions of home-makers regarding various empowerment programmes for women.
3. To make suggestions for effective implementation of these programmes.

Methodology

The study was conducted in two blocks of Ludhiana district. Two villages, one each from two blocks were selected with the help of CDPO's (Child Development Project Officer) of concerned blocks. Thirty women respondents of age group 20-50 years were randomly selected from each village, thus making a sample of 60 respondents. The data were collected through structured interview schedule and analysed in simple percentages. Scoring technique was used to express opinions of home-makers. It was done by giving 3, 2, and 1 scores to agree, neutral and disagree responses respectively. The mean scores were calculated to express the results.

Results and Discussion

It is evident from the data presented in (Table 1) that in rural

Tabel 1. Distribution of Respondents According to Awareness and use of Women Empowerment Programmes

Programmers	*Yes*	*No*
Knowledge regarding:	11	49
(a) Declaration of year 2001 as women empowerment years.	(18.33)	(81.67)
(b) Importance of year 2001, rights of women	10 (16.66)	50 (83.37)
(c) Kishori Shakti Yojana	7 (11.66)	53 (88.34)
(d) Credit facilities for starting an enterprises.	0 (00.00)	60 (100.00)
(e) Women friendly technology for drudgery reduction	18 (30.00)	42 `(70.00)
(f) Sampooran Shikhsa Programme	10 (16.66)	50 (83.37)

Figures in parenthese indicate percentages.

areas few home- makers (18.33%) were aware of declaration of year 2001 as women empowerment year. The data further revealed that only (16.66%) home- makers were aware of rights of women and Sampooran Shikhsa Programme. There were only (11.66%) home-makers who were aware of Kishori Shakti Yojana, which aimed at empowering the teenaged girls. As regard the women friendly technology (30.00%) of women started using the same in their homes for drudgery reduction and hence improving the quality of life. It was observed that none of the respondents were making use of credit facilities for starting their own enterprise to supplement family income as they were totally ignorant about these schemes. Interestingly schemes like Widow Pension Scheme, Maternity Benefits and Girl Child Benefits were fully utilized by the women as these provide direct ecomomic gains to them.

Scores of opinions of respondents towards to women empowerment programmes are given in Table 2. The results

Table 2. Opinion Scores of Respondents Regarding the Women Empowerment Programmes

Statements	*Scores*
These programmes will:	
— make women aware of their rights	2.63
— help women in fighting against discrimination	2.55
— help in improving health of family members	2.33
— help in getting financial aid from banks	2.16
— enable the women to act as self-sufficient women	2.03
— help in strengthening family relations	1.96
— give women confidence to persue their goals	1.95
— help to improve the status of women	1.93
— provide equality of rights between women and men	1.86
— help to develop ability to make better decisions in the family	1.86

revealed that the respondents strongly agreed to the statements that these programmes make women aware of their rights (score 2.63) will help them in fighting against discrimination (score 2.55) and also help in improving health of family members (score 2.33). Whereas they disagree with the statements that these programmes will help to develop ability to make better decisions and will provide equality of rights between women and men. However, they had no specific idea about whether these programmes will enable women to act as self-sufficient. Similarly statements like help in strengthening family relation, given women confidence goals, help to improve the status of the women could get relatively low scores a terms of attaining overall betterment of the women folk.

Suggestions for proper implementation of these programmes were also invited from the respondents. The data pertaining to this aspect is presented in Table 3.

Table 3. Division of Respondents According to their Suggestions for Proper Implementation of These Programmes

Suggestions	*Yes*	*No*
— Government and Non-government organisations must play role for generating awareness about various schemes	52 (86.66)	8 (13.34)
— Expert guidance should be made available at various stages for improving quality and marketing.	58 (96.66)	2 (3.34)
— Training programmes for elderly men and women of households for changing their rigid attitude towards women work force participation.	56 (93.33)	4 (6.67)
— Training programmes should be conducted for developing entrepreneurial skills	5 (83.33)	10 (16.67)

Figures in parentheses indicate percentages.

The results revealed that the suggestions of respondents for better implementation of these schemes and programmes included provisions for expert guidance (96.66%) as the topmost priority followed by training programme for elderly to change their rigid attitude for women work force participation (93.33%). Empowerment of women also requires the participation and co-operation from men. We can catch up with the rest of the world through changing traditional mind-sets that accord women second class status in society (Jayanthi, C.). Further, (83.33%) wanted training programme for skill development, awareness generation programme (86.66%). All the respondents were of the opinion that these programmes if implemented in true spirit will definitely improve the quality of life and status of women.

Conclusions

Empowerment of women calls for strict and rigid implementation of all the programmes that have a bearing on their lives. Mere passing of laws and launching of welfare schemes have a little meaning for women.

So, it can be concluded that careful planning and implementation of women empowerment programmes on the part of the Government across the country with the cooperation of the civil society will go a long way in empowerment of women.

References

1. Jayanthi, C. (2001). Catching up with Education. *Yojna*. August 2001, New Delhi.

2. Singh, O.R. (2001) "Education and women empowerment" *Social Welfare*, April 2001, New Delhi.

3. Veerbhadraiah, V. and H. Shabanali Fami (1999). Empowerment of women for rural development. *Indian Journal of Extension Education*, New Delhi.

4. Bharati, T. Towards a new direction in women's education *University News*, XXXII (5), Jan. 31, pp. 11, 1994.

5. Gupta, R. Modernity in working women. *Journal of Psychological Researches* 36 (2) pp. 72-77. 1992.

6. Hari, M. Modernisation and Status of women and fertility. *The Journal of Family Welfare* 35 (4) pp. 67-69, Jun 1994.

7. Panigrahi, N.P. Gender inequality in India. *Yogana* 33 (12) pp. 1-15. July, 1989.

14

Empowerment of Women and Environmental Degradation: In Todays Changing Human Values Era

Amiteshwar Ratra, Shivani Bala and Neeti Sharma

All the vital inputs in any field of activity, whether economic, social, cultural, moral or spiritual, are provided by environment. It has been observed that our environment is getting degraded day by day mainly due to changing human values. Man's greediness has subjected him to live in danger and pollution which has made the air, water and food unfit for human consumption.

Environmental degradation has occurred due to uuplanned haphazard industrial growth, industrial waste discharges and factory effluents, increased and non-judicious use of fertilizers, insecticides, herbicides, agricultural and animal wastes.

As a result of degradation of environment, the agricultural production by women, their generation of income from natural resources, and their own and family's nutrition and health status has been adversely affected. Especially in the developing nations which have 470 million of the poorest people living in rural and urban areas that are environmentally degraded or ecologically vulnerable. The majority of this population can be found in Asia, where 60 per cent of that regions poor 327 million marginal farmers, herders and urban squatters live in degraded environments (Leonard, 1989). In most South Asian countries, the status of women is low and their socio-economic conditions are much more depressed than that of men (Chaudhry, 1996).

In India, while the constitutional and legal status of women is equal to that of men in all respects, in reality they suffer in all spheres of social and economic life. According to the 1991 census data, about 27 per cent of the rural women live below the poverty line. Regional variations and disparities alongwith environmental degradation is making women more vulnerable.

Poor women may be particularly vulnerable to environmental degradation because of their already heavy workloads, poorer health status relative to men and close dependency on environmental resources for their productive and reproductive responsibilities.

Poor household, regardless to the region they belong, must extend already long working days to maintain economic production in the face of decreasing fertility of agricultural lands, deforestation and reduced pastures and water services, air pollution and exposure to industrial contaminants increase their risk of infectious diseases, respiratory problems and cancers (World Bank, 1993).

Women perform a lead role in agricultural activities. Thereby environmental degradation vastly affects their empowerment. This paper presents the findings from a comprehensive review of the available literature on the consequences of environmental degradation on women. The discussion focuses on the potential impacts of environmental degradation on women and her income earning skills.

Women perform critical roles in agricultural and livestock production that are dependent on the availability and quality of resources such as land, water, forests and pastures. Women produce the majority of the world's food (Sivard, 1985) and contribute 60-80 per cent of agricultural labour in Africa and Asia and 40 per cent in Latin America (Russo *et al.*, 1989). Women agriculturalists are also decision makers in agricultural production, not only in sub-Saharan Africa (Moock, 1976), but also in parts of North Africa and Asia (Paolisso, 1995). In regions of Nepal, for example, women make 40-80 per cent of decisions regarding seed selection, use of improved seeds and fertilizers (Ahmed, 1987).

In developing countries women agriculturists are also responsible for the care of small and large livestock. For these women, livestock is a source of food for both home consumption and sale. In the hilly areas of India, where animal husbandry is the second most important source of income after agriculture, women consistently spend more time tending livestock than men (Kaur, 1991).

Women farmers may suffer indirect effects on environmental degradation when deforestation and desertification increase the time they must spend collecting fuelwood, fodder and water, reducing their time available for agriculture (UNASYLVA, 1990/91); Monimart, 1991; Rodda, 1991; Centre for Science and Environment, 1985).

Women rely on the collection of plants and animals from forests, rivers and marine habitats to help meet home consumption and income needs. Ireson (1991) found that, in load, women in Bolikhansai Province gather or hunt 141 different forest products, including food plants, medicinal products, household items and small animals for domestic consumption and sale.

Many rural periurban women collect and process a wide range of non-timber forest products. They perform activities like harvesting fruits, nuts, and medicinal herbs; home-based processing of foods, fibres, dyes and liquor; and making crafts for sale in local markets. These no-timber forest products can be major sources of income for poor women, particularly in situations where women have no property rights to land (Sontheimer, 1991). A survey of 100 women in Manipur, India, revealed that two-thirds of them collect minor forest products as their only source of income (FAO, 1987). Women in the Sahel also earn cash incomes from the sale of wild basbab leaves (Clous, 1986).

In Africa and Asia, the involvement of women in marketing fuel wood and charcoal appears to be growing. In India, many of the estimated 4 million head loaders of fuel wood are women, while in Ethiopia upto 70000 women around Addis Ababa depend on the sale of fuel wood for their livelihood. In the Sahelian countries the sale of charcoal is a critical source of income for men and women, with women predominating in its sale in urban areas (Rodda, 1991). In Male the small scale retail trade of fuel wood and charcoal is undertaken by women (FAO, 1988).

Small scale fishing enterprises and the collection of aquatic and marine resources is actively done by women. In the Philippines, they trade in marine products such as oysters, claims, and mussels (UNESCAP, 1985; Francisco & Israel, 1991). In Zimbabwe and Ghana, it is primarily the women who process the market fish (Ardayfio, 1986; Hunder *et al.*, 1990). In Colombia, women earn significant amounts of income from the sale of mollusks (cockles) they collect in mangrove forests (Denkelman & Daidson, 1988).

A study in Brazil, in the state of Marantao, estimated 4,00,000 rural workers make a living from the sale of the palm kernel and its oil. Women predominate (upto 86 per cent in one sample) in collecting and processing the oil-rich kernels for sale to local industries to produce lauric vegetable oil used for soap manufacture, feed cakes and other industrial uses (Hecht *et al.*, 1988).

One of the most significant factors determining whether women can profitably undertake any home-based, value-added processing activities is the cost in time money and efforts to obtain fuel wood (Molnar, 1993).

All these activities are highly dependent on natural resources. So that potential losses from environmental degradation is significant. Deforestation and the conversion of biologically diverse forest systems to directly reduce women's incomes by restricting the range of non-timber forest products available, as well as fuel wood for processing non-timber forest and other products for market sale. Overexploitation and contamination of marine and aquatic habitats will have a similar effect.

Changed Human Values and Environmental Degradation

It is of high importance to regard what all harm has occurred due to changed human values. The values of today's man has changed remarkably from the days of "Vasudevya Katumba" today man puts his needs in front and then may feel the other person's need. His greediness for more and more wealth and his striving to conquer the world has resulted in major environmental changes (degradation to be precise) in forms of deforestation reduced pastures, global warming and reclining ozone layers.

The human habitat has changed dramatically in past few decades, with more people moving towards towns and cities. The number as well as the proportion of the urban people living in slums and squatter settlements has been steadily increasing almost everywhere. There is increased problem of housing water supply, clean and safe drinking water sanitation, adequate food supply transport problem, clear and healthy air to breathe and the list goes on.

To meet the needs of the masses at large, the values of the people have changed. Environmental degradation can be reduced if not stopped by popularly making people aware of their losing hold on their values, once held very dear. There is need to bring change in the types of food intake, throwing up of wastes both toxic and home, use of proper gadgets to reduce pollution and proper disposal of industrial wastes.

Conclusion

There is a conceptional bias in the existing literature on women and environmental degradation towards women's responsibilities for providing fuel wood for home consumption. There is insufficient work done on how environmental degradation affects women's ability to earn income and maintain family and personal health. The activities done by women are so dependent on natural resources and potential losses from environmental degradation are high. Deforestation and the conversion of biologically diverse forest systems to less rich secondary or commercial forests, may directly reduce women's incomes by restricting the range of non-timber forest products available, as well as fuel wood for processing non-timber forest and other products for market sale. Degradation of aquatic habitat has also resulted in reduced capacity of women to make a livelihood.

Suggestions

1. Women should have direct access to extension services so as to improve their agricultural outcomes.
2. Women's access to credit should be increased to enable them purchase pumps or tubing to channel irrigation water to their fields.
3. Constitutional and legal provision should be made to make the women agriculturalists and the land owners.

4. Conservation of forests is necessary, not only to preserve wildlife and old plantations, but also to help the women to be able to use it for their income generation activities.
5. More studies should be done to present data on the degree of deforestation that women are experiencing or the actual costs of fuel wood scarcity in terms of income loss.
6. Studies should directly deal with the potential health impacts by substituting poorer quality fuels for scarce fuel wood on women.
7. Studies should be conducted to obtain data for degree of deforestation and the resulting changes in women's work patterns.
8. Studies should also deal with effect of deforestation and changes in women's health status and social activities participation. Longitudinal investigation across a wide range of environmental and cultural settings be undertaken.
9. Further, research on how gender-based differences in economic and social roles structure women's use of and dependence on the environment. Thereby, taking into account the resources women use, environmental hazards that threaten women's health and determine the losses in women's home production and income caused by environmental degradation.
10. There is need of multidisciplinary research. For the costs to women of environmental degradation extend beyond the research boundaries of any one discipline. Anthropologists, economists, extension workers, nutritionists, public health specialists, home scientists, social workers, and health scientists would benefit from expertise of the others in dealing with this issue.

References

1. Ahmed, Iftikhar, 1987. Technology, production linkages and women's employment in South Asia. *International Labour Review*, 126(1): 21-40.

2. Ardayfio, E. 1986. The rural energy crisis in Ghana: Its implications for women's work and household survival. World Employment Programme Research Paper No.10/ WP 39, Geneva, Switzerland: International Labour Organisation.

3. Center for Science and Environment. 1985. The state of India's Environment. New Delhi, India.

4. Chaudhary, M.A.1996. Empowering strategies for rural women in India. Kurukshetra. March : 18-23.

5. Cloud, Kathleen. 1986 Sex roles in food production and distribution systems in the Sahal. In Lucy E. Creevey, ed., Women *Farmers in Africa : Rural Development in Mali and the Sahal*. Syracuse, NY : Syracuse University Press.

6. Denkelman, I. and Davidson, J. 1988. *Women and Environment in the Third World : Alliance for the future,* London, U. K. Earthxan Publications.

7. FAO (Food and Agriculture Organisation). 1987. Restoring the Balance. Rome, Italy.

8. FAO. 1988. Gestion forestiere et a management desterroirs villageois dans la region de Kouli Kouro Phase II: Project No. GCP/ MLI/019/NET. Rome, Italy.

15
Women and Work-Values

Vijayanthimala Kodali,

Introduction

Value refers to a wide range of motivational phenomena. Any singular state or object for which the individual strives, or approaches, embraces, voluntarily consumes, incurs expense to acquire, it's a positive value. Anything that the individual avoids, escapes from, deplores, rejects, or attacks is a negative value. The concept of value expresses a relationship between a person's emotional feelings and particular cognitive categories. Values are thus cognitive in part and affective in part (Jones and Gerard, 1967 15a).

Recently Patterson (1989) observed how difficult it is to define the concept of value though the term is used universally. Value connotes both a perspective (what is good and should occur) and a proscriptive (what is bad and should not occur) judgement regarding the target of one's attitude (Feather, 1975). There are many definitions of value, but probably the most concise and useful (ef. Kelly, 1990) has been provided by Rokeach (1973) and defines that as "an enduring belief that a specific mode of conduct or end state of existence is personally or socially preferable to an opposite or converse mode of conduct or end state of existence".

Values play an important role at two levels, i.e., individual and social. On individual level, they are acquired due to interaction of one's own concept, status and occupational role whereas social level, they are acquired from cultural conditioning (Agarwal and Pachal, 1986). The main function of value is to establish standards which are necessary for decision making. The standards again are formed on the basis of needs, interest, beliefs, attitudes, personality and so on.

Because the values play a key role in shaping the individual behaviour and also the basis for decision making, the present research is an attempt 'to study the value pattern among the working women'. The study aims at studying the dominant values among the working women of different categories.

Objectives

(i) to study the difference between the high professional and semi-professional women in values; and

(ii) to study to relationship between demographic and socio-economic status variables with values.

Hypotheses

Taking into account the above mentioned objectives the following hypotheses have been formulated:

(i) there is a difference between high-professional and semi-professional women/with respect to their dominant values; and

(ii) there is a difference among women of high-professional and semi-professional with regard to the factors related to values.

Method

Sample : The sample consisted of 58 working women belonging to high-professional group (Group-1) and 74 belonging to semi-professional group (Group-2) from **Andra** University and hospitals in Visakhapatnam.

Procedure

A list of working women who are working in the hospital and the University were contacted personally and they were explained the purpose of the study. For assessing the values of the respondents, the scale prepared by Allport—Vernon—Lindzey was administered. The scale consisted of two parts—the first part of 80 questions and the second part of 15 questions covering six value areas like theoretical, economical, aesthetic, social, political and religious. The data was scored in accordance with the procedure given in the manual.

Result and Discussion

Table 1: Mean, SD and 't' Values of Two Groups of Women in Relation to Value Pattern

Values	*High Professional*		*Semi-Professional*		
	Mean	*S.D.*	*Mean*	*S.D.*	*'t'*
Theoretical	43.83	5.19	45.14	4.52	1.09
Economical	44.86	4.45	42.24	6.74	1.81
Aesthetic	37.31	6.57	39.32	6.70	1.22
Social	39.59	7.49	38.45	4.82	0.74
Political	42.14	6.22	40.95	5.04	0.86
Religious	33.10	4.27	34.97	6.88	1.28

Table 1 shows the comparison of value pattern among the two groups of working women. The Mean difference was tested for significance and the 't' values were insignificant indicating that the groups of women did not differ much from each other with regard to values. The predominant values in both the groups were theoretically followed by economical and political. The lowest mean score was obtained in religious value in both the groups. The value pattern was more or less similar in both the groups particularly in case of social and political values. This indicated that women as a group irrespective of their occupational status follow the same value pattern.

The data was further analyzed in order to find our role of demographic and socio-economic factors in values of high-professional and semi-professional women.

Table 2: Correlation Values Between Values and Demo Graphic Factors in High Professional Women

Demographic factors	*Theore-tical*	*Econimical*	*Aesthetic*	*Social*	*Politicall*	*Religious*
Age	-.15	.31*	-.10	.02	.03	-.002
Education	.03	.52*	.17	-.27	.04	-.180
Income	.03	.22	-.04	.04	-.03	-.16
Occupation	*.19	.28*	.06	-.26	.04	-.17
Order of Birth	-.16	.19	.09	.09	-.04	-.24
Years of married life	-.17	.36**	-.15	-.15	-.06	-.10
Type of marriage	-.02	-.08	.09	-.03	-.14	.13
Husbands'	.08	.27*	.12	-.23	-.13	-.09

(Contd.)

Education						
Husbands'	-.07	.47**	-.16	.03	-.04	-.14
Income						
Husbands'	.05	.39**	-.11	-.01	-.04	-.12
Occupation						

* P<0.05

**P<0.01

The above correlation table indicated that the correlation values ranged from insignificant positive to negative correlation. The exception being in economic values where most of the variables are related in high-professional group.

Table 3: Correlation Values Between Values and DemoGraphic Factors in Semi-professional Women

Demographic factors	*Theore-tical*	*Econimical*	*Aesthetic*	*Social*	*Political*	*Religious*
Age	.06	.03	-.13	-12	.01	.12
Education	-.05	-.02	.05	.09	.07	.02
Income	.05	.0002	-.16	.08	-.33**	.04
Occupation	.03	-.07	.14	.09	-.01	-.16
Order of Birth	-.13	-.35	.29*	-.12	.18	.06
Years of married life	-.01	-.05	-.03	+.15	.02	.14
Type of marriage	.15	.14	-.08	–.15	.16	-.06
Husbands' Educaation	-.11	.25	-.17	.27*	-.04	-.09
Husbands' Income	.19	.03	-.01	.04	-.25	.05
Husbands' Ocupation	-.01	.12	.03	.01	-.18	.05

* P< 0.05

**P<0.01

Table 3 revealed that none of the demographic factors were related to theoretical, economic and religious values in semi-professional women. But the variables like order of birth was related to Aesthetic value, husbands' education to the social value and there was a relationship with working women's income and her political participation. Thus, the values were influenced by demographical and socio-economic factors rather than occupational level in working women. The present study was similar to the conclusion of Pratap and Srivastava (1982).

Conclusion

1. There is no significant difference between the value pattern among the high and semi-professional working women. The predominant values in both the groups are theoretical followed by economic and political. Religious value obtained least mean score in both the groups.
2. Economic value is related to most of the demographic variables in case of high-professional working women.
3. Whereas, in semi-professional women, order of birth is significant to aesthetic value, husband's education to social and her own income to the political value.

References

1. Agarwal, K.G. and Pachal, T.K. (1986). "Moral Orientation, Existential Concern and Work Values of the Trade Union Leaders," *Indian Journal of Applied Psychology*, Vol. 23 (1) pp. 6-9

2. Allport, G.S. and Vernon and Lindzey, G. (1951). A Study of Values, Boston.

3. Bentlu, L.E. and Bergan, J (1991). "Value change in counselling and psychotherapy : A search for scientific credibility", *Journal of counseling psychology*, Vol. 38, No.1, pp. 16-24.

4. Feather, N.T. (1975). *Values in Education and Society*, New York : Free Press.

5. Jones, E.E. and Gerard, H.B. (1967). *Foundations Social Psychology*. Chapter-5. The products of socialisation - pp. 158-159, 1967.

6. Kellly, T.A (1990), The role of values in psychotherapy : Review and methodological critique. *Clinical psychology Review*, 10. pp. 171-186.

7. Patterson, C.H. (1989). *Values in counseling and psychotherapy, counseling and values*, 33, pp. 164-176.

8. Pratap, S. and Srivastav, S.K. (1982). "A Comparative study of value patterns of Technical and Non-technical employees". *Indian Journal of Applied Psychology*, Vol. 19 (2) pp. 51-55.

9. Rokeach, M. (1973). *The Nature of Women Values*. New York: Free Press.

16

Value Education: Empowering the Status of Women

S. Parvathi[1] and C. Karthikeyan[2]

Education plays the role as a means for human resource development for sensitising one's perceptions, awareness and for motivating and changing one's behaviour to suit arising needs, demands and opportunities for survival, growth and development.

Newspapers and magazines provide us with information. Formal training in school, college and university gives us the ability to convert information into knowledge and experience allows us to convert knowledge into wisdom. It follows that what is important as far as education goes, is the nature of information that is made available than the wherewithal for converting this information into knowledge. The curricula and the syllabi will tell us to what extent this information would be converted into useful and worthwhile knowledge. Therefore, from this operational point of view, the curricula, the text books, the teachers, the facilities available in the institution, and the environment of the institution from the point of view of values, are what would determine the status in respect of knowledge and values of those who come out of the system.

In human society, individual is the fundamental unit and hence one should be an embodiment of the intellectual values of rational thinking, scientific attitude and fairness, and the moral values of self-discipline, sacrifice and sincerity, honesty and integrity, gratitude and humanity, etc.

The present education is only a process which makes a person to develop himself as a woman or a man. It helps man to grow in all dimensions. The final result of education is a cultured person. But the long cherished human and spiritual values have suffered a set back in the cultured person. The present education does not guarantee a value based life.

A value can itself be defined as a belief which guides human behaviour and helps in making decisions about choices. Faced with many choices, man makes his decisions, based upon his personal values. In this process, value education has a very crucial role to play. Besides creating awareness, value education helps an individual to opt for choices which would contribute towards integral growth and ultimate happiness of the individual and the society.

Value education should focus on the following areas:

(1) To contribute intellectual, moral, physical and overall personality development.

(2) To make an individual to be a responsible citizen, their role and sense of responsibility towards society, family and the world around him.

(3) To develop the ability to distinguish between the right and wrong.

(4) To live in harmony with nature and the world.

(5) To create an attitude of genuine appreciation for the value and respect for all forms of life.

(6) To be aware of social problems.

(7) To be ready to accept leadership.

(8) To become human and learn to give more, than to take.

The process of education will not be complete without a value content.

In a value-oriented system of education values should be its centre, and they should constitute a centrifugal force with full control over the objectives, content, methodology and management of education. Further, in such a system, the benefits of education should reach beyond the four walls of the classroom to the adult population. It is important particularly in the context when only 52.21 per cent of adults are literate (1991 Census). It implies that in a value- oriented education, non-formal system should supplement the formal system. Once this concept is accepted needless to say that, there is an urgent need to revamp the entire system of education.

Education is thus the means to achieve the goals of progress and prosperity. Thomas Jefferson, former U.S. President once remarked, that Education alone can erode ignorance. One will, however, have to be very cautious and ensure that the content and process of education is strong enough to achieve its objectives.

Human value should be the major objective of education at all levels; and all other objectives of personality development, economic development, total employment, etc.

The close relationship between society and the family, results in certain norms, values and rules of behaviour which are required to be observed in all roles and relationships. These can result in either equity or inequity and affect, especially, the vulnerable groups in the family such as women and children, particularly the girl child. Thus, the problems of our society, such as patriarchy, have had an inexorable effect on the girl child, and consequently, not only on women but on women's role and function as decision makers and influencers in the family.

The status of women, in patriarchal culture, is the first major issue we need to consider as it is the root cause of several problems in the family and society. The early curricula in home science, in fact, stemmed from the patriarchal culture where women's role has to excel in the home such as child care, cooking, clothing and household management. Extension beyond the family did not arise as women's role was conceived within the four walls of the family. The status of women can be measured from the importance given to women's education.

Empowerment is to help a person to acquire self-confidence to become self-reliant and efficient to manage one's own affairs of life. Empowerment can only be acquired through knowledge and knowledge is power. The question before us is how an individual can acquire this knowledge and how the society could impart it to the individual. It requires diligent and proper planning and training. This should start from home.

Women should be given information on the suicidal policy of elimination of girl children through foeticide and infanticide and how it should be avoided.

How to achieve gender justice and gender equality should be taught. Awareness on social evils such as dowry menace, how to be self-reliant to face calamities if encountered in life, to accept responsibilities in life, never to feel inferior to others and to develop positive attitude to life should be created in their minds by giving example and precept. The necessity to be economically independent is to be taught to the girl children. The above aspects are to be taken care of both at home as well as at schools to empower the girl children, as they are our future hope.

Planned parenthood bulletin of the Family Planning Association of India published that the Bangladesh Prime Minister announced National Policy to promote "-equality between men and women in all spheres of life" she said "Nobody will give you your rights. You have to get them through struggle and fight."

To overcome the deficiencies governmental and non-governmental agencies should take immediate action. They are as follows:

1. ***Value education:*** Value oriented education to create environmental awareness, cultural heritage and ethics in personal and social life.
2. ***Women's equality:*** Promote the concept of equality of sex through elimination of sexual bias and ensuring equal participation of women in all walks of life.

The following important actions have to be taken to eliminate gender empowerment :

(1) Education must be made compulsory for boys and girls.

(2) Awareness among parents on the importance of education should be created.

(3) Human values have to be taught to the school children. Children should be taught to respect women and men equally.

(4) Training programmes on health education, small savings, developing skills etc. may be arranged by government and non-governmental organisations for women to realize their responsibilities and to develop character and personality. This will enable the women to command respect by their behaviour.

(5) Use of extension methods to create awareness, attitude change and provide information access as a means to empower women.

(6) Promoting developmental organisations for women.

(7) Providing a two -way linkage between the official agencies and the people (women) and as channels between the

originating and receiving ends of development programmes.

(8) Creating an environment for change by working with the women.

(9) To supplement government efforts so as to offer the women choices and alternatives.

(10) To make them self- reliant as far as possible.

(11) To mobilise financial resources from within themselves (women) with a view to making communities stand on their own feet.

(12) Organise propaganda, campaign, leaflets, posters, cultural activities, drama, folk songs, etc. to impart value-based education.

Conclusion

Education has a vital role to play in increasing the capacity of the family and the community for a better quality of life through the competencies they develop. Not only are they empowered through such competency based career development but, in turn, they can extend it through their work to the community and vulnerable groups, thus leading to social development, and particularly to the development of women through self- awareness and acquiring skills. It is worthwhile to create the awakening among women so that they can come up by taking care of themselves.

References

1. Arun Das Gupta, "Sharing Approaches that Work" *Span*, Vol. XXV, No. 6, p. 43, June 1984.

2. Srilatha Batliwala, The Meaning of Women's Empowerment : New Concept from Action–Population, Policies Reconsidered, UNDP, p. 129.

3. Singh Mina Revices : Crossing the Lakshman Rekha, *Manushi*, Sep-Oct. 1997.

4. UNDP Human Development Report, 1995.

5. Giri, V.M. *Emancipation and Empowerment of Women*, Gyan Publishing House, New Delhi, 1998.

6. Mitra, S.M. *The Position of Women in Indian Life*. Neeraj Publication Delhi, 1981.

7. Sujatha, G. *Status of Women at Work*, Hindustan Offset Co. New Delhi, 1992.

17

Women Empowerment Through Education

Bakhale Rupa, Kalra Nishi and Balasuri Geetu

Introduction

" Asatoma Sadgamaya, Tamaso ma Jyotir gamaya
Mtyyosma Amritam Gamaya"

(O Lord, lead me to righteousness from unrighteousness; from darkness to light and from mortality to immortality)

"The actions of man are the best interpreter of his thoughts."

-E.Lyall.

One of the challenges before a modern teacher is how to shape the character of youth as the best citizens of the nation, as well as to make them the persons of high morality gained high spiritual individuals. But a continuous deterioration and fall in values can be observed in our youth and people of the country. The existing higher education seems to be failure in shaping the character of the youth. N.K. Dutta said that " the values are the pillars of meaningful life and education is the tool which can bring a change."

Concept of Values

In philosophical context, values are those standards or a code for conduct conditioned by one's cultural tenents and guided by conscience, according to which human being is supposed to conduct himself and shape his life patterns by integrating his beliefs, ideas and attitudes to realize cherished ideals and aims of life (Dr. N.L. Gupta). Value is a "Conception explicit or implicit distinctive of our individual or characteristics of a group of those desirable traits which influence the selection from available modes and ends of actions" (Wuchohn, 1957).

All the known society has a value system - a set of rules and goals that guide its conduct and goals that guide its conduct and judgments. The business of social life proceeds on the assumption that the values established in the groups are the ones that must be respected and enforced.

Importance of Value in Education

Learning is not simply passive
But also active.
Is not only receptive,
But also constructive.
Is not only result oriented,
But also process oriented.
Is not only individual,
But also cooperative.
Is not only collective,
But also small- group oriented.
Not only extrinsically motivated,
But also intrinsically motivated.
Not only determined by the teacher,
But also determined by the pupil.

Teaching is not only systematic but also continual, not only related to the material but also related to the project, not only related to the subject, but also interdisciplinary open, not only controlled by the teacher, but also controlled by the pupil, standards and relevance to life. The role of education to promote humanistic outlook, sense of brotherhood and a commitment to ethical and cultural values needs to be reemphasized.

Teaching values through moralising and advising seems to be ineffective today, narrating stories has its charm only for the moment without any attitudinal change. The parents offer one set of values, schools project a different set of values, relation proposes yet another set of moralisation. In a world of confusions and conflict, we have to help our students to develop their own value system. This necessitates on the part of teachers to use various teaching strategies that facilitate the process of value development and value clarification.

India is known for its rich cultural spiritual heritage, and the need for a value system through education, has been felt and recognised through the centuries.

Present Status of Value System in Our Society

Education is a powerful instrument of social change and human progress. It is also a powerful tool to cultivate moral and spiritual values in an individual. Universities are the big educational institutes and hence the responsibility is directly imposed on them. It has not been ever seen in universities. Universities are the part of society or we can call them as mini society. These have their own value systems where most of the:

People talk much on values but do not follow them.

People want to earn money at any cost to make their life lavish.

People run behind the power.

People do not have a clear philosophy towards life.

People do not follow the norms of interpersonal relationships determined by the society.

People do not have faith in each other.

People resolve their personal difficulties. They are not bothered about others.

People are going away from natural life due to competition.

There may be several other things, which are focusing us to do so. Due to this, universities are becoming the targets of criticism. In past, the education was based on Tapa, Tyaga, Namrata and Brahmacharya and pupils worked under the guidance of Guru. All these things made their life meaningful. Today, we ourselves do not know, where we are going and where we are leading our pupils.

The Nationals policy on Education of 1986 has very strongly recommended the need for value education due to the following reasons.Tremendous advance in science and technology has resulted in a complete change in the lifestyle of people. Science and Technology is being used to produce weapons of mass destruction endangering the very existence of the human race instead of using it for the betterment of human life.... Erosion of traditional values.

Types of Values

Personal Values: What is enriching and good for the individual? These are practiced by the individual alone, irrespective of his social relationships.

Community or Social Values: ValuesWhat is good for the society? These values discuss the basis of the relationship of an individuals with other people.

Cultural Values: Values Which involve the survival of the culture. The practice of such values are very essential for the growth and survival of any culture.

Institutional Values: Values Which includes political, moral establishment values.

Status of Women

In the human society, as now organised, is an inherent block to women gaining equal status. The human society is hierarchically organised; the relationship is vertical; the ruler and the ruled; the boss and the subordinate; the senior and the junior; the one to order and the other to obey; even among equals one is accepted as more equal than the other. We have well defined tradition for the vertical relationship of unequal; but we have no legacy for the horizontal relationship of equals; it is still in the process of evolution. In those societies, where "the more equal" status of the husband is recognised, either implicitly or explicitly, the family atmospherse is free from tension and there is no break down. When women claim that they are equal, it is concended in principle; not seriously disputed. Equal status for women is granted to them by menfolk as a precious possession. It is meant to be cherished and preserved, not intended for routine use, but if they take it seriously, think of, and resort to practicing equality, there appear problems and breaking of families.

In general, the solution to the social, economic and political problems of human society is to be sought through appropriate education. Education is not a static phenomenon. It is an organic entity which is dynamic; it changes and develops to meet the demand of the environment and needs of the society.

Women's Empowerment

For more than a decade, the term 'empowerment' has been widely used in relation to women. Today, one hears this term much more often than terms like 'women welfare', 'upliftment,' 'development,' or 'awareness raising.' In many cases, the word empowerment has simply been substituted to describe the same strategies and activities, which were earlier, called 'integrated rural development', 'women's development', community or women's participation, 'conscientisation.' etc.

But, is empowerment merely a synonym for these things ? Or is it different ? If it is, what is this difference and what changes does it demand in strategy? The most important feature of the term empowerment is 'power". So obviously, empowerment is about power, and about changing the balance of power. In every society, there are powerful and powerless groups. Power is exercised in social, economic and political relations between individuals and groups. Power itself can be simply defines as control over resources and control of ideology. Those who have power are those who control material and knowledge resource and the ideology, which governs both public and private life, and are thus in a position to make decisions, which benefit themselves.

According to Paul Freire, "The term empowerment refers to a range of activities from individual self assertion to collective resistance, protest and mobilisation that challenge basic power relations." Empowerment, therefore is a process aimed at changing the nature and direction of systematic forces which marginalize women and other disadvantaged sections in a given context.

Thus, Empowerment is a process....not a product.

The outcome of empowerment would then be a redistribution of power, whether between nations, classes, castes, races, ethnic groups or genders.

So, let us be clear once and for all that women's empowerment, if it is a real success, does it mean the loss of men's traditional power and control over the women of their household; control of her body and her physical mobility; the right to abdicate from all responsibility for housework and care of the children; the right to spend family income on personal pleasures; the right to abandon her or take other wives, the right to take unilateral decisions which affect the whole family; and the countless other ways in which poor men and indeed men of every class—have unjustly confined women.

The process of women's empowerment will also liberate men: they will be freed from the role of oppressor and exploiter and become better human beings. They will be relieved of gender stereotyping, just like women. They will be free to discover, develop and openly express the so called 'feminine' traits within them which have been suppressed or disserted. They will be empowered too, in totally new ways.

Power and rights have to be demanded by the powerless and oppressed, for it is they who have something to gain. Just as Marx exhorted the workers of the world in the Communist Manifesto, we could say "Women of the world unite—you have nothing to lose but your chains." However, the process of demanding justice does not necessarily begin spontaneously, or arise automatically from the very conditions of subjugation. We would not like women's empowerment to result in more taking over men's power within same exploitative and corrupt society, women's empowerment should lead to the liberation of men from false value systems and ideologies to oppression. It should lead to a situation where each one can become a whole being regardless of gender and cause for their fullest potential to construct a more humane society for all.

At the very outset, it is important to state that there is no one magic formula, correct recipe or fail-safe design of empowerment. The entire process is so tentative and experimental, so relatively recent that we do not as yet have enough substantial evidence as to say this or that is the right way.

Psychological Changes Needed for Women's Empowerment

The process of empowerment begins in mind from women's consciousness, from her very beliefs about herself and her rights, capacities and potential, from her self image and awareness of how gender as well as other socio-economic and potential forces are acting on her; from breaking free of the sense of inferiority which has been imprinted since earliest childhood; from recognising her strengths, her knowledge, intelligence and skills; above all, from believing in her innate right to dignity and justice, and realizing that it is she alongwith her sisters, who must assert that right, for no one who holds power will give it away willingly.

Horroine Gutierrez describes the process of empowerment by emphasizing the synergism of four psychological changes:

1. *Increasing self-efficacy* : This consists of the control, mastery and ability to act. It also involves the courage to take certain initiatives. Thus, a woman should possess all these qualities of self-efficacy for self-empowerment.
2. *Development group consciousness* : Development of a group consciousness—'a sense of shared fate'—as the development

of a "critical perspective on society that allows individuals to focus their energies on the causes for their problems, rather than on changing their internal subjective states.

3. ***Reducing Self-Blame*** : A reduction in self blame follows raised consciousness which means that women should stop blaming themselves for each and every act. It may either be related to them directly or indirectly but women do say that, "This all is due to me."
4. ***Assuming Personal Responsibility*** : Assumption of personal responsibility is linked to a transition from passive subject to active participant.

Psychological Changes Needed for Society

Expand women's Horizons :

1. Society should access new information, knowledge and skill, and should equip women with the skills of accessing information, knowledge and skills of their own.
2. Enable women to identify issues for action : Society should expand awareness regarding new information, knowledge, critical analysis and should give power of decision making.
3. Formulate a vision of an alternative society : Include alternate models of social and economic relations and alternate development paradigms.
4. Strengthen women to struggle independently: for
   — their material conditions of existence
   — their personal lives; and
   — their treatment in 'public' sphere.
5. Formation of mass women's organisation: Society should encourage the formation of women's organisation at local, regional, national and international levels in order to bring changes in the structure and function of the society.

A woman's status in the family is the indicator of her status in society. Therefore, a change in the attitude of family members is of significance in improving the status of women in the family. Since the unit of attitudinal change in any society is the family, our best effort has to be directed towards understanding their attitudes and aspiration towards the status of women.

Indicators of Women Empowerment

Empowerment is an active process. Power is not a commodity to be transacted. Power cannot be given away as alms. Power has to be acquired. Once acquired, it needs to be exercised, sustained and preserved. Women have to empower themselves.

Government may offer welfare schemes for women. They may float anti-poverty programmes. They may launch projects for their upliftment. They may enact legislation to safeguard women's right. The government policies can only facilitate the process, reduce the hurdles and create, an atmosphere conductive to transformation. But it is the women who have to empower themselves unless they themselves become conscious of their oppression, show initiative and seize the opportunities. The empowerment mechanism is easily enumerated. We all agree that if a woman has all the following; she can reach towards empowerment:

1. ***Higher Education:*** There is no justification for men to deprive women or to deny them equal rights on the ground of their illiteracy; but education is essential for enabling women to uphold these natural rights, to improve them and to spread them; again, the true knowledge of self is unattainable by the millions who are without such education.

Men and women are of equal rank but they are not identical. They are peerless pair being supplementary to one another; each helps the other. In framing any scheme of women's education this cardinal truth must be constantly kept in mind. Man is supreme in the outward activities of a married pair and therefore, it is in the fitness of things that he should have a greater knowledge thereof. On the other hand, home life is entirely the sphere of woman and, therefore, in domestic affairs, in the upbringing and education of children, women ought to have more knowledge. Not that knowledge should be divided into watertight compartments, or that some branches of knowledge should be closed to any one; but unless courses of instruction are based on a discriminating appreciation of these basic principles, the fullest life of a man and woman cannot be developed.

2. ***Health Care:*** Health can be seen as a complicated web of factors, all of which are interdependent, and no one factor can be understood in isolation. Through the process of empowerment, women can improve their health status. With less expenditure of energy and with available nutritious foods, they may be in a better position to maintain and

improve their health. Women's education has been identified as the most important determinant of children's health. An educated women is also able to follow the small family norm, which in turn helps in national development.

3. *Legal Education :* Women themselves need to develop a self identity so that they can lead a life of security and dignity. This can be achieved by making them aware of their legal rights; and potentials. Legal education should be considered more seriously than anything else, because in recent years, crime against women has assumed giant proportions. Even facts related to figures on crime serve as an eye opener for home scientists whose activities are geared towards betterment of family, community and nation, keeping the women as their focus.

   Today's girls are going to be future women and they may have to face the world where the crime rate increasing day by day. This would also help to create awareness, understanding and sensitivity among them. Awareness of legal right among women and girls is nil, therefore they should be made aware and legal education be provided to them.

4. *Higher Age at Marriage :* When the age of marriage is raised, it opens up new choices like decision making power, maturity and so on. Several evidence suggests that women who start there childbearing at an early age are disadvantaged by educationally and economically for the rest of their lives.

5. *Economic Development :* Social reform legislation is good and to be worked for and welcomed. But all the good legislation will not make a good man or woman a free agent so long as he or she is economically under another's bondage. It is this economic bondage that is the root cause of the troubles of the Indian woman and for the removal of this our energies must be directed. The joint family system of Hindus, a relic of a feudal age, utterly out of keeping with modern conditions, must go and so also many other customs and traditions. But the ultimate solution lies only in a complete refashioning of our society.

6. *Adjustments in the Family:* The problems of accommodating married women with children in the developing structure of the labour market, in terms of part time work, flexibility over

hours, work at home, relenting after a broken career, and the possibility of starting another career after the children have reached school age, or are in other ways less physically or emotionally dependent on her, is one we now discuss in short, the domestic side of the women director's life, in so far as it impinges on her career.

First, however, it is necessary to consider women who do not fall in this category and whose very real domestic problems can be overlooked. In doing so, it becomes immediately apparent than their actual responsibilities, many of the distinctions drawn between single and married women on the one side and believers men and women in business on the other are misleading if not meaningless.

Inculcating Values for Women Empowerment

I. Development and advancement to women in management

Objective

To give knowledge and practice regarding management.

Values

— Home management, a joint responsibility of all members.
— Respect for the roles performed inside and outside the house.
— Equal commitment for work at home and outside by both sexes.
— Decision making process at all levels to be shared by both the sexes.

Can be inculcated through

— Making them practice the responsibility by staying in a house for 6-7 days. For each day make them perform different roles like that of father's, in-laws, daughter's mother's and so on.
— Making them prepare charts and posters on different roles that women perform.
— Students may be asked to collect the income and expenditure figures of their families and to relate them with each other, through a survey conducted by them.
— Discussions with students about their family roles played by each family members, their contribution to the family can also be held.

II. Empowerment through economic and social developments

Objective

— To make students self reliant, gain self respect and dignity among women.

— To create awareness regarding various agencies working for women.

Values

— Equal participation in the development of the nation.

— No dependence syndrome but women to be self-reliant, self-propelled and self-directed.

— Development of vocational skills and competencies for economic dependence.

Can be inculcated through

— Arrange training camps for self-employment, vocational/ technical, career related training, etc. so that they can develop skill and competencies for employment. Even on the job training in agencies can be provided to make students aware of the employment opportunities and to encourage them to be self-dependent and self-reliant in their future life.

— Interview an official of one or more service organisation to find out the contribution it makes for women empowerment.

— Invite resource people explain the function and purpose of some of the community and organisations.

— Visits to bank, post office may be arranged to enable their working and schemes made available by such services.

III. Education for women rights and legal awareness

Objective

— To make them aware about their rights.

— To give awareness regarding legal aids provided by various legal aid cells.

Values

— No degrading of women in matrimony such as bride price, dowry, sati, etc.

— Equal participation in the development of nation.

Can be inculcated through

— Inviting resource people to explain the function and purpose of some of the community organisations.

— Attend meetings of organisations and study their purposes and functions.

— Discuss ways in which girls and their families may

participate in community service projects.
- Organise public meetings in the locality to develop awareness of public on human rights.
- Give assignments to evaluate the state and national programmes on human rights.
- Organise exhibitions on different aspects of constitutional provisions and their violation.

IV. Empowerment through health care and family planning

Objective

- To make them conscious about better health care for herself and family.
- To make them aware of importance of family planning.

Values

- Acceptance of small family norms.

Can be inculcated through

- Visits to rehabilitation centres like AIDS, rehabilitation, leprosy, TB hospitals, etc.
- Conduct exhibitions on family planning and health care practices.
- Conducting workshops and expert talks for better health care.
- Develop booklets, books, cassettes, training and preparing street dramas about girl trafficking and helping these women and girls who are victims of trafficking.
- Develop materials to create awareness on girl trafficking and AIDS through stories and parody and organise training to prevent such things.

V. Education related to communication and modern technology

Objective

To provide theoretical and practical knowledge in the communication education.

Value

- Better communication and modernisation.

Can be inculcated through

- Conduct face to face communication methods and group dynamics.

— Use of information technology as it is a catalyst that transforms information into action and action into reality, generating spontaneously mass consciousness of the need for a fair and just society.
— Give training regarding typing, shorthand, computer, basic accounting, book keeping, public speaking etc.

VI. Education and Development

Objective
— To make students conscious about importance of education.
Value
— Higher education as an aid to material development.

Can be inculcated through
— Giving assignments to interview or make survey of women with different levels of education. List down the problems they face and then in the class discuss the problems and reasons behind those problems, and also try to relate them with educational level.
— Conduct campaigns on importance of education.

VII. Gender Training

Objective
To develop gender consistency and remove gender bias.

Value
— Challenging male attitude.

Can be inculcated through
— Prepare aids like charts and posters, on topics related to gender issues and hold discussions on gender training.
— Through field visits conduct activity to educate rural women for a gender training.
— Encourage co-education so that there is no gender discrimination in education.

Learning Experiences

Field Work

Teacher can organise field work to villages. These can also be organised in urban slums or areas where women are deprived. So that they can carry out their activities in such areas and help women to be empowered.

Film Show

Various films on women issues can be shown and a question sheet can be given to each student which contains few points of the film and how they will relate to the course. A discussion can be held on the questions and solutions present through a socio-drama, a play, a song or a panel discussion, indicating how it can be solved.

Celebrating Days

There are certain days in the year like women's day, mother's day, women empowerment day and so on. Such days if celebrated will create awareness and will leave impact on society.

Expert Talk

Interview an official of one or more service organisations to find out the contribution it makes for women empowerment. Invite resource people to explain the function and purposes of some of the community organisations. Highlight problems of women through expert talks. Councilors can also be appointed so that the problems of rural girls or women can be served, even experts in different fields like saving, investment agencies, etc. can be invited.

Internship

Internship can be provided to students in the government and non-government agencies, so that they get exposure to their programmes. Internship can also be given to students in the factories and industries so that they acquire skills required for the job and are economically independent.

Production of Teaching AIDS

Various teaching aids can be produced like charts, posters, flash cards, etc. so that ideas can be inculcated in the minds of the audience. Through posters one can also show the various roles played by women and have discussion on it. For example, mother cooking or father reading newspapers.

Visits to Organisations

Visits to organisations like NGOs and government organisations can be arranged. Meetings of different organisation can also be attended to study their purposes and function. Even visits to banks can be held to know their function and schemes provided by them.

Debates and Discussions

Debates and discussions on various current issues on women can be held. Teacher can initiate the discussion by illustrating some, day to day life situations and later she can invite the student to participate in this regard. Discussion on the social taboos, superstition, costumes and traditions as obstacles in women empowerment can also be held. Debates on a women's place in home can be organised.

Making Leaders

Women themselves are made leaders and given an opportunity to volunteer various functions. The experience given in the leadership field make them teach confident and them to exercise their power which ultimately leads to women empowerment.

Preparing Sketches and Models

Sketches and models can be prepared on women issues and on subjects like "The home, I would like to live in." The ideal home, joys of smaller family, etc.

Suggestions

For Women

1. Women should exercise their empowerment.
2. Women should know and value their own abilities.
3. Educated women must utilize their education for the development of herself, her family, society and nation.
4. Women should promote self-recognition and positive self-image.
5. Women should come out of the social beliefs and wrong practices and should uplift themselves.
6. Women should demand for equal rights and equal decision making power.

For Society

1. Society should promote co-education.
2. Education should be equal in value and status of girls to that of boys and thus avoid social discrimination.
3. Society should not practice the myth regarding women authority.
4. Society should promote women and should give equal space for decision making.

Other Suggestions

1. Networking of courses should be done so as to apply knowledge of one course to another.
2. Linkages of H.Sc. institutions should be maintained and strengthened alongwith industries.
3. Take help from industries while preparing the curriculum.
4. Intensification of practical and strongly building up theory into practical rather than theory in isolation.
5. Separate column in the daily newspaper should be utilized so as to make cartoons to inculcate women empowerment values.

References

1. A guide for developing a curriculum in senior home making.

IOWA - state of IOWA, Department of public instruction Des Moines, 1961.

2. Jane Stein; *Empowerment and women's health, theory, methods and practice*, ZED Books, London.

3. Social welfare, Women's Empowerment Parv 2001, Vol. 48, No. 3, June 2001.

4. Prospectus, Faculty of Home Science, M.S. University of Baroda Press, Baroda, 2000.

5. Bharati, T. Towards a new directions in women's education. *University News* XXXII (5), pp. 11-15, Jan. 1994.

6. Miridula Bhaduri. *Women in India : Some issues.* APH Publishing corporation, Darya Ganj, New Delhi, 1997.

7. Yoginder Verma, Education for Human Excellence. *University News.* Vol. XXXIII, No. 9, pp. 23-26, Feb. 1995.

8. Vohra, R. and Sen A.K. *Status, Education and Problems of Indian Women*. Akshat Publications, Delhi, 1985.

9. Sunder, P. Characteristics of Female Employment, Implications of Research and Policy. *Economic and Political Weekly*, Vol. XII, No. 16, pp. 863-870, May 1981.

10. Thomas, P. Indian Women through the Ages Asia Publishing House, Bombay, 1980.

18

NGO's and Women Empowerment

Mona A. Mehta and Asha V. Dass

Introduction

Across the world culture, countries, societies, families and individuals are experiencing dramatic changes. As a result, the individual roles in the society are getting transformed. The economic revolutions through industrialisation and globalisation influenced the individual to enter new occupations. The human child is born in a family within a socio-cultural context which is mainly anchored in the cultural myths, epics, symbols, folklore and history. Here education has a vital role to play. Educational opportunities for women brought transformational change in social, home bound and relationship dependent roles to enter into occupational roles with job, career and professional orientation. Entry into organisations generated aspirations, ambitions, achievements and experiences of success. It also generated self-worth, confidence and self-esteem. These women extend superhuman efforts to prove their capabilities and end up with responsibilities of both women's role as educationists and teachers have been acceptable, as educational institutions have been legitimate spaces for women to enter.

The UNESCO world conference on Higher Education (1998) examined the status-quo with regard to the major issues of women and emphasised the promotion, notably through the use of binding legal instruments, of the rights of women to full participation in all areas of social development to ensure that highly qualified women will participate fully in the decision making process of society through their roles in the government, in the community and in the family by strengthening their leadership capabilities. The key dimensions identified in this direction are empowerment, cooperation, equity, sustainability and security.

In the present scenario, education is perceived as a very suitable profession for women as nurturing and caring course natural to them. There is a shift in the conceptualisation of education and educational practices today. In the wake of the Industrial Revolution and mass production. The educational model was that of the factor- time schedules to be followed, syllabus to be completed, examinations to be conducted, student to be declared passed or failed, etc. Luckily, this model is being replaced with a more human and nurturing sort of educator-education relationship in the family model of education.

Transformational Change in Women's Role

Socio-familial context	Work context
LEADERSHIP	
Satisfaction	Roles
WOMEN IN EDUCATIONAL MANAGEMENT	
MOTIVATION	
Performance	Professionalism
Participatory Management ------Work Attitude	

Recent advancement of information technology be if in the cordless telephone, computer, fax machine, e-mail or paging, has freed the executive from having to be confined to the office for operational purposes.

"We must think positively about how the position of women in their own societies and in international affairs could not only be improved but also their large potential contribution be better utilized for the benefit of all."

-Kurt Waldheim Secretary General, UN, 1975.

Equal access to education for women and girls will be ensured, special measures will be taken to eliminate discrimination, universalize education, eradicate illiteracy, create a gender- sensitive educational system, increase enrolment and retention rates of girls and improve the quality of education to facilitate life-long learning as well as development of vocational/ technical skills by women.

Women specific activities continue to be important in bridging gender gaps and empowering women to participate in all spheres of development. The present study was based on voluntary organisations whose aims and objectives were to empower and upgrade different women's programme through their active participation.

Objectives

The main objectives of the present study were:

1. Empowerment of women to achieve their aspirations, self-esteem, dignity and fulfillment.
2. Develop women's capabilities, abilities and skills through training and education.
3. Foster understanding communication and provide support services to improve women's effectiveness in dealing with their roles.
4. Educating and motivating women in developing their skills to generate income.
5. Generating income to sustain the project and empower the women to meet their basic family needs.
6. To enable them to develop personal attributes gained from their employment.

Ways for Empowerment

There are two ways in which education and employment improve woman power.

(i) By imparting skills and
(ii) By generally raising the capability through greater discipline, responsiveness to challenges, conscientiousness, pride in workship, etc.

Methodology

For the present investigation, descriptive research design with interview schedule was thought to be the best and questionnaire was employed to collect data for the study. Simple random sampling was chosen as the mode for identification of respondents. Descriptive statistics of mean, standard deviation and percentage was used for statistical analysis.Canonical correlation and multiple regression analysis were applied for the present investigation.

Major Findings of the Study

There were 5 selected income generating activities carried out by 3 voluntary organisations of Baroda only. The number of respondents who were satisfied by the way the training was given to them and helped them to acquire certain personal attributes from the training as shown in the table below:

Sr. No.	*Personal attributes*	*Frequency*	*Percentage*
1	Better confidence	83	69.2
2	Better knowledge	88	73.3
3	Better self-esteem	11	9.2
4	Better ability to socialise	111	92.5
5	Better problem solver	56	46.7
6	Better decision maker	50	41.7
7	Better planner	45	37.5
8	Better organiser	30	25.0
9	Better proficiency in the skill	50	41.7
10	Better use of time	90	75.0

The data revealed that majority of the respondents could develop good ability to socialise with others. This may be because the jobs required working in groups and team work. Also, there was a majority of them who found they could make use of time more fruitfully by working and earning rather than idling, gossiping, etc. or by remaining at home. A majority of them became more knowledgeable and also acquired confidence due to status gained by earning and participating in making the ends meet. Nearly half of the respondents acquired good proficiency in the skill which helped them to become better decision makers and planners as the job required selection and purchase of materials and planning for it and so it also lead half of the respondents to be better problem solvers considerably small number of respondents could become better organisers.

This may be due to their positions as workers not supervisors who may be doing the job of organising. A very small number could develop self-esteem may be because of their submissive role due to the gender in the family and society. It may be also due to lower level of education and job designation. The respondents gained many personal attributes due to their exposure to training and employment.

Conclusion :

These are not isolated problems falling under the purview of this or that discipline. Naturally any one discipline cannot claim to find lasting solutions to them. Their study therefore assumes an inter-disciplinary character. Disciplines like Social Sciences, Humanities, Education etc; all have something to contribute to this effort. It has to be a combined effort on the part of all these to conduct serious and in-depth study to find out the root cause of this malaise that has set in. The value of independent research efforts bereft of any political, ideological leaning therefore assumes great importance in this serious effort to rid our social life of this cancerous growth.

Suggestions and Recommendations

The last decade of the century has recognized that women's empowerment needs constitute a significant group in monitoring of education for all targets. Focus has to be on the qualitative levels to be attained through imparting education by the government and non government organizations for their development. This can be only resolved through concrete suggestions:

(1) Motivate students to do more researches on issues related to women's empowerment.

(2) National and International NGO's and agencies support can be enhanced through proper planning and congenial atmosphere as this cannot be achieved without proper support from all sectors.

(3) Attempts have been made to promote integration. The challenge therefore is to convert small scale experiments/ projects into a mass implementation programmes.

(4) Information Technology avenues may also be expanded to cover this group of learners. Internet facilities can overcome this requirement.

References

1. Dr. Annorett Bascamisa (1964) - "How Developmental are Voluntary Organisations" A paper presented in All India Conference on Tribals of India.

2. Chandrasekhar Raj Kumar (1989) - " A book on women's resource and national development".

3. Dayal Rekha (1987)- "Resource Book on women's development; cooperation with government donors and voluntary organisations".

4. Gansalves, S.L. (1989) - *Development and Voluntary Agencies* Vol. 3.

5. Dr. Goeta Usha (1986) - "Contribution of selected voluntary organizations on women's development".

6. Harichandran C. - "Let Voluntary Agency Play a Positive Role" *Yojana* Vol. 32, No. 12.

7. Irminia Mary (1965)- " A study of the reasons why married homemakers accept gainful employment outside the home in the city of Ernakulam, Kerala" Faculty of Home Science, Baroda.

8. Vijay Kaushik and Bela Rani Sharma (1998)- "Women Power and Development" *Encyclopaedia of Human Rights and Women's Development*. Sarup and Sons.

9. Dr. (Mrs.) V. Mochini Giri (1998)- "Emancipation and Empowerment of Women" Gyan Publishing House, New Delhi.

10. Sneha Joshi and Pushpanadham K. (2001) - "Empowering Women for Educational Management," National Policy for Empowerment of Women - 2001, Courtesy - Department of Women and Child Development, Ministry of Human Resource Development, Govt. of India, Shastri Bhavan (A 'wing', New Delhi.

19

Empowerment of Rural Women in Agriculture

P. R. Kanani, P. D. Verma & V. J. Savliya

The prosperity of a nation depends on the status and development of women. Women are the potential source to development as pointed out by our first Prime Minister Shri Jawaharlal Nehru who said that to awaken the people, it is the woman who should be awakened. Once she is on the move the family moves, the village moves and ultimately the nation moves. Thus, she is the main architect of change in the society.

Despite the fact that most of the agricultural operations performed by the women, nearly 84 per cent of all economically active women in India are engaged in agriculture and allied activities. They constitute one - third of the agriculture labour force and 48 per cent of self-employed farmers. There are 75 million women (as against 15 million men) in dairying. The women engaged in animal husbandry account for 20 million (as against 5 million men). Since, they have not been actively involved in the main stream of development and there is hardly any appreciation and recognition of their extensive contribution. By and large, they have remained as "invisible workers." The agricultural policy is still dominated by the false view that farmers are men and women are housewives. The farm women are generally neglected in farm decision process. The sole reason for such behaviour is that the empowerment base of farm women is very narrow. If we want to improve the agriculture sector as a whole, it is perhaps the woman who needs utmost attention.

The real issue therefore, is the need for comprehensiveness and holistic policy on women. The policy should consider social, cultural, and political factors that inhibit women's efficient participation in agriculture and allied sctors.

To empower the rural/ farm women, the proposed policy and programming should focus on the following:

A. Women as a Critical agent of Change

The following are the areas in which women can work as change agent.

1. Literacy Campaign

About 50 per cent of women are illiterate. The literate women can play pivotal role to over come this social taboo.

2. Decision- Making

Women can play a significant role in breaking male headed decision making process in agriculture, provided that they are exposed and trained through effective and systematic extension tools.

3. Extension system

There should be increased involvement of female extension workers to speed-up the effective communication between the extension workers and farm women.

B. Involvement of Women

Generally, decision regarding the activities requiring technical competency and money related matters are handled by male members. Since knowledge and economic independence are the parameters of women empowerment enhancing the technical knowledge skills and building greater access to the various resources will develop self-confidence among them and would automatically lead to their greater involvement in various agricultural activities.

The direct involvement of women in various phases of development projects such as planning, implementation and decision-making should be encouraged to share and reap the benefits of the projects effectively.

C. Decentralisation

This system was conceived in the hope that the bureaucracy will change its attitude and behaviour to fulfili the objectives of development and administration and to motivate the people to avail of the opportunities available to them through plans and schemes of the government. The constitution with special reference to the (73rd Amendment Act 1992 which came into effect on April 1993, makes villages the focus of development efforts and gives special importance to local communities in deciding priorities and programmes. It is a fact that one- third of the elected representatives at village, block and district level are going to be women provides the right opportunities for decentralized planning and programming as well as community participation for making an effort on poverty removal among women.

Decentralised decision-making powers can ensure accountability and sustained agriculture development. A community based monitoring system involving all acts of social change especially women should be set up at all level; village, block and district. Besides, women should be involved in determining priorities, choice and diffusion of agricultural innovations and decision-making process related to agricultural and rural development.

The factors of change would need to be empowered through training, awareness and advocacy. The NGOs could play a very crucial role in the process of empowerment as facilitators.

D. Organizing Women's Groups for Participatory Approach

The participatory approach is assumed to develop self confidence, competence and managerial capacity. It enables women to discover their innate potential. increase their aspiration level and mobilize their resources for productive purposes.

The aims of poverty alleviation and empowerment of women can be effectively achieved if the weaker sections of women could organise into groups for community participation as well as use their rights in various services related to their economic and social well being. For this training would become critical for building organisations of the weaker sections of farm women and undertaking essential social services promotional programmes, credit and loan servicing as well as leadership skills. Their creative potential shall have to be achieved by mobilising, expending and organising them through a participatory process. This would enable them to participate in various programmes as effective partners and articulate their hopes and aspirations.

Creating equal access to and control over resources and

products of their labour, attacking patriarchal structures in family and community, creating adequate opportunities and institutions for rural women / farm women's participation are some of the main concerns to be tackled when we consider the issue of empowering farm women.

E. Reorganisation of Society

The ignored status of women is the outcome of a variety of causes in which devoted values reinforced by traditional media and other socio-political institutions play a pivotal role. It is high time women's oppression has to be sensitized to accept the gender equality. Reorientation of society, reorientation for gender just society would require a radical transformation through awareness about gender issues and their importance in the well being of the community and society. The perception of the women would also need to be changed. To overcome this issue governmental and non-governmental organisations, formal and non-formal leadership, print and electronic media can shoulder this responsibility effectively. National level literacy campaign can also play a key role in raising awareness of gender equality. For effective feedback and monitoring, a dog watch monitoring mechanism has to be built to ensure the systematic progress towards this delicate social change.

F. Holistic Approach

Several exercises, programmes and studies have shown and confirmed that women can make, manage and do the things better for thier own society's development. Women as one half of the human population have had a tremendous role to play in the dynamic process of social change. The policy makers must realize the needs of the women as holistic and response to their problems should be taken into account, women's poverty as both a cause and effect of their backwardness. Poverty reduction appears to be the right approach for raising the status of women in general but alongwith these strategies, other schemes for promoting literacy, social awareness, better nutrition and health and social security etc. should be strengthened to improve the condition and status of women in India.

The farm women would need to get mobilised into sub-villages and village level groups. The groups perception about their health, nutritional educational and economic status as well as their needs should determine the mode and content of the services and interventions. This would enable them ot reduce not only operational cost but also opportunity costs for using these services.

The strategy should aim at changing society's attitudes for women, which in turn would improve their self-perception, institutional and legal environment, faster economic empowerment and improve economic generation opportunities. The ultimate outcome would be a gender just society, which will certainly shift share in country's development through the empowerment of women.

References

1. Committee on Status of Women in India (1971-74).

2. Department of Women and Child Development 2001. "Women's Empowerment Year" Delhi Ministry of Human Resource Development.

3. Kumari, R. *Women in decision making*. New Delhi, Vikas Publishing House Pvt. Ltd., 1992.

4. Malti, M. et. al. Value Orientation of rural women. *Maharashtra Journal of Extension Education,* 8 Oct. 1989.

5. Mathew, P.M. and Nair, M.S. *Women's Organisation and Women's Interests,* New Delhi, Punjabi Bangh. 1986.

6. Programme of Action. Ministry of Human Resource Development, Govt. of India, 1992.

7. Schuler, Margaret, ed. *Empowerment and the Law; Strategies of Third World Women,* Washington, D.C. OEF International, 1986.

8. Swarnkar, G.P. Women Participation in Rural Environment. Chugh Publication, Allahabad, U.P., 1988.

20

Gender Equality for Adolescents : A Pedagogic Value

Sangeeta Chaudhary and Bhamini Mehta

Introduction

The term value education brings forth three basic qualities of life that are considered as an essence of the cultural notions and beliefs. Gender equality, as a value, is a resultant of the recent phenomenon of development. It becomes a pertinent value in the contemporary situation because of the dynamics of modernisation.

Traditionally, the roles and responsibilities of an individual have been divided on the basis of construction of gender norms. But in the last few decades, people have started questioning. It has been observed that there is a visible change in the prescibed gender roles, with more number of women going in for attaining higher education and opting for gainful employment in the organised sectors. On the other hand, development has unfolded various issues of gender which were never considered before. The issues of marginalisation and disempowerment of women as a result of lack of recognition of women's contribution to the household and the economy has led to the evolution of the concept of gender and development to address equal opportunities for women [Bharin, 2000].

Meaning of Gender Equality

To understand the intricacies related to gender equality, let us first disintegrate the terminology. Gender is a socially constructed term depicting the various aspects of life. It connotes how a person will behave, expresses his/her emotion etc. It is embedded within the wider social context of kinship. The terms sex refers to the biological differences between men and women, whereas gender is a term/construct/concept, which is used to represent dominant and subordinate status of the human being depending on their sex. Sex is natural, whereas gender is a variable, it keeps changing from time to time, (Duke, 98; Bharin, 2000).

Gender Equality refers to the divison of labour based on individual abilities which in reality diversify people (Vianello & Slemenska, 1990).

Understanding or an egalitarian society lies on the basis of gender equality and for this it is imperative to recognize gender (GE) as an impinging factor on human life.

Gender Equality as an Important Value

Gender equality becomes an important value in the present context because, gender, as a construct has never been recognized by the society. The idea of natural difference has been forced upon individuals, which has a major impact on the development of the very conception of femininity and masculinity. Socialisation plays a very important role in preparing girls for submissive roles and boys for dominant roles in all spheres of life reflecting adverse consequences for women in the long run (Vianello & Siemienska, 1990).

In the wake of the new century women seem to have more opportunities and greater awareness, whereas the factual statistics show/depict a grim/depressive picture. The female-male ratio in India has trickled down to 927/ 1000. Apart from this violence against women, dowry deaths, cases of sex determination against females, etc. and other similar issues have been increasing (Bharin. 2000: Karkal, 1991). This has given rise to the present need to focus on gender and development, gender relation and makes one realize the lack of representation of women in the process of development.

The Intricacies of Gender and Inequality

The day a child is born, her/his fate is decided by the society on the basis of the genitals she/he does/ doesn't possess. The society moulds the child into the preferable stereo typical—normative standards of behaviour with a vicious cycle of deprivation and pain for the female child. Her very ability to reproduce makes her suffer by having lesser access to food, people and education and recreations and early induction into domestic chores followed by early marriage and motherhood (Karkal, 1991).

Socialism of the child is geared towards gendering the boy into a strong autonomous, self-reliant and if need be aggressive personality whereas the girl child is made to become into a self-sacrificing tolerant, nutrient and caring individual so that they can bear the tortures inflicted on them in the form of dowry, sexual abuse, domestic violence and inequality in all the spheres of life.

Gender Equality and Adolescence

Adolescence is the phase of life during which major changes in the physical, sexual, psychological, social and emotional arena's occur as well as there are changes in the social demands and expectations. In the process of meeting these challenges of adolescence, an individual gradually develops a philosophy of life and a sense of identity. In Eriksons's theory, the core concept is the acquisition of an ego-identity and the identity crisis is the most essential characteristics of adolescence. According to him, ego-identity is never "established"as an "achievement" as something as static or unchangeable but is a forever, to be revised, sense of reality (Chaudhary, 1999).

Thus, adolescence is the second phase of socialisation, the first being childhood, when the values and ideas concerning self and the society/others are imbibed strongly by the individual. It is during this phase that the adolescents are strongly initiated into their gender norms to suit the ideology of patriarchy. The study of Kumar, (1986) supports this by focusing on the traditional ethos in India, which separates boys from girls as soon as they enter the secondary level of education. Further stressing the concept of gender identity a study by Ryhal (1988) revealed that the traits like aggressive, bold, assertive, were associated to males and traits like beautiful, charming, etc. were highly associated to females.

This rigid acceptance of gender identity is explained/ enumerated by Bandura and Walter (1963) by the term "Identification", modeling of behaviour of significant people in the environment. It includes the incorporation of the models, values, beliefs, roles and attitudes. Thus, these notions of gender inequality are perpetuated unknowingly. This asks for a conscious effort to bring about changes in the thinking regarding gender an adolescence, is the stage when they are in the process of building their ideas, attitudes and values, which will last with them throughout the life as a foundation stone. Thus, it becomes imperative to create awareness amongst the adolescents regarding the basic issues concerning gender.

Gender Equality as Pedagogic Value

The education system like all other organisations, is very patriarchal because they are products of the same culture. For this "massive changes are required in thinking, in organisational structures and policies, in planning and implementing development programmes for real social change to take place." People have made efforts to bring about a change in the school curricula.

The Programme Experience

The present programme for adolescent children was originally conceptualized by Women's health, Training, Research Training and Advocacy Centre (WHOTRAC) a project within Women's Studies Research center of the M.S. University of Baroda which was further taken over by the Department of HDFS, Faculty of Home Science, the M.S. University of Baroda, as a part of the one research programme of the department.

The third year students of the Department of HDFS, as a part of their fieldwork course, implemented this package on the students of 8th and 9th standards in the various schools of Vadodara City.

This was the programme of "responsible sexual behaviour" among adolescents. It includes various concepts regarding self, self-concept, understanding of gender and the gender identity and roles related to that, as a major part of the package. The concepts were implemented through various games, exercises and discussions among the group.

At the end of each programme, the written feedback from the students had been received.

The present information has been gathered on the basis of the feedback by the adolescents.

Results

The feedback from the students had indicated that they have

a stereotypical notion about gender and sex. Almost all of them lack and does not posses an understanding of equalisation concept of gender and are provided with the stereotypical role models prevalent in the society.

The adolescents had shown their reluctance when they were exposed to the meaning and concept of gender and sex. The meaning were not readily acceptable to them, though they were told now these roles are not natural but socially constructed.

The students have rigid concept regarding role allocations in the family. For example, female are meant for cooking, managing household and looking after the children and males are there to take care of the family and earning a livelihood.

Students were carrying the preconceived ideas of inferior status of women than men. They consider fathers, job, outside work more important than mothers work at home. Alongwith this, if the mother is employed outside and earning for the family, even then her responsibilities were never given as much importance as for the father. It was so, because father's role is always depicted as more responsible, more burdensome and therefore more important.

When an effort was made to make them to realize regarding the role of women through discussions, it was found that indeed that was a difficult exercise. The adolescents not only denied but presented so many reasons and logics for their beliefs and ideas. In all the schools, this particular topic, used to gain maximum attention and participation from the students. The debates and discussion always continued for longer hours. The students initially always disagreed but by the end of the sessions, they were compelled to think about the women's role and responsibilities, which were equally important.

The experience at the various schools has really led to thoughtful situations and calls for developing a strategy to combat this misunderstanding of gender roles in the society. It was felt that adolescents should be given some exposure by incorporating these in their curriculum through various exercises by the teacher, developing the concept of gender equality.

The misconception regarding gender, sex, and its roles etc. might lead to further severe following concerns in the society.

1. Lack of understanding is occurring between sexes.
2. The disparity—difference is widening because of the

inequality due to patriarchy prevailing in the society.

3. All these may result in domestic violence, divorce, dowry, deaths, abuse, etc., which are malignant for sustaining any society.
4. All these are dangerous for the survival of the family unit.

Therefore the following suggestions can be taken for consideration to include the Gender Equality in teaching learning process during adolescence.

1. First, of all, teachers need to scrutinize for gender equality through various learning programmes and packages.
2. Rigorous parent education programmes need to be implemented advocating for gender education.

Last, but not the least, school curricula, needs a thorough reviewing. The topics of Gender Equality, apart from teaching them directly could be weaved alongwith various chapters and examples in the textbooks.

The interwovenness of these concepts, in the curriculum, would influence indirectly the adolescents to understand the issues related to gender equality in deeper sense which would definitely be reflected in their thinking and behaviour.

REFERENCES

1. Bhasin, K. (2000) Understanding Gender, New Delhi: Kali for women.
2. Bronfrenbrenner, U (1979). The ecology of human development. Experiments by nature and design. Cambridge: Harvard University Press.
3. Chaudhary, S. (1999). Television Viewing Pattern in Relation to Perception of Family Role Portrayals and Consumer Behaviour Among Adolescents. (15-18 years) An unpublished Ph. D Thesis. the M.S. University of Baroda.
4. Erikson, E.H. (1963). identity, Youth and Crisis, New York, Norton.
5. Karkal, M (1991). The Indian Journal of Social Work: Special Issue on the girl child, LII (1)
6. Kumar, K (1986) Growing up male, Seminar, 318, 21-23.
7. Ryhal, P.C. (1988). A study of sex stereotypes among school and university students. Indian journal of Psychology, 63 (1-4), 59-69.
8. Vianelo, M & Siemienska, R. (1990). Gender Inequality: A comparative study of discrimination land participation. London: Sage.

21

Financial Empowerment of Hill Women Through their Active Participation in Food Processing Units of Nainital District, Uttaranchal, India

Meeta Agarwal and Promila Sharma

Introduction

Women are important human resource for every household for their selfless contribution towards the development and progress of the family. Food processing is a sector with good economic potential for hill women. However, this potential should be exploited to the full with a forward looking strategy not merely as temporary income generation measures. Women workers in food processing units are either semiskilled or unskilled. These hill women are making various type of edible items like bari, papad, sauces pickles etc. These women are spending lots of their time in preparation of these food products, but unfortunately working conditions in which these hill women are working are very poor. Due to poor working conditions time spent by these hill women in making various items is very long. Since the food processing units of hill region of Uttaranchal, i.e., fruitage are excellent industries to provide income generation/ productive work to the women of hill and best source of income to the families of hills of Uttaranchal, efforts were made to suggest remedial measure to improve the working conditions of units so that large number of women of hills of Uttaranchal can be attracted towards these food processing units.

Table 1: Income of the Women Respondents

Sr. No.	*Family Characteristics*	*Women Respondents* 16-25 years (n=18)	26-35 years (n=12)	36-45 years (n=10)	Total N=40
1.	**Land holding of the family**				
a.	Landless (0 acres)	14(77.77)	07(58.33)	04(40.00)	25 (62.50)
b.	Marginal farmers (<1 acre)	01(05.55)	01(08.33)	02 (20.00)	04 (10.00)
c.	Small Farmer (1-4 acres)	01(05.55)	03(25.00)	01(10.00)	05(12.50)
d.	Large farmers (4 acres and above)	02(11.11)	01(08.33)	03(30.00)	06(15.00)
2.	**Monthly income of respondents (Rs.)**				
a.	500-800	11(61.11)	07(58.33)	03(30.00)	21 (52.50)
b.	801-1250	03(16.66)	02(16.66)	02(50.00)	10(25.00)
c.	1251-1500	04(22.22)	03(25.00)	02(20.00)	09(22.50)
d.	Mean ± S.D.	802.94 ± 283.65	866.36 ± 300.74	783.33 ± 277.76	846.40 ± 299.32
3	**Monthly income of the family (Rs.)**				
a.	1200-1500	08 (44.44)	05(41.66)	06 (60.00)	19(47.50)
b.	1501-2000	06(33.33)	04(33.33)	02(20.00)	12(30.00)
c.	2001-5000	04 (22.22)	03(25.00)	02(20.00)	09(22.50)
d.	Mean ± S.D.	1588.23 ± 365.51	1559.09 ± 36.93	1494.44 ± 407.31	1669.23 ± 673.26

* Figures in brackets represent the percentage

* N=sample size

Material and Methods

Descriptive research design was selected to find out income of these women respondents, and time spent in performing different activities. The precoded interview schedule was constructed for collection of data. The instrument prepared initially was distributed to a panel of judges for establishing its content validity. A pilot study was conducted to establish feasibility of instrument. Purposive-cum simple random sampling was employed to select the total sample size of forty women respondents from different blocks of Nainital district.

Statistical Analysis

Descriptive statistical analysis was used including frequency, percentage and mean.

Results and Discussion

Monthly Income of Women Respondents

Mean monthly income of the women respondents was Rs. 846. 40. Monthly income of the women respondents ranged from Rs. 500—Rs. 1500 per month. More than half of women respondents, i.e., 52.50 per cent were falling under the range of Rs. 500—Rs. 800 per month and very few, i.e., 22.50 per cent were falling under the range of Rs. 1251—Rs.1500/-per month. Mean income of the women respondents belonging to age group of 16—25 years was Rs. 802.94. Mean income of the women respondents belonging to age group of 26—35 years was Rs. 866.36. Mean income of the women respondents belonging to age group of 36—45 years was Rs. 788.33 (Table 1).

Time Spent by the Women Respondents while Performing Different Activities

As shown in Table 2 for carrying out the activity of washing average time spent by all the women respondents was 170 minutes, women respondents belonging to age group of 16-25 years were spending less time, i.e., 120 minutes, whereas the women respondents belonging to age group of 36-45 years were spending more time, i.e., 210 minutes, it was noted that average time spent by all the women respondents while performing the activity of peeling was 240 minutes. Women respondents beloning to age group of 16-25 years were spending less time i.e, 210 minutes, whereas the women respondents belonging to age group of 36-45 years were spending more time i.e., 270 minutes. It was found that while carrying out the activity of packing average time spent by all the women respondents were comparatively 'less than in other activities i.e., 45 minutes. Women respondents belonging to age group of 16-25 years were spending less time, i.e., 30 minutes than the women respondents belonging to the above age group of 36-45 years, i.e., 60 minutes.

Table 2: Average Time Spent by the Women Respondent While Performing Different Activities

Sr. No.	*Selected Activity characteristics*	*Average time spent in particular activity (Minutes)*			
		16-25 years (n=18)	*26-35 years (n=12)*	*36-45 years (n=10)*	*Total N=40*
1.	Washing	120 min.	180 min.	210 min.	170 min.
2.	Peeling	210 min.	240 min.	270 min.	240 min.
3.	Cutting	270 min.	330 min.	390 min.	330 min.
4.	Boiling	180 min.	180 min.	180 min.	180 min.
5.	Cooking	240 min.	270 min.	330 min.	280 min.
6.	Bottling	60 min.	750 min.	100 min.	78.33 min.
7.	Packing	30 min.	45 min.	60 min.	45 min.

N=Sample size

Conclusion and Recommendations

The research focused on financial empowerment of hill women through their active participation in food processing units. For analyzing this problem, we collected data from the procedure of reliable and valid questionnaire. From this reserach following results were obtained :

1. Mean monthly income of women respondent was Rs. 846.40. Monthly income of the women respondents ranged from Rs. 500 to Rs. 1500 per month.
2. For carrying out the activity of washing average time spent by all women respondent was 170 minutes, for peeling—240 minutes, for cutting—330 minutes, for boiling—180 minutes, for cooking 280 minutes, for bottling 78.33 minutes and for packing—45 minutes.

After conducting study investigator reached at following conclusions:

The food processing units of hill region of Uttaranchal are excellent units providing ample opportunities of income generation to hill women on one hand and on the other hand due to poor working conditions time spent by these hill women in various activities, viz. washing, peeling, cutting, cooking, etc. is very long. Therefore, there is an urgent need to improve the working conditions of these units so that large number of women of hills of Uttaranchal can be attracted towards there food processing units and enhance their quality of life, shall be improved.

References

1. Arahi, 1999. "The change of rural society and its revitalizing movement." *J. of Rural Planning Association* 18 (3): 1991-2000.

2. Abey Wardane, P. 1995 "Food processing in Srilanka. Do—it herself women and technical in motivation" pp. 275-297.

3. Asian and Pacific centre for transfer of technology A.P.C.T.T. 1997. *Worship on Small-Scale food processing technology for rural women May,* 3-5.

4. Bureau of labour statistic, 1990. *A report on the survey of occupational injuries and illness U.S. Department of labour* 92: 731-732.

5. Desai, N.L. and Gopalan, P. 1990. *Women food processors' work without reward*: Pandey, D. (ed). Before the farm and thali women and food processing, Bombay research centre for women studies, pp. 82-88.

6. Gopalan, S. 1990. *Women and Employment in India.* Ewha Women's University, p. 312.

7. Lyer, Lalita 1990. Overview of employment in the food drink industries. *Economics Survey,* pp. 99-114.

8. Krishnaswamy, L. 1990. Food Processing activity and self employed women. M. Panday, D. and Sarana, M. Between the farm and thali women and food processing. Bombay Research Centre for Women Studies, pp. 115-118.

9. Mehrotra, J.N. 1990. Corporate level and food processing. The Problems and potential for women. M. Pandey, D. and Savara, M. Between the farm and thali women and food processing. Bombay Research Centre for Women Studies, pp. 119-120.

10. Sahoo, A. 2000. *Food processing A boost to rural economy.* Kurukshetra. pp. 29-31.

22
Discrimination of Girl Child

Anita P. Patel

Women constitute nearly half of a country's human resource. An effective management of a country's human and non-human resource leading to their optimum utilization, is vital for its growth and development.

No society can progress if awareness and developmental urge are absent among the women. As compared to boys, girls have always been a neglected part of the family. The birth of a girl child does not arouse as much ado excitement as the birth of a boy. Scientific test as aminocentesis is being abused to conveniently get rid of female foetuses and like a forest fire, it is spreadcing fast among the various segments of our society.

A daughter is never regarded as a full member of her family and she is kept under much more discipline and restriction as compared to the son. Preference for son, this is increasing day by day and hence there is an increase in discrimination of girl child. Thus, it has become a matter of concern for the social scientists to examine the status of a girl child in the present socio-economic conditions who can act as a catalyst in the development process. Thus, the study was undertaken in this area to focus the discrimination towards girl child and the factors which directly or indirectly effects her growth and development.

The objectives for the present study were:

1. To study the factors associated with discrimination of girl child in the family, with special reference to:
   (a) Demographic factors (Family type, family size)
   (b) Socio-economic factors (income, education, occupation)
   (c) Personal factor of mother (age, education, attitude)
2. To assess the attitude of mother towards girl child.

3. To study the effect of selected variables on attitude of mother:
   (a) Age
   (b) Income
   (c) Educational level
   (d) Type of family
   (e) Size of family
4. To assess the extent of opportunities given to a girl child for her own growth and development.

Hypothesis was formulated to test the relationship between the treatment of girl child and attitude of mothers towards girl child with the selected demographic variables.

HYPOTHESES TESTED: DEMOGRAPHIC FACTORS

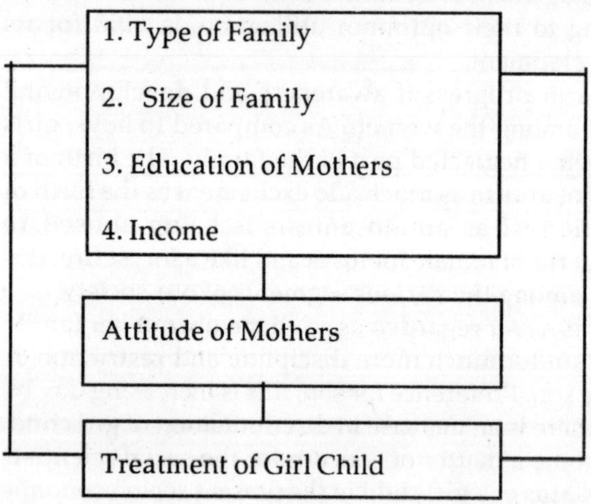

The interview schedule was used to elicit the data for the present study. The investigator approached each home personally having at least one girl child and one boy child and the homemakers who were non-employed from the three different income groups. The content validity and reliability of the instrument were already established. The reliability coefficient obtained was 0.90 which showed that the tool was highly reliable. The tool was pretested and necessary improvements were made. The data was then tabulated and analysed in terms of simple frequencies, percentage and chi-square tests to test the relationship between the independent and dependent variables.

Following conclusions were drawn from the findings of the present study.

1. Overall the study showed that extent of discrimination in treatment towards girl child observed in LIG was greater than that in MIG and HIG.
2. In the case of attitudes of mothers towards girl child, it was found that majority of the respondents in the LIG had negative attitude towards girl child and majority of the respondents in the MIG and HIG had neutral attitude towards girl child.
3. A striking difference in the treatment of mothers towards girl child was also found between low educated mother and higly educated mothers. Low discrimination was observed in highly educated mothers.
4. The discrimination in treatment of mothers towards girl child was also observed high in joint families than in nuclear families.
5. Low discrimination was observed in majority of small families and high discrimination was observed in large families.
6. Majority of the respondents had welcoming attitude towards the birth of girl child.
7. It was also found that there was positive relationship between the income and attitude of mother towards girl child. Therefore, it can be said that as the income increased, the attitude of mothers became favourable towards girls child.

References

1. Angndelakshmi, S. The female child in Family setting. *Indian Journal of Social Work.* Vol. 529, No. 1, Jan. 1991.

2. Deepika Vig and Paramjeet Nanda. Status of Women Maternal Attitude Towards Girl Child. *Social Welfare,* Vol. 49, No. 12, pp. 20-23. Mar. 2000.

3. Leelamma Devesia. *Cild Child in India.* APH Publishing Corp., New Delhi, 1991.

4. Madhumita Majumdar. "The Girl Child and the Family" in *Yogana* Vol. 34, No. 160, Sep. 1990.

5. Nander K. Singh. "Gender inequality. A Theoretical Construct in Anit," (ed) "Quest of Equality" Sterling Publication, Delhi, 1998.

23

Self-Help Group As a Strategy for the Empowerment of Women

K.C. Leelavathy

"Women must be directed to solve their own problems in their own ways. Our Indian women are as capable of doing as any in the world."

Swamy Vivekananda

Empowerment is an active, multi-dimensional process which should enable women to realize their full identity and powers in all spheres of life. It would consist of greater access to knowledge, resources, greater autonomy in decision-making, greater ability to plan their lives have greater control over the circumstance that influence their lives and free them from sackles imposed on them by custom, belief and practice. Generally development with justice is expected to generate the force lead to empowerment for various sections of population in a country and to realize their status (Bhatnagar, 1995).

What is Women's Empowerment ?

The term "empowerment" is frequently heard today, whether in the media or among development workers or in the classroom. It is clearly connected to the word "power." Simplistically speaking, empowerment is derived from the word "empower" meaning to give or to acquire power or to increase power. Thus, the word empowerment also implies a change in the equation or level of power. It can therefore be viewed as both a process as well as a result of social change.

The term "power" in turn connotes control. In the context of human society, it means control over resources. These resources could be materials such as natural resources and financial resources, human resources such as skills, labour, people, etc. or intellectual resources including information, idea and knowledge. Power is a relational dynamic between individuals or between groups of people and is often unequally distributed. This inequality results in control or domination. Many a time the domination accompanies exploitation.

At the overall level, women's empowerment aims at chaning the balance of power between the sexes so as to create a more equitable distribution of power in society. However, when we examine this overall process of women's empowerment more closely, we become aware of the economic, social, political and legal dimensions of the process. Each of these dimensions is interlinked to the other, and have bearing on each other.

Indicators of Women's Empowerment

Indicators of women's empowerment are the measurable changes that occur in the position and status of women. Identifying the indicators of the empowerment process is a complex task. Much depends on who is examining this subject, and at what point of time. It would however be fair to say that women who are engaged in the process of empowerment themselves are in the best position to decide such indicators. In such as case, the indicators would be based on the actual life experiences of the women. Some examples of the indicators of women's empowerment are: change in women's self-perception from negative to positive, increase in self-esteem and self-confidence, clear increase in level of women's knowledge, education, skills and overall awareness of her rights, a positive change in her capacity to take decisions independently, and the development of her ability to speak out and to defend herself against the violations of her human rights.

Who Empowers ?

The question "Who Empowers?" is asked quite often. From what has been said earlier, it may be seen that there is no one person or institution or agency, which alone empowers women. The creation of an enabling environment through strong polity support, the work of voluntary organisations, women's groups, academicians and researchers, committed bureaucrats and other support groups are among the multitude or agents who can provide support to take forward the agenda of empowerment of women. And yet, ultimately it is the women herself who has to empower herself within the family and outside the home. The others can only facilitate the process of empowerment. All the external agents or forces can only help the motivated women to transform themselves and their reality. Organising and empowerment of women at the grassroots in rural and urban areas has now become a key task of field based development workers. The mobilisation of women to form Self Help Groups or SHGs is a widely popular method of organising and empowering them. SHGs bring together underpriveleged women from a common socio-economic background. It then helps poor women to meet regularly to discuss about common problems and to work tighter for their collective empowerment. Mature SHGs also help to develop local women leaders who can contribute to the development of the entire community.

There are clear advantages of the collective approach to women's empowerment since no one single woman alone has to face the obstacles that may arise. Further, the SHG allows women to pool together their material (savings) and human resources, reduces individual risk, and promotes democratic ways of working. SHGs can also serve as a voice for negotiating access to various resources for women struggling to overcome their class and gender oppression.

However, it must be remembered that the empowerment process takes place in the larger social and political environment in which women live, this larger context both supports and hinders the empowerment process. The influential leaders, institutions, policy and laws which are part of the larger environment, must provide continuing support and the movement for empowerment must in turn advocate and lobby for the transformation of the key elements, which form the environment.

Self-help Group can be formed or promoted, in the manner in which the group can work for a positive impact

Definition of a Self-Help Group

A self-help is a collection of people who have common problems that cannot be solved individually, and have therefore decided to form a group and take joint action to solve the problems. The group may be known by different names in different places. Some of the terms used are—Sngha, Samooh,

Mandal, Sangham, etc. depending upon the region.

Conditions for an Effective SHG

There are some conditions for self-help group to be workable. These are:

- Each member of the group should be facing a similar, crucial problem.
- Only when each member realizes that the problem cannot be solved individually will the member cooperate to act as a group.
- Persons who have the resources or power to solve problems on their own should not be part of the self-help group.
- For a joint and collective action to have the best possible chance of success, each and every person must be convinced that the action being taken is the best possible one. For this a great deal of discussion is required.

Main Features of a Self-Help Group

As the above example indicates the main features of a Self-Help Group are:

- Members are a set of people, who come together voluntarily.
- Purpose of members is to solve crucial problems which cannot be solved individually.
- Members act Aollectively to bring about positive change in the lives.
- SHG Members can support each other and strengthen their collective position in dealing with external agencies.
- Often Self-Help Groups begin around a small issue but with increasing confidence and experience the group is able to tackle issues that are much larger and more complex.

Women are most Affected and Marginalized in Society

- Women are overworked
- Women are underfed
- Women hardly control any assets or income.
- Women are socially discriminated
- Women are excluded from 'public spheres'
- The self-help group model has shown that it results in women's empowerment as well as improves the situation of the entire family. Thus, the SHG strategy is more often used for organizing women.

The Changing Development Model

Until recently, development agencies focused upon solving all the problems of the poor communities, mostly without involving them in the process. This was based upon the belief that these agencies know what the needs of the poor people were and therefore were in the best position to provide the necessary help to them. This approach known as the 'top-down' approach, in which the development agencies provided resources, information and services to the poor.

Limitations of the Top-Down Approach

(i) Development agencies decided which problems needed to be tackled.
(ii) Solutions decided by development agencies are often not the best suited for the area or the people.
(iii) Development agencies try to solve all the problems of all the people but they do not have enough money or the knowledge to do so.
(iv) Development agencies make people permanently dependent upon them by not encouraging the latter to use their own resources.
(v) Development agencies top-down approach tended to ignore women even though they form the largest number of poor.

Role of SHG in New Community Based Approach

As the 'top down' approach was not having any impact in defeating poverty, development agencies realized that a new approach was needed. This was the bottom-up approach. The following are the characteristics of this new model, which has become the basis of development policy worldwide. Self-help groups form an important part of all development programmes, whether it is education, income generation, health, use of common assets such as land, water service delivery of existing public institutions such as schools, health centres, Anganwadi centres, etc.

Economic Empowerment

- Financial Resources
- Material Resources
- Cooperating for mutual economic benefit
- Access to external resources.

Political Empowerment

- Participation in election process.
- Influencing programmes of development agencies.
- Influencing policies of banks.
- Monitoring public service delivery agencies.
- Fear of being marginalized.
- Quality of leadership.
- Conflicts within groups.
- Politicisation and vested interest.

In India where poverty still remains a major problem with about 320 million people forming 36 per cent of the population living below the poverty line. NGOs recognized micro finance as one of the tools to attack poverty. They took the Self- Help Group approach promoting peoples organisation and functioning as feeder banks linking unleased and served rural poor. They have facilitated the organisation of SHGs for a common - cause through a process of social mobilisation with varying entry points like removal of illiteracy, basic health care, access to local resources, removal of social evils, resolution of social conflict, protection of the environment and thrift and credit.

What is SHG?

It is a small economical and homogeneous and affinity group of rural or urban poor voluntarily formed to save and contribute to a common fund to be and to its member as per group decision and for working together for social and economic uplift of the families and communities.

Research Thrust

A study was conducted by Sharmila Devi and Sithalakshmi (1998) on "initiating self help groups (SHGs) among urban and rural women". The major findings of the study were evaluated in quantitative and qualitative dimensions; a total of 462 women from the urban and 364 women from the rural areas had benefited out of the internal lending. Hence, the SHG starting income-generative activities for socio-economic upliftment of members and streamlining the procedure of repayment.

A study was conducted by Sudha and Jothimani (1999) on profile of self-help groups (SHGs) in Karamadi block. The qualitative aspects included group dynamics, collective action and articulation and awareness generated. It provides values about the SHGs. Efforts are being channalised in organising women into group for group cohesion and dynamism. The group dynamism should become infectious and spread in all spheres in all phases of development.

A study was conducted by Sangeetha and Thangamani on initiating self-help groups for urban women. "The investigator used the techniques AIDCAS (Wilson & Galup, 1995) for motivating the women to join SHGs. The attention of the women was derived through public meeting and demonstration, empowerment traits such as group attitude and desire to improve standard of living scored better.

Linkages with other Financial Resources

Sr. No. Area	Revolving	NABARD	RMK	LFS	Others	Total
1. Karamadai	3,00,000	8,00,000	1,00,000	41,000	-	12,41,000
2. PNP	2,75,000	-	-	2,47,000	-	5,22,000
3. Coimbatore Corporation	-	-	1,00,000	3,08,000	89,000 (UBSP)	4,97,000
Total	5,75,000	8,00,000	2,00,000	5,96,000	89,000	22,60,000

Selection of Trade

Majority of the members had undertook self- employment as their mode of trade and other doing common activity and the reasons expressed revealed that they had their own specific reasons for choice of trade.

Marketing Outlets

Of the total 1843 members, most of them resorted to weekly shandies, Uzhavar Sandhi, Town and Village Markets.

Investment on Trade and Business

Eighty per cent of the selected samples had invested within Rs. 1,000/- to Rs. 1,500/- whereas 13.3 per cent if them had invested within the range of Rs. 2,500/- to Rs. 5,000/- and 6.7 per cent of them had invested with the range of Rs. 5,000/- to Rs.10,000/-.

Training Imparted to SHGs

The Mahalir Thittam provides different type of training to all project agences on various topics.The different types of training imparted by the SHFs (12) were.

1. Animator and representative training.
2. Skill training for SHG members and
3. NGO staff training.

Linkages with other Agencies

DRDA	:	District Rural Development Agencies.
NGOs	:	Non-Government Organisations.
TTC	:	Trainers Training Centre.
WOBEDA	:	Women Business Enterprise Development Association.
THADCO	:	Tamil Nadu Adi Dravida Development Corporation.
CWS	:	Centre for Women Studies.
DSWO	:	District Social Welfare Office.
MT	:	Mahalir Thittam.
KKID	:	Kari Kubel Institution Development Education.
AJSS	:	Avinashilingam Jon Shikshan Sansthan.
ASETI	:	Ambedkar Self Employment Training Institute

Conclusion

Efforts are being channelised in organising women into group for group cohesion and dynamism. This effort will go a long way in due eradication of poverty and thereby improve due standard of living of the poor and rural mass. Women must be empowered economically, politically, educationally and scientifically in its true prospective and spread in all phases of development to attain holistic development.

References

1. Almelu. S. Vocational training for women placement within easy reach. *Social Welfare* 38 (8) pp. 34-38, Nov. 1987.

2. Ann, V. and Pillai N.C. Women entreprenews in Kerala. *Social Change* 20(2) pp. 61-29, June 1990.

3. Ganesan S. Duraipandian R. *Women entrepreneurship-Issues and strategies*. Kanisk Publishers, 1999.

4. Goela Usha. Training Schemes for Women in Govt. of India. 1989.

5. Moin Qazi. Self Help Groups : A Novel approach to Rural Development, State Bank of India, *Monthly Review*, Sep. 1997.

6. R.K. Mukherjee. Self Help groups- and bank. *The Economic Times*, May 26, 1999.

7. S.S. Sangwan, Financing through Self Help group–An Experience of a Commercial Bank in Dehradun. *The Journal of the Indian Institute of Bankers*. April-June 1997.

Part III
Health

24

Factors Responsible for the Living Conditions of Urban Elderly Women of Punjab

P. Sandhu R. Bakhshi and M.K. Sindhu

Factors which are affecting the living conditions, benefits enjoyed by elderly women in urban Punjab and the drawbacks of the changing times were studied on 120 randomly selected elderly women from 6 cities of Punjab. Data was collected through personal interview method. Major factors affecting health, social life, financial position, home living and working pattern were studied. Results of the study revealed that most prominent factor which was affecting their health was immunization, medical facilities and life saving drugs. They also agreed to other factors i.e., "Life is better" nowadays because of many outcomes of these advancements like spectacles, dentures, walkers, hearing aids and wheel chair and that due to better transportation and communication ; "medical emergencies"are handled successfully these days and elderly are able to overcome many of age-related problems. Most convincing factor as viewed by respondents regarding changing times and its effect on their social life was that "better communication system viz, telephones and mass media has brought elderly people closer" and that transportation facilities like cars and other vehicles have made "carrying out social obligations easier and more frequent" for elderly people. They gave some evidence to agreeing to few financial advantages bestowed by today's society and government to elderly women. Respondents also agreed to certain factors contributing to mental well-being of elderly negatively viz. "loneliness and alienation in the lives of elderly is fast growing" due to changing society."Elderly are more sad and depressed in the materialistic world and feeling of mental insecurity is more due to lack of moral support from children these days.

They identified that "home life of elderly had become very comfortable " due to technological advancements, followed by the view that these days "leisure time is spent more effectively" by them due to vast variety in entertainment and indoor games viz, satellite TV, internet. They also agreed that " improved ways of work has made their routine simpler" viz. ready made food stuffs, outside help, hired assistance, gadgets and home services.

The scenario is changing and creating its impact on elderly. According to National Sample Survey Organisation, reported by Narula(1998), 36.7 per cent of 70 million elderly people want to shift to old age homes because they can't manage alone. Saraswati (1976) concluded in his study that the old age has started emerging as the social problem in Indian society due to the socio-cultural changes brought about bv industrial revolution. Rao (1979) observed that because of better health facilities people lived longer in India and its typical socio-economic conditions like poverty, breaking up of joint family system and after care of the aged persons posed a threat to them. Keeping in view, the changes which have taken place with time, a need was felt to examine it's impact on way of life of elderly in India. Hence, the present study was undertaken with the following objective:

To identify the factors which affect health, social life, financial position, home living and working pattern of elderly women in urban Punjab.

Methodology

For field survey two cities from each of the three cultural regions of Punjab were randomly selected. Followed by the random selection of four localities from each city. A sample of five elderly women (60 years and above) was selected from each locality on random basis. Pre-tested interview schedule was used to get relevant information from the selected sample of 120 respondents. Simple averages, percentages and weighted scores were used to analyse the data. Five point scale for " agreement level" was used viz. Strongly agree—2; Agree- 1; Neutral— 0; Disagree—1; Strongly disagree—2.

Results and Discussions

1. Impact of changing scenario on health of elderly

Table 1 indicates agreement level of respondents on positive impact of changing times on health of elderly. Maximum agreement of respondents was on the view that "life expectancy has increased due to immunization" (mean score 1.83) and also because of Medical facilities and life saving drugs' (mean score 1.82) which are the result of advancement of science and technology of recent times. They also agreed that the "life is better" nowadays because of many outcomes of these advancements like spectacles, dentures, walkers, hearing aids and wheel chair (mean score 1.35) and that due to better transportation and communication; "medical emergencies" are handled successfully these days and elderly are able to overcome many of age-related problems (mean score 1.06). "Infections and communicable diseases are less fatal" now because of medical advancement and "terminal sickness is a rare phenomenon in old age" in present times was also agreed by respondents with mean of score .83 and . 74 respectively.

Respondents also agreed that "old age ailmets are treated more effectively" nowadays and that 'life is safer' these days because of scientific innovations hospitals and mobile services (mean score 61 and 50 respectively).

The negative effects of these advancements on health as viewed by respondents were that there are increased life risks and disabilities " due to accident hazards caused by heavy road traffic and elderly are at greater risk (mean score 1.23) closely followed by the feeling that there are "increased diseases" viz, asthma, bronchitis, allergy and water borne diseases due to environmental pollution (mean score 1.22). Even 'food adulteration and trace of toxic elements directly harm the health, specially the health of fragile people like elderly; and 'health in general (specifically for elderly) is adversely affected due to deteriorating living conditions in third world (underdeveloped countries) was also expressed by respondents with mean scores .63 and .50 respecitively. They also felt that ideadly diseased viz. AIDS and cancer are also more' due to harmful living styles in modern world and that 'cardiovascular disorders are on increase' due to sedentary way of living and elderly are getting. affected maximum (mean socre. 29). Average score of .75 for positive impact on health as viewed by respondents was higher than average score of. 69 for negative impact as given by them about the changing times and its' effect on their health, gave an overall impression of a positive effect on health (as viewed by respondents).

2. Impact of changing scenario on the social life

It is clear from Table 2 that most convincing positive view of respondents regarding changing times and its effect on their social life was that 'better communication system viz. telephones and mass media has brought elderly people close' and that transporation facilities like cars and other vehicles have made 'carrying out social obligations easier and more frequent' for elderly people (mean score 1.31) followed by their feeling that eradication of social evils (child marriage, polygamy and sati system) has brought relief in general to women (mean score 83). 'People are more prosperous and uplifted' viz. abolishing *Zamindari* system, land reforms and shift in occupational structure; and that 'emergence of social reforms' (widow remarriage, universal education to females, dowry ban, legal protection and right of women to ancestral property) has strengthened women's position in general was also agreed by respondents with mean scores of. 83, 44 and. 37 respectively.

Views regarding the negative impact of changing times on the lives of elderly people clearly indicates that respondents felt most strongly that in modern society 'respect for elderly has diluted' (mean score. 93) followed by the feeling that 'isolation among elderly has increased' due to dying out of close knit relations in the society (mean score. 79). Respondents also felt that 'pleasures of outdoor life for the are less' these days due to growing self-sufficiency within families viz. television and other kind of indoor entertainment (mean socre. 75). 'Society is less interactive with elderly' these days affecting their well being (mean score. 73); and that the migration of children to work place and their desire to settle separately after marriage leave elderly to fend for themselves alone (mean score 5.0) was also felt by respondents.

Average score of . 57 for positive feelings of respondents was higher than the average score of .11 for negative views agreed upon by them. So it may be concluded that generally respondents felt that with changing scenario their social life is also benefited.

Results of Dayal (1978), Prasad (1983) and Nagesh (1987) also point out some changes in the social life of elderly people.

3. Impact of changing scenario on financial position and mental well being

Thorough perusal of the Table 3 indicates that respondents disagreed on the positive views regarding the strengthened position of elderly women and felt that there is 'no secure financial position' for them viz. wide variety and availability of saving and investment schemes; and 'no significant financial relief' to them viz. maintenance through court and income tax relief (mean score. 69 and . 47). Disagreement was also there for the feeling that 'financial position of elderly women has improved' due to ancestral right over property and other legal protections for women and that there is 'relief to elderly due to old age pension and concessions' like concession for bus train and train concession provided by government nowadays (mean score-08).

Disagreement was also there regarding negative impact of changing times on financial position with the views viz. 'control of finances by elderly has decreased' due to their decreased importance, influence and authority these days, 'allowances of elderly has decreased' because of increased cost of living in recent times, 'assets of elderly are devalued' due to fast changing trends and fashions; and 'demand of elderly remain unfulfilled' since headship of households is not more with elderly (mean scores—-86, 81, 75 and 65 respectively). Average score of—64 for disagreement of respondents with negative impact was higher than average score of 33 for positive impact which give some evidence to agreeing to few financial advantages bestowed by today's society and government to elderly women.

Responses on impact of changing conditions on mental well being are also presented in Table 3. It can be clearly seen that there was disagreement by the respondents on the view that 'required' importance has come through because elderly population is getting attention internationally' (mean score. 37). However respondents agreed to certain views regarding negative impact of changing times on mental well-being of elderly viz. 'lone lines and alienation in the lives of elderly is fast growing' due to changing society, 'elderly are more sad and depressed in the materialistic world' and 'feeling of mental insecurity is more due to lack of moral support from children these days' with mean score of. 79,. 39 and. 37 respectively. 'They also agreed that elderly are more mentally stressed in today's competitive world and have more worries and tensions due to growing uncertainties these days (mean score. 36) and that peace of mind of elderly is adversely affected in noisy environment (mean score. 06). Average score was-.18 for the positive views and for negative views average score was. 15; depicting the feeling that respondents did not agree to any good signs of mental well-being of elderly in today's life.

4. Impact of changing scenario on home living and working pattern

Respondents agreement to views regarding positive and negative changes in home living which have taken place with changing scenario are presented in Table 4. They agreed maximum to the view that 'home life of elderly has become very comfortable' due to technological advancements (mean score 1.24) followed by view that these days 'leisure time is spent more effectively' by them due to vast variety in entertainment and indoor games viz. satellite, TV. internet (means score. 65). They also agreed that 'awareness of elderly to surroundings has increased' due to better communication, transportation, information technologies and mass media; and that there is 'better home environment' due to technological changes (mean score .55 and .25 respectively). However, there was agreement of respondents for the negative changes too as they felt that technological advancement has ill effects also and maximum agreement was with the view that 'elderly lack company of family members because family members' time and work pressures do not allow them to spent more time with elderly (mean score. 86) followed by view that they feel 'lonely and are left to fend for themselves' due to growing trend of outside employment of women, specially daughters-in-law (mean score. 79). They also agreed that elderly are 'deprived of attention' due to highly competitive goals of children these days as they have no time for their elders; and that cultural values have eroded and thus 'significance of elderly has decreased' also due to invasion of satellite, TV and other media and its impact on younger generation with means score of.53 and .52 respectively.

Average score of. 67 about the positive impact was higher as compared to feeling of respondents about negative impact with average score of. 49 thus clearly indicating a positive role of changing conditions on home living of elderly women.

Impact of working pattern of elderly has also been viewed very positive by respondents as it can be clearly observed in Table 4. They generally agreed that 'improved ways of work has made their routine simpler' viz. readymade food stuffs, outside help, hired assistance, gadgets and home services (mean score 1.23) as compared to the lower mean score of. 85 for their agreeing on the negative aspect of these changes on working pattern of elderly with the realisation that 'elderly's home responsibilities have increased these days due to women's outside employment; especially due to daughters-in-law's absence for work.

Table 1: Impact of Changing Scenario on Health of Respondents

Impact	*Weighted score*
Positive Impact	
— Life expectancy increased due to Immunization	1.83
— Life expectancy increased due to Life saving drugs	1.82
— Life expectancy increased due to better medical facilities	1.82
— Life easier viz., spectacles, denture, walker, hearing aids, wheel chair	1.35
— Medical emergencies handled more successfully	1.06
— Infections and communicable diseases less fatal	.83
— Terminal sickness a rare phenomenon	.74
— Life expectancy increased due to better diet	.71
— Deficiency diseases checked	.68
— Old age ailments treated more effectively	.61
— Life safer	.50
— Better health due to vitamin-mineral supplements and fortified foods	-.06
— Aging delayed	-.48
— Better life viz. readymade foods, easy to cook stuffs	-.82

(Contd.)

Average Score	-.75
Negative Impact	
— Increased life risks and disabilities viz accidents	1.23
— Increased diseases due to environmental pollution	1.22
— Health harmed due to food adulteration and toxic elements	.63
— Health deteriorated in under-developed countries	-.50
— Deadly diseases increased viz AIDS and Cancer	.29
— Cardiovascular disorder increased	.29
Average score	.69

Table 2: Impact of Changing Scenario on Social Life of Respondents

Impact	*Weighted Score*
Positive Impact	
— Better communication system brought people closer	1.31
— Transportation facilities made carrying social obligations easier and frequent	1.31
— Eradication of social evils brought relief to women	.83
— People more prosperous and uplifted socially too	.44
— Social reforms strengthened women's position	.37
— Emergence of progressive thinking and liberal society	-.01
— Society interactive with elderly	-.24
Average Score	.57
Negative Impact	
— Respect for elderly diluted	.93
— Isolation among elderly increased	.79
— Pleasures of outdoor life decreased for elderly	.75
— Society less interactive with elderly	.73
— Elderly left alone to fend for themselves	.50
— Status of elderly sharply declined	-.10
— Traditional role of elderly uprooted	-.16
— Importance of elderly decreased	-.27
— Elderly felt as they are no more reservoir of knowledge and experience	-.53
— No place of elderly in modern definition of family	-.65
— 'Headship' in family shifted from elderly to powerful	-.73
Average Score	.11

(Contd.)

Table 3: Impact of Changing Scenario on Financial Position and Mental Well-being of Respondents

Impact	*Weighted score*
• Impact on Financial Position	
Positive Impact	
— Financial position of elderly has improved	-.08
— Relief of elderly due to old age pension and concessions	-.08
— Secure financial position for elderly	-.47
— Financial relief to elderly	-.69
Average score	**-.33**
Negative Impact	
— Control on Finances by elderly has decreased	-86
— Allowances of elderly has decreased	-.81
— Assets of elderly have devalued	-.75
— Demands of elderly remain unfulfilled	-.65
— Level of living of elderly has declined	-.14
Average score	**-.64**
• Impact of Mental Well-Being	
Positive Impact	
— Elderly more mentally sound	0
— Required importance has come through international recognition of geriatric population	-.37
Average score	**-.18**
Negative Impact	
— Loneliness and alienation among elderly fast growing	.79
— Elderly more sad and depressed	39
— Increased feeling of mental insecurity among elderly	.37
— Elderly more mentally stressed	.36
— Elderly have more worries and tensions	.36
— Peace of mind adversely affected	.06
— Elderly feel useless and a burden on society	-.24
— Cannot perform *'puja'* peacefully due to small houses	-.29
— Frustration in elderly has increased	-.38
Average Score	**-.16**

Table 4: Impact of Changing Scenario on Home Living and Working Pattern of Respondents

Impact	*Weighted Score*
• Impact on Home Living	
Positive Impact	
— Home life for elderly became very comfortable	1.24
— Awareness of elderly to surroundings increased	.65
— Leisure time spent more effectively by elders	.55
— Elderly have better home environment	.25
Average score	**.67**
Negative Impact	
— Elderly lack company of family members	.86
— Elderly feel lonely and left to fend for themselves	.79
— Elderly feel deprived of attention	.53
— Significance of elderly decreased	.52
— Elderly's small pleasures of life adversely affected	.29
— Elderly's living space annexed	-.01
Average Score	**.49**
Impact of Working Pattern	
Positive Impact	
Improved way of work made elderly's routine simpler	1.23
Negative Impact	
– Elderly's home responsibilities increased	.85
Average Score	**.38**

REFERENCES

1. Nagesh, H.V. (1987). Care of the aged in Karnataka, *J Social Welfare* 34: 4-6.

2. Naurla, R. (1998) The nowwhere people. *The Tribune; Saturday Plus* 118 (253): 1.

3. *National Sample Survey Organisation* (1989) 42nd round, Government of India.

4. Prasad. P. (1983). Problems of the Aged in Rural India. *J Social Research* 32: 12-15.

5. Saraswati, H. (1976). The changing relationship between the young and the old. *J Social Welfare* 24: 29-32.

6. Singh, R. Singh, K. and Sharma, M. K. (1987). Economic problems of aged women.HAU *Journal of Research* 17: 199-202.

25
School Health Education–Today's Concern

Sonia Thakur& Monika Sharma

Health has been designated as a quality of life more comprehensive than an absence of disease, as that state of well-being which will enable to live most fully. Health education is a discipline in its own right derived from the health and behavioural sciences. It touches upon every phase of living. School health education aims to conserve or improve the health of school age youth and give them guidelines for healthful living all over their lives. A teacher presents the basic factors or concepts of health and disease as a continuum throughout the school years in such a way that a youth is stimulated to strive constantly for the best personal health, including a healthy emotional life. School health education is that which is conducted through teaching in the schools-elementary, secondary, and higher. The health education programme in a school is no longer a hit-or-miss. Instead, it is a planned, basic area of the curriculum in the same way as are other subjects such as language, science, arithmetic, social studies, art, music and physical education.

Health education is a continuous process and so cannot be completely compartmentalized within a definite subject area or within a specific class period. It should embrace all the activities and subjects that are a part of the child's life.

Role of the School in Health Education

1. To learn effectively, a child or youth needs good health. Health is a basic goal of all education, for the student can hardly achieve any other goal without having his health.
2. Children and youth tend to respond better than do older

people to health education in the development of desirable health attitudes and desirable health practices. The earlier, therefore, that an individual learns the elements of healthful living the more likely it is that they will be applied.

3. There cannot be a fully adequate community programme without the schools contributing to the overall effort. Therefore, what the school does in matters of health affectsthe community and conversely, what the community does affect the school population. All those who are concerned with children must work together to plan and carry on the total health programme so that children can apply in their whole living what they are learning in school.
4. The more the school has done before an individual reaches adulthood, the easier it will be for official and voluntary health agencies.

There are three levels of curriculum planning for the subject matter that is to be taught: (1) health area (2) teaching unit (3) the individual lesson plan.

Curriculum planning in the school involves a number of factors of which consideration is given to pupils needs and interest, principles, the content of health instruction, time allotment, and the function of the teacher in health teaching.

Integration and correlation of health education represent degrees and phases of the plan of including health teaching in other subjects and programmes. Integration implies an organisation of health learning experiences in the school curriculum around a central objective with several subjects and programmes contributing to that objective, whereas correlation refers to the inclusion of health teaching in specific non-health courses and programmes. All the health opportunities affecting learning and behaviour of children and youth in the total school curriculum is school health education curriculum. Almost every activity in the school program can be correlated with health teaching.

- **Language Arts** : Health topics can be included in connection with writing and speaking assignments. School magazines can publish health articles written by pupils.
- **Art** : Posters, free drawing and paper cutting can deal with many specific health topics.
- **Arithmetic** : Simple arithmetic is involved in a number of

health activities such as determining the amount of food eaten and the numbers of hours of sleep and exercise obtained and the keeping of height and weight records.

- **General Science** : The best suited for inclusion in general science are human physiology, sense organs and physical environment.
- **Biology** : Many topics of personal health fit logically, e.g., human growth, non-communicable diseases such as circulatory disorders, body's responses to the physical environment such as sunlight, air, humidity and temperature.
- **Chemistry** : Certain aspects of human physiology such as a study of the composition of blood and bones, the chemical changes in respiration, osmosis, drugs and chemical changes during exercise.
- **Physics** : Certain principles of physics are needed to be understood such as ventilation, heating, humidity, the mechanism of the eye and ear.
- **Social Studies** : In these classes there can be included a consideration of the personal hygiene habits as reflected in the way people lived during different periods in history, the effects of the industrial revolution on healthy practices.
- **Physical Education** : Many of the topics can be applied, i.e., sleep, fatigue, skills in play and recreation, cleanliness, perspiration and posture.
- **Home economics** : Certain topics can be included, i.e., grooming, cleanliness, cosmetics, posture, nutritional disorders, etc. consideration can be given to the improvements in home furnishings and equipment that contribute to more healthful living.

Health as a quality of life involves every aspects of living. Therefore, the content of a health education curriculum is wide and involves many and diversified areas of learning, a range from a healthful school environment and the health aspects of daily classroom living to subjects which deal directly with health and health information.

Health education derives its content from the biological and physical science, behavioural or social sciences. Knowledge along these lines promotes understanding the man's needs and adjustments in his environment and can indicate means to be used in motivating desirable health behaviour. The primary purpose of a health education curriculum is using this knowledge to provide learning experiences which will influence the attitudes and practices relating to individual and community health.

Selection of content of a health education curriculum will be determined by many factors:

- The physical, emotional, social and intellectual needs of children.
- The health interests of children.
- The personal experiences of children.
- The capacities and levels of comprehension of children at each age level.
- The objectives of health education.
- The contributions of specialists in health education.

The planned, organised, direct approach to health teaching and curriculum development recognises health education as a discipline and provides basic knowledge for healthful living.

Following Methods are Suggested for Imparting Health Education

- **Lecture Method :** Factual information can be made concisely and fairly quickly.
- **Discussion :** These are valuable at junior and senior high school levels. Talks on health topic should encourage students to express themselves effectively.
- **Guest speakers** : Physicians, nurses, counselors for professional organisation can make valuable contributions.
- **Demonstrations** : They add to the interest of a lecture and help motivate students. It can be used to emphasize basic facts in nutrition. A table can be set with a well-balanced lunch. Children may demonstrate butter making. If possible, after demonstration pupils should be offered the opportunity to develop their skills, e.g., preparing a sandwich, handling a doll to demonstrate bathing or diapering a baby.
- **Experiments** : Use of vegetable coloring in detection of plaque deposited on teeth serves to emphasize the need for correct and regular brushing of teeth. Penicillin molds can also be grown on agar plates.
- **Field Trips** : There may be visits to dairies, hospitals, health

museums, dental clinics, health departments, pasteurization plants, water purification plants and other health oriented establishments. A field trip must have educational value.

- **Role playing** : Children may act out many situations, i.e., a scene in the restaurant where the food if being selected and a visit to the dentist.
- **Dramatizations** : Simulated radio or television programmes, puppet shows, skits, and plays can be used successfully.

The whole area a of health information is dynamic, continually being changed by new discoveries in medicine and science and a teaching must keep uptodate on his knowledge and interpretations. Health education curriculum must be under continuous scrutiny to determine whether the objectives of health education are being fulfilled. Content may be integrated or correlated with related subject matter areas. A health curriculum is a guide and aid in the health education process. When the components relevant curriculum and a creative and committed health educator are plugged into each other, there will be generated electricity, excitement, enthusiasm and vibration in the student to turn him on to health learning. Planning a health education curriculum should be continuous throughout the year and from year to year, with a coordinated programme.

References

1. Bedworth, D. and Bedworth, B. *Health Education - A process for Human Effectiveness,* Harper & Row Pvt Ltd., New York.

2. Bibby, C. *Health Education - A guide to principle and practices.* William Heinemann Ltd., London, 1967.

3. Elliot, D.S. and Elaine, T.M. *Health Education-Patterns for Teaching* St. Martin's Press, New York, 1990.

4. Humphrey, J.H. Johnson, W.R. *Elementry School Health Education.* Harper and Brothers, Publishers, New York, 1999.

5. Kilander, H.F. *School Health Education-A Study of Content, Methods and Materials.* The Macmillan Company, New York, 1985.

6. Neimer, A and Schaller, W.E. *The School health programme,* W.B. Saunders Company Philadelphia, 1975.

7. Prakash, R. *Research and Counselling in Health Education.* Sarup and Sons. New Delhi 1998.

8. Ramachandran, L. and Dharmalingam, T. *Health Education-A new approach,* Vikas Publishing House Pvt Ltd., Delhi, 1993.

26

Nutritional Education to Eradicate Malnutrition Among the Rural Children

K.N. Balapurkar, M.V. Bonde, Ch. Balamoni, V.R. Bonde, V.B. Sutar

Introduction

The principle aim of Krishi Vigyan Kendra (KVK) is to develop the rural people by educating them with modern technologies developed by the scientists of research and development division of ICAR. KVK includes all the faculties that are engaged in all-round development of the rural population. The home science division of KVK is engaged in development of rural women and children by modifying their daily activities of home like food, clothing, finance, health, child-care, home beautification etc. The rural population of this area is almost completely occupied by the population of different tribes like Pawara, Mauchi, Kokani and Bhil. These tribals follow the old habits for food preparation and unhygienic ways of living. Though their children go to school they won't follow the habits of personal hygiene. Their schooling is nominal.

The rural areas are with sporadic small water bodies. Their main occupation is agriculture. They grow all the varieties of vegetables of the area but they are reluctant to utilize them in their daily diet. The staple food includes the pancakes of cereal alongwith pickles and small quantities of dals of legumes. Their reluctance for green vegetables as stated by women of the village was because children won't prefer to eat and hence the children are main bait for malnutrition because of complete absence of essential nutrients like vitamins and minerals and inadequate quantity of proteins in their daily diet. Besides improper food habits they lag behind in personal hygiene too. Especially the children are not taken care of whether they clean their hands before meals. The parents won't give importance towards basic needs of healthy living. The people are unaware of clean surroundings. But the value of health, and comfort are interdependent and help guide the conduct of individuals and family members and health is one of the motivating values of intrinsic and instrumental worth.

Materials and Methods

The village Nakane was selected for the programmes as its population is tribal people and most of the children of the village are malnourished.

The Anganwadi workers of the village were consulted for identifying the children suffering from malnutrition. 26 such children aged 2-5 years were identified. These children were given a medical check up by a pediatrician for the enquiry of any other ailment apart from the malnutrition problem.

To start with, the parents, i.e., the mothers of children were consulted to know about the food habits of the children. It was learnt that almost all the children were on diet of pancakes of cereal, pickles and little dal. They were mainly on carbohydrate diet. On behalf of Krishi Vigyan Kendra the children were fed with supplementary diet of pancakes prepared by adding the minced green vegetables, like spinach, fenugreek, amaranths, cabbage, bottle gourd, carrot, cucumber, radish, etc. alongwith sprouted legume and fruits, groundnut/sesame mixed with jaggery.

Sr. No.	*Name of foodstuff*	*Protein (gm)*	*Fat (gm)*	*Energy (cal)*	*Ca (mg)*	*Fe (mg)*	*Carotene (mg)*	*Vit B_1 (mg)*	*Vit B_2 (mg)*	*Vit B_3 (mg)*
1.	Wheat	11.8	1.5	346	41	4.9	64	0.45	0.17	5.5
2.	Bengal-gram	17.1	5.3	360	202	10.2	189	0.30	0.15	2.9
3.	Green-gram	24.0	1.3	334	124	7.3	94	0.47	0.27	2.1
4.	Amarath	3.0	0.3	43	800	22.9	3564			
5.	Cabbage	1.8	0.1	27	39	0.8	120	0.06	0.09	0.4
6.	Coriander	3.3	0.6	44	184	18.5	6918	0.05	0.06	1.9
7.	Spinach	2.0	0.7	26	73	10.9	5580	0.03	0.26	0.5
8.	Carrot	0.9	0.2	48	80	2.2	1890	0.04	0.02	0.6
9.	Radish	0.5	0.1	16	20	1.0	4	0.02	0.03	1.4
10.	Bottle Gourd	0.2	0.1	12	20	0.7	0	0.03	0.01	0.2
11.	Cauliflower	2.6	0.4	30	33	1.5	30	0.04	0.10	1.0
12.	Cucumber	0.4	0.1	13	10	1.5	0	0.03	0.0	0.2
13.	Groundnut	25.3	40.1	567	90	2.8	37	0.90	0.13	19.9
14.	Banana	1.2	0.3	116	17	0.9	78	0.05	0.08	0.5
15.	Guava	0.9	0.3	51	10	1.4	0	0.03	0.03	0.4
16.	Papaya	0.6	0.1	32	17	0.5	666	0.04	0.25	0.2

The children were kept on this diet for a period of 3 months and the weight improvement studies were conducted in every eight days interval. Children were rechecked by the pediatrician at the end of the programme and were found to be healthy. The results are discussed below.

Result and Discussion

The growth parameter especially the weight of the children was measured once in a week to appraise the nutritional efficiency of the diet supplied to them. There were 11 children of 2-3 age group; 7 children of 3-4 age agroup and 8 children of 4-5 age group among the 25 children selected for the programme. The average weight was recorded at the end of every month. (Table 2).

Table 2: Age and Weight Parameters Obtained During the Study

Sr. No.	*Age*	*St.d Wt. (kg)*	*Wi (kg)*	*W1 (kg)*	*W2(kg)*	*W3(kg)*
1	2-3	8-12	7.0	8.5	10.08	11.5
2	3-4	10-14	9.0	10.0	10.8	12.7
3	4-5	12-16	10.0	10.7	12.2	13.0

Std. Wt. (kg) — Standard weight in kg.
Wi (kg) — Average initial weight of the children
W1(kg) — Average weight of children after one month of programme
W2(kg) — Average weight of children after two month of programme
W3(kg) — Average weight of children after three month of programme

An average weight increase of 1.5 kg, 3.08 kg and 4.5 kg after one month, two months and three months of programme respectively in children of 2-3 years age-group. An average weight 1 kg, 1.8 kg and 3.7 kg after one month, two months and three months of programme respectively in children of 3.4 years age group. Similarly, an average weight increase of 0.7 kg, 2.2 kg and 3.0 kg after one month, two months and three months of programme respectively in children of 4—5 years age group.

From the table it is clear that the children of 2—3 year age-group were mostly malnourished. The mothers casually give the pancakes in the hands of the children and leave themselves to eat. The children of smaller age groups perhaps have difficulties eating the pancakes and the spicy pickles and dals or may have lesser preference. Hence, they remain malnourished. The children of 3 to 4 year age group and 4 to 5 year age group are less in number in the malnutrition list. This may be due to the reason that the children with age have adapted to the food habits slowly. But if the children in growing stage are malnourished, this may lead to serious ailments of inadequate nutrition and nutritional deficiency diseases. Hence, the skills of preparing the food items that are nutritionally balanced, utilize available ingredient and above all the preparations likely to be preferred by the children of above mentioned age groups were taught to the women of the village. As the method of preparation of these items were similar to their traditional ones and less time consuming the results were appreciable.

Conclusion

It is said that the nutritional educational changes the attitudes, beliefs and understandings about the food into practices which are nutritionally sound and consistent with an individual's needs, purchasing power, available food sources and socio-cultural background. To reflect this, the women of the village have adopted the skills taught to them. But the effective nutritional education results not only in the acquisition of knowledge and skills, but also in the changes desired in the eating habits and behaviour of the learners. The impact assessment studies and appraisal of the programme after 3 years has shown that 69 per cent i.e., 18 children out of 26 of the children who were taught the good habit of personal hygiene and eating habits follow them till date and they are adapted to them. We can say that the home is the place from where the seeds of education are sown and home science is an appropriate and effective tool that makes the home an environment for the sprouting of the seeds of education and grow healthily thereafter.

References

1. Extension education in community development, pp. 307, 398 (Directorate of Extension, Ministry of Food and Agriculture, Govt. of India).

2. Proceedings of the International Symposium, p. 282. (Agricultural Research and Education Systems for Development) (C.A.R.).

3. Handbook on Integrated Nutrition Education. (Food and Nutrition Board, Govt. of India).

4. Nutritive value of Indian foods, National Institute of Nutrition, ICMR, New Delhi, 1985.

5. Savile, A.H. *Extension in rural communities*, University Press, Toronto, 1968.

6. Supe, S.V. *Introduction to Extension Education*, Oxford and IBH Publishing Co. New Delhi, 1982.

7. Waghmare, S.K. *Teaching Extension Education*, Vallabh Vidyanagar Anand, Gujarat, 1980.

8. Chaubey, B.K. *A Handbook of Education Extension*. Jyoti Prakashan, Allahabad, 1979.

9. Dhama, O.P., Bhatnagar, O. *Education and Communication for Development*. Oxford and IBH. Publishing Co. New Delhi, 1980.

10. Devi Rameshwari and Ravi Prakash. *Social Work and Social Welfare Administration*, Vol.1 Mangal Deep Publications, Jaipur, 1998.

27

Child Rearing Practices with Special Emphasis on Health and Dietary Habits of Children

Ila Jogi

With the advancement of science and technology, the progress in the field of health and hygiene has become inevitable. In the health improvement programme of people, health of women and children became focus of central attraction. Therefore, quite a large number of programmes for the welfare of women in general and children in particular have been introduced by the Government from time to time. Functionaries responsible for implementation of different schemes and programmes are trying their best to give benefits thereunder. However, it has become obligatory on the part of parents to make use of most appropriate, desirable and ideal health and diet schedule particularly for children in the age group of right from birth to 3 years.

Health and diet schedule, it is a matter of common observation and experience as well, differs from, and it is quite natural from family to family and for that matter mother to mother in the context of their differing socio-economic and psychological context. As a matter of curiosity and concern, author was very much interested in understanding health and diet pattern prevailing in the study area. In the present paper an attempt has been made to report health and diet situation as perceived and followed by the parents for children in between 0 to 3 years of age. Specific objectives of the present investigation however were as under:

1. To present personal, economic and psychological profile of

the parents.
2. To understand personal hygiene prevalent in rural area as reported by the respondents for their children.
3. To analyze and report dietary habits of children according to parent respondents.
4. To enlist difficulties encountered by the mother respondents in observing health, hygiene and dietary habits in their true manner.

Methodology

Findings emerged were based on the data collected from 138 mother respondents randomly selected from one purposively selected village Malkapur in Karad Taluka of Satara district from Western Maharashtra region of Maharashtra state. For the purpose of selection of mother respondents, author had to do a survey of houses wherein children in the age range of 0-3 years were there. From amongst the list, 138 mother respondents were randomly selected with the help of lottery method of random sampling.

Comprhensive and systematic schedule was developed which contained aspects otherwise necessary for inclusion and were within the purview of objectives set-forth for the study at hand. Data were personally collected with the help of schedule through personal interview. Data were subsequently tabulated, analyzed and presented in suitable manner for interpretation.

Findings and Discussions

Results that emerged out of the present investigation have been presented below under suitable sections.

1. **Personal, economic and psychological characteristics of the parents:** Personal, economic and pyschological; characteristic of the mother respondents has great deal to do with awareness and adoption of personal hygiene and dietary habits of children and therefore, it was essential to collect information pertaining to these characteristics of the mother respondents. Mother respondents were, therefore, asked to furnish information about their selected characteristics included in the study. Information received during the course of an interview is presented in the Table 1.

N=138

Table 1

Sr. No.	Character and Category	Respondents reporting No. (N=138)	Percentage
1	**Age**		
	(i) Upto 30 years	38	27.56
	(ii) 31 to 40 years	73	52.85
	(iii) 41 years and above	27	19.59
2.	**Education**		
	(i) Illiterate	11	9.00
	(ii) Primary	14	11.00
	(iii) High school	91	70.00
	(iv) Graduate	13	10.00
3.	**Type of Family**		
	(i) Joint	94	68.00
	(ii) Nuclear	44	32.00
4.	**No. of Children**		
	(i) One	48	36.00
	(ii) Two and more	90	64.00
5.	**Attitude of Mothers towards Health and Dietary Habits**		
	(i) Favourable	30	21.72
	(ii) Unfavourable	70	50.67
	(iii) Undecided	38	27.61

Data presented in table above have clearly brought out, that majority (52.85 per cent) of mother respondents fall in the age category of 31 to 40 years followed by those (27.56 per cent) who were less than 30 years of age. Minimum of the respondents, however, reported to be above 41 years of age.

So far as formal education mother respondents have undergone is concerned, it was served that as many as 91 mother respondents were observed to be educated upto high school. Number of mother respondents receiving primary education and graducation is almost equal. Even at this stage of development however, it is surprising that 11 mother respondents however, were found to be illiterate. This could be justified firstly due to the fact that the sample mother respondents originally came from rural area where probably educational facilities might not have been available and secondly due to poverty and domestic situation.

As regards number of children with mother respondents was concerned, it was revealed that majority of the mother respondents came from joint family system. Only 44 being the members of nuclear family. Data supported the presumption that joint family system is still a matter of common observation in area unlike urban area.

In an attempt to understand number of issues the mother respondents have given birth to, it was noticed that majority (64 per cent) of the respondents had two and more children. This could be taken to mean that in spite of repeated inculcation of importance of family planning, mother respondents from rural area probably have not realized.

Researchers have clearly brought out that attitude towards a particular practice has to do a lot for its adoption. In the present study therefore, attitude of mother respondents towards personal hygiene and dietary habits of children was obtained. It was observed that majority (50.67 per cent) of the respondents had expressed their unfavourable attitude towards personal hygiene and dietary habits of children. As many as 38 respondents had no response in terms of favourable and unfavourable to record, 30 of them being in the category of favourable attitude towards personal hygiene and dietary habits. This could be attributed to prevailing rural customs, traditions and values besides absence of education on these aspects.

Dietary Habits

In consonance with one of the objectives, author wanted to understand dietary habits of children from the respective mother respondents. It was therefore, essential to operationally define the term dietary habits. In the present situation, the term dietary habits has been taken to mean as diet components of children including breast feeding, bottle feeding and supplementary food comprising of variety of products depends upon, preferences suitability and affording capacity of the parents.

Mother respondents were therefore, asked to furnish

appropriate response for the questions asked. Information furnished by the respondents is depicted in Table 2

Table 2: Dietary habits of children as reported by mother respondents

Sr. No.	*Dietary Habits*	*Respondents reporting No.*	*Per cent*
1.	**Breast Feeding**		
(i)	Upto 1 year	26	18.82
(ii)	Upto 1 ½ year	71	51.40
(iii)	More than 1 ½ Year	35	25.34
(iv)	No response	06	04.44
2.	**Milk Feeding Practices**		
(i)	Bottle feeding	75	54.30
(ii)	Spoon feeding	97	70.02
(iii)	Glass feeding	19	13.75
3.	**Supplementary Food**		
(i)	Cow/Buffalo's Milk	80	54.92
(ii)	Soup	54	39.09
(iii)	Fruit Juice	21	15.20
(iv)	Milk powder/instant food	10	07.24
(v)	Pysum	26	18.82
(vi)	Soji	05	03.62
(vii)	Dal and Rice	66	47.78
(viii)	Chapati-sabji	21	15.20
(ix)	Bread	12	08.68

From the Table 2 above, dietary habits in terms of breast feeding, milk feeding practices and supplementary food including various aspects contained there in under is perspicuous. Under the aspect of breast feeding it was further observed that the number of mother respondents reporting breast feeding upto one year, upto 1 ½ year and more than ½ year worked out to be 26, 71 and 35 respectively togerther with six respondents with no response received. Variability in the period of breast feeding could probably be due to the non-availability of the period of breast feeding could probably be due to the non.availability of supplementary food with mother, lack of knowledge on the part of mother about continuation of breast feeding, health of mother and finally aggressive demand of child for breast feeding.

Information regarding milk feeding practices reported by the mother respondents revealed that majority of the mother respondents resorted to spoon feeding as a milk feeding practice followed by those who had done for bottle feeding. As many as 19 mother respondents reported to have used glass feeding. Usefulness of this method is probably governed by the factors such as ease, convenience, availability of time at the disposal of mother and preference of choice of child.

Further, probing as regards washing methods for bottles and type of nipple used for bottle revealed that out of total sample of 138 mother respondents only 75 respondents reported to have habit of washing milk bottles after their use, which includes 42 mother respondents using cold water, 21 mother respondents hot water and 12 respondents making use of soap for washing of bottles. Further it was noted that 26 mother respondents used simple nipple for their bottle, five mother respondents however, were very meticulous in using nipple of any particular company of their own choice. It is interesting to note that eight mother respondents were using nipple of any company and of any specification whichever is available on the spot.

So far as timing for milk feeding is concerned, 73 mother respondents reported specific timings for milk feeding and 62 mother respondents reporting no specific timings for milk feeding. In spite of author's effort three respondents were reluctant to respond for this type of information.

Very interesting information was sought from the mother respondents stating that they however switched on from one milk feeding practice to other in course of time and according to the vagary of child.

Supplementary Food

The concept of supplementary food stem from variety of reasons such as increasing nutritional demand of child with the advancement of age, non-availability of breast milk and choice and preferences of child. In an attempt to understand the type of supplementary food consumed by the children and subsequently reported by the mother respondents revealed that majority (57.92 per cent) reported cows/ buffalo's milk which was followed by dal-rice (47.78 per cent) which was again followed by soup (39.09 per cent).

The number of respondents reporting fruit juice, milk powder/instant food, pysum, chapati-sabji and bread as supplementary food worked out to be 21, 10, 26, 21 and 12 respectively. Very few (3.62 per cent) mother respondents however, reported to have fed soji as supplementary food to their children. Differential dietary habits particularly for supplementary food probably would depend on nutritional awareness of the mother respondents, financial position, availability, traditional values and liking of childrens.

Personal Hygiene

Importance of personal hygiene in the life of an individual needs no special emphasis. The significance of personal hygiene needs to be inculcated in the minds of children from their early period of childhood. This responsibility naturally has to be shouldered by the mother. As enunciated in one of the objectives, author wanted to understand how far and to what extent mother respondents are conscious about hygiene of their respective wards, besides the aspects and method used for the same.

The term personal hygiene in the present study has been operationally defined as an atmosphere characterised by a spirit of healthy life and adequate emphasis on activities such as bath, masage, care of skin and cleanliness of ear, eyes, nails, clothes and tongue besides toilet training and preventive and control measures including care during illness.

Mother respondents were therefore, asked as to whether they follow different aspects covered under the operational definition of the term."Personal hygiene"and responses received in turn are tabulated in the Table 3 Below:

Table 3 : Mother Respondents Reporting Adopting of Methods of Personal Hygiene

Sr. No.	*Aspects of personal Hygiens*	*Respondents No.*	*Reporting Per cent*
1.	**Bath:**		
(i)	**Regularity**		
	(a) Regular	110	79.72
	(b) Irregular	28	20.28
(ii)	**Type of Water**		
	(a) Cold	03	2.17
	(b) Warm	72	52.
	(c) Hot	63	45.66
(iii)	**Number**		
	(a) Once	120	86.95
	(b) Twice	18	13.05
2.	**Massage:**		
(i)	Upto 6 months	85	61.59
(ii)	Upto 12 Months	53	38.41
3.	**Care of the skin:**		
(i)	Daily bath	128	92.74
(ii)	Massage with application of oil	90	65.21
(iii)	Soap	108	78.25
(iv)	Gram dal flour	09	06.52
(v)	Talcum Powder	73	52.89
(vi)	Washing of skin 2-3 times a day	46	33.33
4.	**Cleanliness of Ears:**		
(i)	Hair pin	10	7.24
(ii)	Stick	14	10.14
(iii)	Cotton bud	102	73.84
5.	**Application of 'Kajal' for:**		
(i)	Healthy eyes	75	54.34
(ii)	For big look	31	22.46
6.	**Periodicity for cutting nails:**		
(i)	Regularly	33	23.90

(Contd.)

(ii) With particular period of interval	45	32.58
(iii) Occasionally	60	43.52
7. Cleanliness of clothes:		
(a) Type of Water		
(i) Cold water	113	81.91
(ii) With hot water	16	11.58
(iii) With dettol water	09	06.51
(b) Washing clothes of children's with clothes of other family members.	**105**	**76.02**
(C) Type of clothes used for children:		
(i) Cotton	117	84.70
(ii) Wool	07	5.06
(iii) Silk	14	10.12
(iv) Polyester	35	25.34
8. Cleaning tongue:		
(i) With the help of finger	53	38.47
(ii) With tongue cleaner	46	33.60
(iii) No cleaning	39	28.23
9. Toilet habits:		
(i) (a) Regular	58	42.00
(b) Irregular	80	58.00
(ii) **Place for toilet training:**		
(a) Bath place	36	26.18
(b) Road	87	63.04
(c) Potty	08	5.78
10. Casual illness:		
(i) Fever	54	39.12
(ii) Cold	94	68.11
(iii) Cough	51	36.95
(iv) Stomachache	5	03.62
(v) Ear pains	5	03.62
11. Vaccination:	132	95.64

Table 3 above clearly delineates methods of personal hygiene employed by the mother respondents for their respective children.

Data depicted in the table above denote that majority of the mothers provide regular bath to their children particularly with warm water. Almost an equal number of mothers used hot water for bathing their children. Only three mother respondents however, reported to have used cold water for bathing their children. In an attempt to understand number of times bathing is provided to their children revealed that, majority of the mother respondents provided bath only once a day, few of them providing bath twice a day. Bathing once a day is a common practice obviously because bathing has been considered as one of the important component in personal hygiene. Bathing twice a day is a matter of occasion and happens only after when child returns home after playing or any other such occasion.

Massage also has been taken care of as one of the aspects of personal hygiene and regularly followed by majority of respondents upto the age of six months only, followed by the number of mother respondents who had followed the practice of massage after six months and upto 12 months.

In the initial stage of the development of child, care of skin assumes a greater importance in the process of personal hygiene. The number of respondent reporting various methods for care of skin such as daily bath, massage with application of oil, use of soap for bath, gram dal flour, talcum powder and washing of skin two to three times a day worked out to be 128, 90,108, 09, 73 and 46 respectively. Method used for caring the skin naturally differ with the development, outlook, financial position, availability of time at the disposal of mother and mothers awareness about modern child rearing practices.

Cleaning of ear is also an important aspect in personal hygiene. With a view to understand how ears are cleaned ; mother respondents were requested to state methods they are using for. It was observed that majority of the mother respondents are using cotton bud (match box stick with cotton surrounded) for cleaning. As many as 14 and 10 mother respondents reported any stick and hairpin for cleaning ears of their child respectively.

Use of 'Kajal' for application in eyes although a traditional practice for improvement of not only the size but also sight, is a matter of controversy, yet many of the mothers seem to have regular practice of its application. In the present survey, as many as 75 mothers had used 'Kajal' for improving health of eyes and

31 for big look, in terms of size of the eyes.

As far as the periodicity for cutting nails is concerned, data denoted that majority of the mothers are cutting nails of their child occasionally, followed by those who are cutting nails of their children with a particular period of interval. This operation is very regularly being performed by only 33 mothers. Considering of nature of this aspect would reveal that this activity has not been assigned that priority as compared to that of other activities under personal hygiene. Secondly depending upon the availability of time at the disposal of mother, operation of nail cutting is performed.

As regards cleanliness of clothes is concerned it is vivid from the above that majority (81.91per cent) mother respondents are washing clothes of their children with cold water. The number of mother respondents using hot water and dettol for washing clothes of their children worked out to be 16 and 9 respectively.

Substantial number of mother respondents observed to be washing clothes of their children with the clothes of other family members.

In an attempt to understand type of clothes being used by the children, it was noted that types included cotton, wool, silk and polyester. Maximum number of respondents reported to have used cotton followed by polyester. About 10 and 5 per cent of mother respondents reported to have used silk and wool clothes for their children.

During the course of an interrogation mother respondents were specifically asked about cleaning of tongue and in turn it was observed that majority of the mother respondents reported that tongue of the children is cleaned with the help of fingers followed by those who seem to have used tongue cleaner. It is very interesting and surprising as well that 39 mothers reported 'no cleaning' at all.

Toilet habits assume a greater significance in personal hygiene.However, unfortunately 80 mothers reported irregularity, 58 mother respondents reporting regularity.

From the point of view of sanitation, it was thought essential to know the place of toilet training. In this connection it was made known to the author that 87 mother respondents reported road as a place for toilet while 36 mother respondents were reported to have used bath place for toilet.According to only eight mother respondents reported to have used potty for toilet.

Illness, be that of a casual nature or otherwise is a significant indicator of personal hygiene. What are the different types of illness was therefore a matter of concern and curiosity. It was found in the present study that fever, cold, cough, stomachache and ear pains were some of the casual illnesses mother respondents reported for their children. When the question of number of mother reporting comes, it worked out to be 54, 94, 51, 5, and 5 respectively.

Out of the total sample of, about 96 per cent of mother respondents were cautious and careful in getting their children vaccinated against different diseases as a preventive measure.This may be due to the fact that the advantage of different schemes implemented by Department of Health appropriately availed by the mother respondents.

Conclusion

Based on the strength of findings emerged out of the present investigation, it can be concluded that-

1. Although different schemes for improving health and dietary conditions of rural poor in particular are under implementation, yet benefits not only reached but also have not been availed by thc scheme beneficiaries by the rural poor in general and schemer beneficiaries in particular.

2. Mothers are unaware of the real know-how pertaining to personal hygiene and dietary conditions in true perspective and therefore, it is necessary to organise training programmes to educate them.

References

1. Anand, D. and Rama Rao, A. Feeding Practices of infants and toddlers in Najafgara area Delhi. *Indian Journal of Child Health* 11: 172, 1988.

2. Jain, S. A Study on the indigenous Knowledge system of child health and care (0-2yrs) prevalent in the tribal area of Girwa Panchayat Samiti. An M.Sc Thesis. Rajasthan University, 1995.

3. Madhavi V. Prahalada. N. and Mathur V.C. A survey of infant feeding and weaning practices in the village Fathepura. Hyderabad. *Indian Pediatrics.* 9: 480-484, 1972.

4. Mead, M. Culture and change in relation to Nutrition, Burgess and Lane. 50-62, 1962.

5. Dhillon, M.S. Health begins at home. Swasth Hind Vol. VI No. 1982.

28

A Study on Health Awareness in Women Residents of Chak, Kamed and Surasa Village (Madhya Pradesh)

Madhu Gautam, Preeti Gupta

Education is not only an aspect of development but more significantly, it is a primary instrument for the achievement of other aspects of development, i.e., economical, social and political. It is the basic minimum requirement for creating awareness that itself is vital for the accelerated and effective participation of women.

There are deep-rooted cultural forces, outdated value systems and discriminatory socialisation process that obstruct the development of women in India. Despite attempts through many government policies, academic and activist interventions like Raja Ram Mohan Roy, Ishwar Chandra Vidhyasagar and M.C. Ranade, education still remains a poor area for women. The rate of literacy is still very low and seems to be hastening very slowly. The 1991 survey reports of "M.P. literacy campaign" shows that, there is a marked (21 per cent) increase in women literacy in the state but the results of our survey shows us a different picture.

Besides it, extension and communication has an important inter relationship with home science. It enables us to understand better the conditions surrounding us and finding solutions to the problems faced by the whole community. The study conducted by the authors was basically centered on married women, of different age groups of Chak, Kamed and Surasa

Villages, which are near about 13 kms away from Ujjain city. The people residing in the village mainly belonged to Scheduled Caste and OBC, and most of them were small farmers and landless labourers.

To see the Health awareness in these Women and the causes interfering with their healthy living, subjects were selected at random and were subjected to the prepared questionnaire.

Firstly, was studied women literacy level of village Chak, Kamed and Surasa. It was found that 82 per cent women were illiterate and 6 per cent women were literate. Remaining only 12 per cent studied till that school level.

Women Literacy Level of Village Chak, Kamed and Surasa (Madhya Pradesh)

Sr. No.	*Literacy Level*	*Percentage*
1.	Illiterate	82
2.	Literate	6
3.	Primary	6
4.	Middle	4
5.	Higher Secondary	2
	Total	100

Contrary to the belief, that illiterate women of Indian villages do not know anything about health problems facing them, study showed a marked awareness about the issues related to health as 92 per cent women were quite keen on caring for their health and cleanliness, as 74 per cent women took bath daily, even though there was a marked shortage of water in this area of M.P. It was also found that 92 per cent of women cleaned their teeth daily but 70 per cent of the women were not very particular about their daily exercise, this may be due to the hard work done by them.

Health Awareness in Women of Villages Chak, Kamed and Surasa (M.P.)

[Figure in percentage]

Sr. Opinion	*Taking Care*	*Hair Cleanliness*	*Daily Bath*	*Teeth Cleanliness*	*Daily Exercise*
1. Yes	92	92	74	92	26
2. No	-	6	26	8	70
3. No Answer 2	-	-	-	4	
4. Not Known 6	2	-	-	-	
Total	100	100	100	100	100

Health awareness in women brings naturally, awareness for vaccination for their young kids. The Govt of India has launched many such programmes through many Govt. and Non -Govt. organisations. Since 1966, the need for vaccination was felt, to decrease the infant mortality rate and to ensure the safety of small children from tuberculosis and small pox.

In this respect it was found that 80 per cent women were aware of vaccines given to small children, whereas, 70 per cent had actually got vaccinated their kids. Although only 56 per cent women knew the actual benefits of the vaccination among small children, rest of 44 per cent were not aware of the benefits of these vaccines.

Awareness for Vaccination and Familly Planning Methods in women of Chak, Kamed and Surasa

[Figure in percentage]

Sr. No.	*Opinion*	*Vaccine know-how*	*Children vaccinated*	*Benefits of vaccination*	*Family planning methods*
1.	Yes	80	70	56	38
2.	No	18	28	44	54
3.	No answer	02 -	-	-	04
4.	Not known-	-	02	-	04
	Total	100	100	100	100

The central and the state Government is spending crores of rupees on Family Planning Programme scheme at village level in India, but the sad truth which comes out of the study showed that 52 per cent women of Chak, Kamed and Surasa were not knowing about the various methods used for family planning. We are talking of population explosion in India and at top level various facilities and incentives are offered for decreasing the population growth rate, but due to poor communication between the organisation and a general man, hinders the expected results of these organisations. To gain the effective results educated people of the villages have to come forward to propagate and extend the know-how to other unaware people of their villages.

A balanced diet is must for maintaining proper health. Diseases often upset health. Diseases may be either due to imbalances in diet or infection by microrganisms. The diet consumed in our country is based on, mainly energy yielding foods and contains only small amount of protective foods. Recent developments in telecommunication have made it possible for the common people to get the knowledge of balanced diet.

Balanced Diet Awareness in Women of Chak, Kamed and Surasa

[Figure in percentage]

Sr No.	Opinion Consumption	Daily dal consumption	Daily milk leafy	Daily green balanced vegetables consumption	What is a diet
1.	Yes	74	68	68	24
2	No	26	32	32	
3	Don't know	-	-	-	74
4	No answer	-	-	-	2
	Total	100	100	100	100

The study conducted to see the awareness in the women regarding a balanced diet showed a marked awareness regarding use of pulses as 74 per cent of them were consuming it daily. When asked about giving milk to the small kids, 68 per cent women replied affirmatively. Even they were aware of importance of green leafy vegetables. When asked those women about a balanced diet, they were not as knowledgeable about its whole concept.

Diet Awareness During Pregnancy in the Women of Chak, Kamed and Surasa

[Figure in percentage]

Sr. No.	*Opinion*	*To consult Doctor*	*Knowing about extra diet*	*Use of odized salt*	*use of toxic sub*	*Keeping fast*
1.	Yes	86	56	68	14	72
2.	No	14	32	26	86	28
3.	Don't Know		2	-	-	-
4.	No answer.	-	10	6	-	-
	Total	100	100	100	100	100

We also studied diet awareness during pregnancy in women of these villages. It was found that 86 per cent women consult doctor and 56 per cent women knew about extra food required by them. 68 per cent women were aware of importance of iodine in salt and were actually using iodized salt; 86 per cent women refrained from taking tobacco in any form during pregnancy. But due to pressure in the village society of cultural and social beliefs 72 per cent women kept fast on various occasions even during pregnancy.

The major factor, of course, was the persistence of socio-cultural norms and socialisation process. But due to the lack of adequate educational facilities, poor implementation of incentive and provision of supporting infrastructure services like drinking water, fuel, fodder, health, childcare etc, added to it.

The foundation of good health is exercise, good habits and correct knowledge of balanced diet and their importance in our daily life. All these have to be imparted to the common women of our village, so that they can keep themselves as well as their family healthy. Without good health, an individual can not perform any work efficiently and cannot contribute to the common good as a member of his community.

Benjamin Disraeli has rightly said, "The health of the people is really the foundation upon which all their happiness and all their power as a state depend."

Conclusion

The findings of this study showed marked, health awareness in them due to advantages of telecommunication and other sources of extension methods.

Thus, Extension education will be used as an agent of basic change in the status of women. In order to neutralize the accumulated distortions of the past; there will be a well-conceived edge in favour of women.

The method of imparting knowledge to the common women is also important. The value of dialogue has assumed great importance in the later half of the 20th century. Dialogue helps people to grow in mutual understanding and love . There should be a mass educational movement.

Extension education to college students is also an important medium in imparting knowledge to village women by conducting various shows, plays, lectures and use of audio-visual aids. "Where there is a will, there is a way." So it is upto us to help our gender to come forward and make a strong nation.

References

1. Denver Public Schools. Health interests of children 1980. In Denis Pirrie and Dalzelliward, Arthur, A Textbook of Health Education.

2. Dhillon, M.S. Health begins at Home. *Swasth Hind* Vol. VI No. 8, 1972.

3. Mark Vande M. A study on dietry habits and food consumption patterns of teenage families. *American Journal of Home Economics.* Vol. 63. No. 7, pp. 540, 1977.

4. Park J.E. *Text book of Preventive and social Medicine a Treatise on community health.* Jabalpur, pp. 86-170, 1971.

5. Sinha Archana. Nutrition and Women's Health. Health for the Millions. Voluntary Health Association of India. Publication. Nov-Dec., pp. 42-46, 1999.

6. Sherry. MA. *Health Education.* Ramprasan Sons, Agra, 1980.

7. Swaminath, M. and Bhagwan R.K. *Our Food.* Ganesh & Co., Madras, 1990.

8. World Health Organization Tech Rep ser No. 409. Geneva 1969.

9. Longree, K. *Sanitary Techniques in Food Service.* John Wiley and Sons. Inc. New York, 1971.

Part IV
Human Rights

29

Self-Concept of Orphan Adolescents in Delhi

*Neeti Sharma*and Priyanka Aeri*

One of the most dominant aspects of human experience is the compelling sense of one' unique existence, what philosophers have traditionally called, the issue of personal identity or the self. Self is viewed as a component of the psyche which serves as an introspective function. Operationally, self is the complex set of physical, behavioural and psychological processess, characteristic of the individual and self-concept is the individual's personal views about him/ herself. Mead (1934) called self-concept."social creation which results from one's relationship with others"

The importance of home in the development of an individual is very significant. Healthy homes cast healthy impact on the growing body, mind and heart of the child. But with the absence of both presents, the child is deprived of healthy home environment. In the earlier ages due to the prevalence of joint family system, the orphans were looked after in the home or were adopted by some relative, but abandoning of orphan children is becoming more common these days.

An individual needs a stable and secure environment for development of positive attitude towards oneself, which an orphan may be deprived of we associate environment with the development of self-concept of an adolescent. It is human baby's right to have an enriching environment for his /her proper development. Setting up of orphanages or children's homes as they are now called, look into these children's needs and provide care and protection at times of stress.

The present study was conducted with the following specific objectives.

1. To find out the reasons of abandonment of children at orphanages.
2. To assess the self-concept of adolescents who are reared up in orphanages.

Methodology

The study was conducted in the Government schools of NCT Delhi, which admitted both orphan and non-orphan students. A sample of fifty orphan respondent's both boys and girls in equal proportion, in age range of 14-16 years was selected.

To achieve the objectives of the present study, a general in formation proforma was prepared. Also, Self-Concept Questionnaire (SCQ) by Dr. Raj Kumar Sarawat (1992) was used. The scores obtained were categorized into five levels of self-concept, that is high, above average, average, below average and low.

Data collected was suitably analyzed using frequencies and percentages.

Analysis

More than half of the respondents (58%) had joined orphanage after five years of age, followed by 22 per cent who had joined at 2-5 years of birth, 10 per cent in between 6-12 months of birth, 6 per cent at the age of 7-30 days of birth and only 4 per cent at the age of 1-2 year of birth Table 1.

Most of the orphans had some knowledge regarding their parents education and occupation Table-2. This knoledge was imparted to them through orphanage attendants. Most of the respondent's father's were educated till graduation (60%), while 20 per cent did not know about their educational status. A majority of respondents' mother's were illiterate (44%) with 22 per cent of respondents were unaware about their mother's educational status. A large number of respondents father's were in service (46%) and a few respondents were unaware of their father's occupation (26%). Half of the respondents believed that their mother's were housewives (52%) and only a small proportion were unaware of their mother's occupation (16%).

Majority of the orphan respondents had above average self-concept (Table 3). Comparatively, male respondents had better physical self-concept, though only a few had high physical self-concept (20%). While none of the female respondents had high physical self-concept. Majority of both boys (68%) and girls (30%) had above average physical self-concept. As compared to girl orphans (4%), boys had high social self-concept (20%). Though the majority of both boys and girls (80% and 88%, respectively) had above average social self-concept. Both, boys and girls had equal proportion (16%) for average temperamental self-concept, though, boys (12%) had better high temperamental self-concept as compared to girls (4%). Only in the educational component girls self-concept was high (28%) as compared to boys (24%) for high educational self-concept. But, again only girls showed average educational self-concept (4%). Except, for 4% of boys all the respondents had above average moral self-concept. A large percentage of both boys (68%) and girls (76%) had above average moral self-concept. Only a few boys (8%) had high intellectual self-concept and, also, below average intellectual self-concept (4%). Majority of girls (72%) had average intellectual self-concept, while boys (64%) had above average intellectual self-concept. Boys also faired better than girls on total self concept, with only boys having high total self-concept (12%). Majority of both the respondents (88% boys and 96%) had above average total self-concept.

Conculsions and Implications

From the present study, it can be concluded, that, majority of orphan respondents joined the orphanage after the age of 5 years. A large proportion of the respondents were aware of their parents' educational and occupational status. This information was imparted to the respondents through orphanage attendants. Majority of the orphans fathers' were educated till graduation and mothers' were illiterate. A large number of orphans father's were in service and mothers' were housewives. Most of the respondents had above average self-concept, though boys on the whole had better self-concept compared to girls, especially in components like physical, social, temperamental, intellectual and total self-concept and only for educational self-concept girls scored better. But for moral self-concept both boys and girls had similar self-concept. Also, only boys showed below average self-concept in intellectual component.

It can be concluded that there exists positive relationship between self-concept of an individual and his/herecology. The self-concept of an adolescent is affected by people who play significant role in his/her life and relationships develped with them. There is need to provide enriching environment to orphan adolescents who are in double risk, to develop negative self-concept girls being at more risk, should be provided encouraging interactions by the caretakers.

Orphanages should be visited by home science extension specialists, counsellors and human development experts to provide healthy interaction communication channels to both orphans and orphanage personnels. Visits to schools in which they study and interaction with their respective teachers is also necessary.

With the changing priorities and our family values, people should be made more aware and conscious to the needs of the orphan children, so that they can be better taken care of. Also, our National Planners, Parliament and State legislators must give due importance to orphans and safeguard for their rights as privileged human resources should be made.

Table 1: Percentage Distribution of Age of Orphans at which they Joined the Orphanage

N=50

S. No.	*Age of joining of orphanage*	*Percentage distribution*
1.	7-30 days of birth	6
2.	6-12 months of birth	10
3.	1-2 years of birth	4
4.	2-5 years of birth	22
5.	5 years onwards	58

Table 2: Percentage Distribution of Orphans Parents According to their Education and Occupation Status

N=50

S. No.	Parental education and Occupation	Percentage distribution
1.	Father's educational status	
	(i) Illiterate	20
	(ii) Till graduation	60
	(iii) Post graduation and above	-
	(iv) Unknown to self	20
2.	Mother's educational status	
	(i) Illiterate	44
	(ii) Till graduation	34
	(iii) Post graduation and above	-
	(iv) Unknown to self	22
3.	Father's occupational status	
	(i) Service	46
	(ii) Business	28
	(iii) Professional	-
	(iv) Unknown to self	26
4.	Mother's occupational status	
	(i) Housewife	52
	(ii) Service	18
	(iii) Business	14
	(iv) Professional	4
	(v) Unknown to self	26

Table 3: Percentage Distribution of Orphan Adolescents on Various Levels of Self-concept

N=50

Sr.	*Variables*	*Sample*	*Self-Concept* *High above average* *F*	*Average* *%*	*Below average* *F*	*Low* *%*	*F*	*%*	*F*	*%*	*F*	*%*
1.	Physical	Boys	5	20	17	68	3	12	-	-	-	-
		Girls	-	-	20	80	5	20	-	-	-	-
2.	Social	Boys	5	20	20	80	-	-	-	-	-	-
		Girls	1	4	22	88	2	8	-	-	-	-
3.	Temperamental	Boys	3	12	18	72	4	16	-	-	-	
		Girls	1	4	20	80	4	16	-	-	-	-
4	Educational	Boys	6	24	19	76	-		-	-	-	
		Girls	7	28	17	68	1	4	-	-	-	-
5.	Moral	Boys	7	28	17	68	1	4	-	-	-	-
		Girls	6	24	19	76	-	-	-	-	-	-
6.	Intellectual	Boys	2	8	16	64	6	24	1	4	-	-
		Girls	-	-	7	28	18	72	-	-	-	-
7.	Total	Boys	3	12	22	88	-	-	-	-	-	-
		Girls	-	-	24	96	1	4	-	-	-	-

References

1. Saraswat, R.K. 1992. Manual for Self-Concept Questionnaire (SCQ). National Psychological Co-operation. Kacheria Gate, Agra, India.

2. Meda, 1994, Cited by Morgan *Introduction to Psychology*. 6th edition, Mc Graw Hill Inc. New York: 384.

3. Siddiqui, Noor Jahan 1997. *Adolescent orphan girls in Delhi A sociological profile*. Regency Publication, New Delhi.

4. Bandura, Albert and Walters, Richard, H. *Adolescent Aggression*, The Ronald Press Company, New York, 1980.

5. Berkowitz, L. *Aggressison : A Social Psychological Analysis*. Mc Graw-Hill, New York, 1990.

6. Browing Charles, J. *Differential Impact of Family Disorganization on Male Adolescents, Social Problems*, 8, No. 1, Summer 1960.

7. James, Howard. *Children in Trouble*. David Mckay Co. In, 1975.

8. Nair, K. *Blossoms in the dust*. Lond : Duck Worth, 1995.

9. S.P. Chaube, *Psychology of Adolescents in India*; Concept Publishing Company, New Delhi, 2000.

10. Singh, O.P; Verma, Reeta; Arora, Meenakshi and Agrawal Padma, Self image of institutionalized male deliquent adolescents *Journal of Human Development*, Vol. 22, 7-13, 1986.

30
Misuse of Human Rights and Our Changing Values

Neeti Sharma, Amiteshwar Ratra and Shivani Bala

Today, the society has a strong feeling that woman is ill-treated. She is not dealt equally in both her parental and in-laws home. They face a great deal of cruelty both mental and physical,. Harassment for dowry related demands in their husband's homes. Bride burning and women dying under mysterious circumstances is quite common.

With the advent of too much torture on married woman, dowry related harassments and deaths, the government has passed various acts from time to time. These acts are:—

1. The Dowry Prohibition Act 1861;
2. Sections 498A, 406, 304B, 306, 323, 506 of IPC; and
3. Section 113A and 113B, of the Indian Evidence Act.

Woman has always lived in subservience. She has suffered injustice and atrocities. It is heart breaking when one hears of young innocent brides being tortured physically and mentally. Despite special protective laws for women, cases of dowry deaths, harassment, torture and cruelty are on the rise. This is indeed horrendous. The agony of the family whose daughter has suffered atrocities can well be imagined. The shock and trauma of those who have lost their daughter cannot be described in words. The whole family is ruined and wrecked. The parents shudder to think of the marriage of their other daughters and always live in a state of fear.

The real victims of dowry related crimes are crippled by the attitude of their parents, who keep forcing their daughters to go back to their in-laws and husband's homes even when there is enough evidence of terrible ill treatment of these women at the hands of the in-laws or husband. Societal pressure and age old belief of husband's home being the girl's ultimate destination, forces girl's parents' to ask their daughter to keep on adjusting there.

Girl's parents only rise to the situation when there is a case of bride burning or a suicide by the daughter in desperation. It often takes the death of their daughter to wake the parents, who then start lodging police complaints against the whole family of the girls in-laws, indiscriminately, whether all of them are guilty or not.

The problem that is arising is that there is a growing widespread belief that many people (the bride, her parents and maternal family and especially their lawyers) are misusing these laws to gain an unfair advantage over the husband and his family. The lawyers advise and teach them how to take advantage of the current provisions of the laws. However, the decision to misuse or not, rests with the girl and her family.

The laws relating to dowry are needed in society and no one can deny that these provisions are widely misused by wives and her relatives for many reasons. It may be claimed that the most common and extreme form of exploitation of a husband and his family by his wife is to make false charges of harassment for dowry, ill treatment and abetment to suicide is presented as a case of homicide specially when the death is due to burn injuries. Every problem in the family may be attributed to dowry demands made by the husband and his relations. In most of the cases, womens's versions is inevitably believed by both society at large and the judge. All this leads to a bad effect on the so-called accused person's reputation, profession, career, health and self-respect.

There are some court cases, where in, fake implications by the parents of the girl, with a view to harass and blackmail innocent spouse and his relations is fast emerging.

These Acts have made women very powerful. They got a edged weapon with which to harass their husbands and his family members. To achieve their utmost interests they used these provisions of law, which are meant primarily, for the benefit of the sufferers of dowry demands and harassment.

There is no denying the fact that every strata of society praises all these statutory and other special measures. What is, however, disturbing is the misuse of this provision. Dowry is being made a scapegoat for all problems in the family. A man, whose wife is not happy in her marriage for whatever reasons, is placed in a very vulnerable position.

It is true that in many of these cases a woman may be a victim of dowry harassment but surely not all cases can be attributed to dowry harassment. A woman may feel harassed and frustrated for many other reaons, like lack of privacy or living in a joint family, incompatibility, drinking, smoking or other habits of the husband or financial stresses and so on.

The basic reasons responsible for misuse of the dowry related laws by the relatives of the bride, as well as, by the brides themselves, are:

1. Extra marital affair
2. Premarital affair
3. Incompatibility—Education, culture difference, ego, the desire to live separately, class difference, manipulation to coerce the husbands to obey their wishes
4. Hunger for money/greed for material goods
5. Vengeance
6. Rejoinder to a husband's petition for restitution of conjugal right
7. Shortcomings in the divorce law.

Conclusion

There is no denying the fact that women are still the oppressed class in many parts of the country-especially amongst certain sections of society and they need protective laws and procedures. What is distressing is that some laws and procedures have the potential to be misused and so cause great harm. Often we find today that husbands are harassed too. It is submitted that the courts and society should not proceed on a prior assumption that the devil of the game is always the man and his family. The constitution and our law makers have jealously guarded the interests of wives by way of special statutory provisions, which are edged weapons and if these provisions are misused, not only is harassment caused to the other party but also a complete embargo is put on any efforts towards reconciliation.

A permanent social stigma is attached to the so-called accused's family, the amount of humiliation, tension, harassment and embarrassment is indescribable. There are cases where due to shock or humiliation, people have died or have committed suicide.

The working of the women protection laws, in the in-laws house, needs to be examined minutely. If the guilty are escaping punishment, or the innocent are wrongly charged and placed in judicial custody lasting several years till their acquittal, then, there is need to take appropriate action that ensures some changes made in the laws to prevent their misuse and also to ensure that the guilty are punished.

References

1. Garg, T.L. 2001. In Laws must not always be implicated in dowry cases. *Delhi Age*, May, 31.

2. 2000. Man says his in-laws troubling him for dowry. *Indian Express*. June, 26.

3. 2000. Three commit suicide fearing implication in dowry case. *The Hindustan Times*, August, 30.

4. Devendra, Kiran, *Status and Position of Women in India : With Special reference to women in contemporary India*. Shakti Books. New Delhi, 1985.

5. Ilaish, J. Women in development. The Andhra Pradesh Situation. Unpublished paper presented at the "National Conference on Women's Status" held at S.N.D.T. University Compus, Bombay, 1981.

6. Glen, N.D. and Weavers, C.N. A multivariate study of marital happiness. *Journal of Marriage and the Family*, 40. 269-282, 1978.

7. Kumar Pramod. Marital adjustment : A study of some related factors. *Indian Journal of Clinical Psychology*. 23 (2), 112-116, 1996.

8. Mehta Sushila. *Revolution and the Status of Women in India*. Metropolitian Book. New Delhi, 1982.

9. Sreenivas Rao, K. and Jahwari, S. Human Rights Education and the role of Universities. Experiments in Education. 27, 3, 47-49. March, 1999.

10. Starkey, H. The Challenge of Human Rights Education. Council of Europe. Strasbourg, 1991.

31

My Views About Human Rights

Arya Gupta

Introduction

Our National Pledge

We the people of India (irrespective of caste, creed, race, sex, place of birth) solemnly resolve—

To constitute India into a Sovereign Socialist Secular Democratic Republic, and to secure all citizens:

JUSTICE, Social, Economic and Political, LIBERTY of thought, expression, belief, faith and worship; EQUALITY of status and of opportunity; and to promote among all, FRATERNITY, assuring the dignity of the individual and the unity and the integrity of the nation.

(Legal News & Views, 2001)

Human Rights

Human Rights means the rights relating to life, liberty, equality and dignity of the individual guaranteed by the Constitution or embodied in the international covenants and enforceable by courts in India.

The major international documents on human rights include? *doynets* of kinds of rights, often artifically divided into, civil, political, social, cultural, and economic rights.

Human Rights Courts

Human Rights courts are for the purpose of providing for speedy trial of offences arising out of violation of human rights, the state Government may with the concurrence of the chief justice of the high court, by notification, specify for each district a court of session to be a Human Right Court to try the said offences.

(a) a court session in already specified as a special court; or
(b) a special court is already constituted.

Meaning of Human Rights

First, there is a right to be free from governmental violation of the integrity of the person. Such violations include torture, cruel, inhuman or degrading treatment or punishment and arbitary arrest or imprisonment. And they include denial of fair public trial, and invasion of the home.

Second, there is the right to the fulfillment of such vital needs as food, shelter, health care and education. We recognize that the fulfillment of the right will depend, in part upon the stage of a nation's economic development. But we also know that this right can be violated by a government's action or inaction—for example, through corrupt official process which divert resources to our elite at the expense of the needy, or through in difference to the plight of the poor.

Third, there is the right to enjoy civil and political liberties.

Quality of life cannot be improved in developing countries unless they check population growth. India's population has already crossed the one billion mark. And the net addition to the population every year is around 17 million people. Our national priorities should also be reoriented with sufficient stress on public health, family welfare literacy, rural development and employment generation.

"People must work to rid society of everything that offends the dignity of a person or violates human rights. There can be no place for intimidation and domination of the poor and weak."

Pope John Paul II

In developing or least developed countries the problem for the protection of human rights is quite different. They are fighting for providing basic necessities of life to their people because of their poor economic conditions.

How can a state think of providing civil and political rights to its people unless food, shelter and clothing are made available? Speaking of human rights without speaking of developmental issues or the new international economic order is to take precisely one sided approach.

Rammohan Roy emphasized that if we want India to occupy her rightful place in the company of nations we have to reorient our present and future keeping in mind that the fundamental inspiration for human progress comes from the demand for human rights and human dignity. In fact, these are cultural values which are eternal as well as spiritual and without such values there will be no human heritage worth cherishing. It is regrettable that not much well-informed discussion on this aspect of human rights education in India, in the light of this perspetive, has taken place. Such discussions have not been common even among human rights and civil liberties groups and activists in our country.

In the modern period the first intellectual activist was Raja Rammohan Roy. This movement for freedom, social justice, human dignity—in short that all are born equal—spread in other parts of India. This intellectual movement, unfortunately, paled into insignificance during the freedom movement in the 20th century particularly since the early twenties. It is regrettable that after independence too there has not been any such movement. It is precisely for this reason that our human rights educationists and social activists ought to give the utmost importance to our intellectual heritage. Research in the field of human rights must begin with the positive aspects of our own heritage and revive them, and prepare a course of study based on that heritage. We must, however, guard ourselves against romanticizing the past, we must raise our voice of reason and wisdom, which means that we must revive only that past which can guide us to respect the individual's dignity and human rights with a view to building a future of which we can be proud. Which further means that we must discard those aspects of our past, like for example the laws of Manu, the theory of Karma, the principle of hierarchical division of society and so on which hamper our progress and which go against the philosophy of human rights. In fact, we must discard all that seeks to persuade the poor, the depressed, the oppressed and the exploited to reconcile their lot to suffering, sacrifice and voluntary poverty—all that signify complete surrender and the absence of the spirit of revolt. What is most important is to accept the fact that the highest appreciation of our past is to find out how it could generate in us the spirit of revolt against social injustice and human rights violation and to inculcate that spirit.

Kinds of Human Rights

Human rights are indivisible and interdependent, and therefore precisely there cannot be different kinds of human rights. All human rights are equal in importance and are inherent in all human beings. The Universal Declaration of Human Rights therefore did not categorize the different kinds of human rights. It simply enumerated them in different articles. However, the subsequent developments made in the human rights field under the United Nations system make it clear that human rights are of two kinds, viz., (1) Civil and Political Rights, and (2) Economic, Social and Cultural Rights.

Civil and Political Rights

Civil rights or liberties are referred to those rights which are related to the protection of the right to life and personal liberty. They are essential for a person so that he may live a dignified life. Such rights include right to life, liberty and security of persons, right to privacy, home and correspondence, right to own property, freedom from torture, inhuman and degrading treatment, freedom of thought, conscience and religion and freedom of movement.

Political rights may be referred to those rights which allow a person to participate in the Government of a state. Thus, right to vote, right to be elected at genuine periodic elections, right to take part in the conduct of public affairs, directly or through chosen representatives are instance of political rights.

It is to be noted that the nature of the civil and political rights may be different but they are interrelated and interwoven, and therefore, it does not appear logical to differentiate them. This reason alone led to the formulation of one covenant covering both civil and political rights into one covenant, i.e., International Covenant on Civil and Political Rights.

Economic, Social and Cultural Rights

Economic, social and cultural rights are related to the guarantee of minimum necessities of life to human beings. In the absence of these rights the existence of the human beings is likely to be endangered. Right to adequate food, clothing, housing and adequate standard of living and freedom from hunger, right to work, right to social security, right to physical and mental health and right to education are included in this category of rights. These rights are included in the International Covenant on Economic, Social and Cultural Rights.

Although the United Nations has recognized the above two sets of right in two separate covenants, there is a close relationship between them. It has been rightly realized especially by the developing countries that civil and political rights can have no meaning unless they are accompanied by social, economic and cultural rights. Thus, both the categories of rights are equally important and where civil and political rights do not exit, there cannot be full realization of economic, social and cultural rights and vice versa. The relationship of the two categories of rights was recognized by the International Human Rights Conference held in 1968 which declared in the final proclamation that—

Since human rights and fundamental freedom are indivisible, the full realization of civil and political rights without the enjoyment of economic, social and cultural rights is impossible. The General Assembly in 1977 reiterated that all human rights and fundamental freedom are indivisible and interdependent and equal attention and protection of both civil and political rights, and economic, social and cultual rights is necessary. The resolution also stated that civil and political rights are the means to the social and economic rights of the people. The Vienna Conference of 1993 again, emphasized that there is no difference between the two sets of rights by stating that all human rights are universal, indivisible and interdependent and interrelated. The international community must treat human rights globally in a fair and equal manner on the same footing and with same emphasis.

Value Education

The growing concern over the erosion of essential values and an increasing cynicism in society has brought to focus the need for readjustments in the curriculum in order to make education a forceful tool for the cultivation of social and moral values.

In our culturally plural society, education should foster universal and eternal values, oriented towards the unity and integration of our people, such value education should help eliminate obscurantism, religious fanaticism, violence, superstition and fatalism.

Apart from this combative role, value education has a profound positive content, based on our heritage, national and universal goals and perceptions. It should lay primary emphasis on this aspect.

"Everyone has the right to education." To achieve this goal, the following principles are laid down:

1. Education shall be free, at least in the elementary and fundamental stages. Elementary Education shall be compulsory.
2. Technical and professional education shall be made generally available and higher education shall be equally accessible to all on the basis of merit.
3. Education shall be directed to the full development of the human personality.
4. Education shall be directed to the strengthening of respect for human rights and fundamental freedoms.
5. Education shall promote understanding, tolerance and friendship among all nations, racial or religious groups.
6. Education shall undertake activities for the maintenance of peace.
7. Parents have a prior right to choose the kind of education that shall be given to their children.

Why Human Rights Education ?

Human Rights Education is the only guarantee of demonstrating our commitment to human dignity, promotion of an adequate standard of life to everyone and finally for the promotion of world peace and prosperity for all.

Human Rights Education guarantees fundamental human rights and freedoms to all without distinction of creed, race, sex, economic or political status.

Human Rights Education guarantees gender equality and women empowerment to enable women to contribute equally to peace and prosperity.

Human Rights Education brings awareness of fundamental freedoms enshrined in the Constitution of India in 1950. India's most precious gift to world culture is "Vasudhaiva Kutumbhakam," the whole worlds is a family. The need of the hour is that we learn to live like the members of one big family.

Human Rights Education is committed to the achievement of goals of UN Decade for Human Rights Education 1995-2005. The United Nations has provided the best chance to mankind to uphold Universal Declaration of Human Rights; and all other instruments put forth by the UN since 1948.

Human Rights Education

Towards a Culture-Centric Pedagogy

Violation of human rights has become an every day event in our "civilized societies." The path from violation of rights to redress is littered with barriers and alternative paths. Most of these barriers and alternative paths are anchored on cultural variables.

The Context of Culture-centricity

We are in the decade of Human Rights Education for empowerment launched in 1991 by the World Non-governmental Organisation's Coalition. It may also be noted that we have just completed the United Nations' Decade on Cultural Development launched in 1983.

This is an uphill task because teaching of human rights as a cultural issue is recongnised as a weakly defined area by academic circles. Whatever methodological and theoretical exercises done already are in the area of jurisprudence which itself is a non-priority item on the educational/research agenda of most governments and universities in India and abroad. Given the limitations, it is time to make an attempt to evolve basic ideas for a culture centric pedagogy which can act as basic bricks in building a new educational process, particularly to develop a culturist curriculum for teaching human rights. The time is ripe due to the ongoing realities of human life the power of state as protector of life and liberty is going down the drain due to globalisation and marketisation in the name of 'free trade'. Conservation and preservation of basic human rights will be left to the individual and small, issue based groups. Individuals and small groups have to prioritise their human rights agenda' if they want to survive in this era of global hegemony by a few economic and political elites. This prioritisation needs an educational base for its efficient performance because knowledge and information are the two vital inputs for concerted action in this era of information economy. A culture-centric curriculum to teach human rights is a vital element in the new 'human rights agenda.'

The Present Scenario

Human rights is not an item on the educational agenda of state Governments which possess control over the school curriculum. It will be foolish to propose an extension of school curriculum at this stage because most of the state governments are trying to reduce their budgetary allocation for school education.

Human rights and its wider implications are usually enveloped by the social science curriculum of universities, particularly by disciplines such as political science, law and sociology. Human rights as a curricular component in these disciplines is limited to a bare minimum and follow a non-critical mode in the process of teaching. This is a natural fallout of the westoxified, colonial pattern of education, enforced and sanctified by academic elites for parochial reasons. Non-critical devouring of facts and theories is the mainstay of this pedagogical process which is current in most of our educational institutions including the so called centres of excellence.

A positive trend favouring the changing realities is the increasing focus on law and related issues by all concerned-media, universities and non-governmental groups. Feminist and minority scholarship and activism are acting as great catalysts in legitimizing the new consciousness as they try to subvert the existing, oppressive and unequal settings through asserting difference. There is a growing opposition all over the world against the homogenizing, unidimensional, highly centrist attitude of the political and economic elites. This positive trend is evident in the increasing attempts by under privileges and marginalized to use the legal and political mechanisms to their advantage. These attempts are following different methods as dictated by the peculiarity of the situation—it may be in the form of spontaneous protest, either peaceful or violent or it may be in the form of bio-political action, like the sit-in protest, conducted by the activists of Narmada Bachao Andolan or by the farmers of Karnataka during recent past. A large number of peoples movements have already altered their cynical views concerning the legal system. They are mobilizing force from all sides to change the attitudes of the legal system.

The multi-cultural society of India offers a great challenge to those involved in developing a culture centric/specific pedagogy for human rights education. Anthropological exoticity and confusion should not be viewed as stumbling blocks preventing theoretical elaborations concerning the process of evolution of human rights consciousness. They should be made as offering great challenges to the committed researcher and activist.

The externalities of the realm need an appraisal before embarking upon a search for an altered pedagogy. Globalisation, marketisation and privatisation are the current slogans, flashed on every vintage point as the magical cures for the sickness of the welfare state. This is coupled with necessary ventilations to push out people's protests against an increasingly irresponsible state machinery—this ranges from outright state lawlessness to that of state sponsored catharsis including cricketisation, karsevisation, tinelisation, carnivalisation and 'golden handshake in front of the gates of graveyards.' Democracy remains on the political agenda as an essential mythical drug to keep masses waiting on the surgical table of poverty and powerlessness, to be operated upon by the politicians and priests whenever they wanted a blotting on the ballot or a mythical'moksha march' to keep their chairs intact. Recently the Government of India initiated the people into a 'new cargoism' as a solution for the age old ailments of the welfare state—the government is bringing the foreign saviours (the kith and kin of those colonial invaders who left India in 1947) through the 'open door' to save the hungry millions.

The individualistic perspective of human rights no longer holds good as it is proved to be counter to the experience of urban and rural masses who are perpetually under the process of marginalisation' enforced and effected in the name of 'development' in which they are not participants. Among these communities the question of survival as a group, against the socio-politico- economic onslaught by a mythical elite minority, became the focal point of all rights discourses. The resulting debates are still ongoing but a transitional consensus confirms the culture- centricity/ specificity of human rights.

The new pedagogy for human rights education is to take off

from the affirmation of culture specificity/centricity of human rights. Assertion of heterogeneity should precede the search for homogeneity because homogenisation (mostly, in the name of non-existing harmony or unity) always followed hegemonical instruments and resulted in total destruction of the beauty of diversity. Assertion of difference is not intended to negate the universality of those fundamental principles cherished everywhere since the dawn of humans. It is intended to highlight the fact that the basic elements of human society are still threatened from within the society itself. The search for an alternative pedagogy should start from a deep focusing of our observations on the inner contradictions of humanity as a whole.

Mass Media and Human Rights Education

The world has come to recognise that a free, flourishing, independent and responsible mass media plays an essential role in the functioning of a democratic society. By informing the nation on important developments and issues, by monitoring and reporting on government activities, and by encouraging public debate on key issues, print and broadcast media contribute to such basic democratic necessities as governmental transparency and accountability, popular participation in community decision-making, and ultimately, the education of the people. Think about the importance of the role played by the media in reporting about daily events upto the point of influencing the work of the Security Council in world affairs.

As a tool for the promotion and protection of human rights, a free mass media can greatly facilitate the building of a culture of human rights, by reporting on the content of international human rights, by encouraging tolerance between various national ethnic, religious and linguistic groups and by exposing rights violations wherever and whenever they occur.

Media for human rights means the strengthening of free expression, of independence and of non-interference with the world's publishers and broadcasters. Media for human rights means information dissemination which combats propaganda for war, intolerance or racism. Media for human rights means publications and broadcasts which serve not the interests of powers, but father of empowerment for neglected senior citizens; for persecuted minorities; for vulnerable children, for oppressed women, for silenced indigenous peoples; and for the desperately impoverished.

Role of family and Parents

1. Parents should be careful regarding the choice of the school or any academic institution.
2. They themselves should try to inculcate values and awareness regarding basic human rights and responsibilities.
3. They should take their children to such places and events where informations is being given.
4. They should encourage their children for participating in different events.

Role of Society

1. Everyone should raise voice whenever he/she sees something wrong and should support the right.
2. Regular meetings and discussions should be conducted on these topics of general concerns of the values and human rights, etc.
3. Clubs and groups should be formed for protection of human rights.

Role of Teachers

1. Teachers should educate students regarding rights and responsibilities.
2. She should plan the curriculum in such a way so that equal weightage is given to maths, science and social science.
3. They should plan talks, seminars, rallies, exhibitions, workshops, etc., on Human Rights.
4. They should motivate children to conduct activities related to such topics.

Objectives of NGO'S Programme for Human Rights Education

A. Participants (both men and women) / citizens understand that all Human Rights could be enjoyed by them:

(1) They know the human rights spelt out in the International Charter.
(2) They understand the conceptual meaning of Human Rights.
(3) They understand that human rights education is essential for their socio-economic and political empowerment.
(4) They understand that discrimination between man and man

on the basis of Race, Religion, Language and Nationality, and others should be eliminated.

(5) In the midst of social, political and ethnic problems, citizens understand and apply, justice, equality and fraternity.

B. Participants/Citizens develop Positive Attitude towards life and living :

(1) Healthy attitude to gender- equality, to members of the family, neighbours and society is developed.

(2) Favourable Attitude towards one's job or profession and to the people working in institutions or organisation is developed.

(3) Motivation to Achievement by Self and for Self is developed.

(4) Growth of personality is effected.

(5) Welfare of society and its well being are understood with healthy attitude.

(6) Proper attitude towards all the Human Rights is developed.

C. Action plans are developed and implemented by Participants/ Citizens, NGOs' and members plan activities, which bring about social change and which include:

(1) Participation in general and local elections relating to political governance of the country.

(2) Planning and Implementation of activities, in a phased manner, which bring social justice, economic prosperity and religious tolerance.

(3) (i) Planning visits of Citizens from other nations to NGO participants.

(ii) Planning visits of a few nations, outside India, depending on the Fund-Sufficiency.

(4) Planning strategies to fight against and eliminate evils such as corruption, abuse of power and violation of Human Rights.

(5) Others: Curriculum for Human Rights Education for Personality Growth and Social Change by NGOs, focussed on the need for a clear understanding of the Human Rights concept.

As per the report of NGO's Seminar on 'Content and Methods of Education for Human Rights' convened by the Standing Committee of International NGOs in Consultative Relationship with UNESCO in October, 1978, the seminar made the following suggestions:

(1) That NGOs intensify among themselves the exchange of information regarding:
   (a) The procedures within the United Nations system for dealing with alleged violations of human rights;
   (b) The extent to which such procedures are used and are adequate to meet the needs of those whose rights are violated; and
   (c) Situations where human rights are being violated.

(2) That NGOs urge their Government to ractify or accede to:
   (a) International Covenant on Economic, Social and Cultural Rights;
   (b) International Covenant on Civil and Political Rights;
   (c) International convention on Elimination of All Forms of Racial Discrimination, and
   (d) International Convention on Suppression and Punishment of Crime Apartheid.

(3) That NGO's intensify their effort to promote:
   (a) The widest dissemination of international instruments on Human Rights.
   (b) Their adaptation into forms which may be used effectively in programmes of education for human rights all levels of society.

(4) That NGOs promote full access to legal systems for all sectors of society as well as to knowledge of the existence of machinery (national/regional/international) for the protection of human rights.

(5) That NGOs promote the acceptance and implementation of national and international codes of conduct for law enforcement, medical and other personnel directly at risk.

(6) That NGOs, particularly through their national affiliates, promote the exchange of experience regarding the development of mechanisms at the national level for the evaluation of the realization of Human Rights.

(7) The UNESCO and NGOs, in their programmes of human rights education devote larger resources to regional meetings on these questions and in regions where no regional machinery for the protection of Human Rights exists, promote discussion of the desirability of such machinery.

Role of NGOs

Today the society is more or less violence striven. Concern with human rights can not stop with the enunciation alone. There is need for more positive and operational steps. In order to carry the work of promotion of HR's various non-governmental organisations have started the work in every part of the world. NGOs are the voice of the people of the world. It is gratifying to note that in spite of sharp differences among themselves, the NGOs managed during the Vienna Summit to reach an agreement among themselves for their joint proposals. NGOs have made their impact on the civil society of Asia, Africa and Latin America in the preparatory conferences in Tunis, San Jose, Bang Kong and the Asian Conference. Now the people in general no longer leave their problems to Government alone to see the violence and injustice but depend on the NGOs. NGOs have a share in the responsibility of greater accountability to their own and their future generations.

Suggested Functions of the NGOs

The non-governmental organisations can play a very important role. The important functions may be,

(1) Collection of information about the violation of HRs and monitoring the same
(2) Education
(3) Legislation
(4) Preventing HR abuses and rendering humanitarian help to the victims
(5) Solidarity
(6) Working in the areas of social rights.

• The Inclusion Of HRE: Higher Levels

During the decade years and till such time, the school going generation of today enter college, university, professional institutions.

• College/University

As a component of all Science, Humanities, Social Sciences and languages, Arts, with a specialisation component for those who may like to take it.

• Professional courses

As a part of the basic-core, compulsory, curriculum

integrated with an existing foundational paper or separate units added in all teacher Education and Education-related degree, diplomas, certificate courses.

- **Professional courses**

As an orientation component in the professional training courses of personnel dealing with human beings, life needs problems such as medicine, nursing, architecture, business, management, journalism, computer sciences.

(a) Specialized Training Programmes for Services: As an orientation component in National Defense and Police Training Academy Centres.

(b) For Civil Services: As a component of the short term training, orientation of the law, IAS, IPS, IES in time and Central Services entrants.

Immediate Prime Goals

UN Decade and Human Rights votaries suggest early action for certain definite purposes, viewed as short-term goals to lead to the realization of the long-term ideal vision. Here is a statement on some which stand out boldly.

literacy

Eradication of illiteracy, provision of total literacy not feasible through the school system alone due to limited access: crash programmes, non-formal settings; alternative channels, non-conventional methods.

Information

Wildest possible information through educational institutions, alternative channels, all available for and technique.

Awareness

Much emphasized: Simultaneouly through the educational system, non-formal set ups, community centres and agencies, all available channels, for a multi-media approaches as appropriate.

Knowledge and Understanding

Development of common understandings, essentially based on literacy, information and awareness but to be attempted simultaneously as for awareness, people will begin to know and understand, may not be literate in the given sense but there are non-conventional methods and now the massmedia to get messages across.

Empowerment

Of weaker sections, field work in progress, credit cooperatives for self-help, different kinds of work opportunities being provided, but new ways and means must be found for the empowerment of the needy in different spheres of life.

Human Development

Full development of human personality based on desirable values, nurtured at home, by the school and the community, facilitated by governing agencies.

Reflection and Action

Primarily a function of the major agencies of education training in thought development and the capacity to reflect and act will be fostered as the UN Decade HRE drive proceeds forward.

Commitment

To rights, duties and values, individual and collective; fostered through the home, the school, the community, the use of all available channels, for and techniques, particularly through example and demonstration of committed.

Solidarity

Of people, of peers, of families, citizens and communities, of committed leaders to stand together for common human rights, causes on the basis of shared values and help others to do the same education system can contribute but essentially it would be of, by and for the people, cultivated as in above particularly by example, demonstrated solidarity of action.

Implementation Enforcement

This is one major factor on which the success of HRE depends: even persons with required qualities may not be able to achieve implementation it has in the hands of others: Enforcement agencies regulate day-to-day life in so many ways. Heightened consciousness without the means of protection and redress may cause unrest, conflicts true, committed people prepared to stand together, and make sacrifices may eventually obtain the implementation of the right.

Supportive: Complementary Activities

To strengthen the overall HRE endeavour from different directions with suitable inputs some more supportive activities may be considered.

Establishment of HRE-HR Cells

In educational Institutions Enforcement Agencies to focus attention on HR needs to collect and disseminate information, prepare and distribute materials: collaborate with other agencies: some WCCI AIHRE motivated sponsored ones being established in educational set ups: one police department recently initiated action for an HR cell.

Celebration of Important Events Days

Involvement of key functionaries: such as the International Human Rights Day and Human Rights activities Birthday Jubilees, centennials for their popular appeal, as a rallying point for promotion, awareness and solidarity of action. This approach will be quite effective with the participation of known. HR champions persons with some kind of star celebrity status and key functionaries dealing with different aspects of HR.

Establish Human Rights Watch

Human Rights Commissions: HRW points, centres should be initiated in addition to HR National and State Commissions, some of which are in the process of being established: these to keep watch on brewing trouble, bring cases to notice of the concerned and raise with the HR Commissions, public authorities, community leaders for the prevention of HR violations and for seeking remedial action.

Final Word of Caution

In the strong pursuit of the protection of Human Rights in the world two discordant notes are heard:

(i) Within the International Commissions on Human Rights, some sub-committees, adopt a biased approach or Dichotomy of approach in interpreting Human Rights Violations, one standard for wealthy and western nations and another for poor Asian Nations.

(ii) More dangerously, it is linking Aid for Development of poor or Developing nations to the perception of Human Rights violations in those nations. All nations have to fight against this unjust dichotomy as otherwise, it will be a violation of the Right to Equality by a body which professes to protect this right.

Promotion and Protection of Human Rights by the United Nations

Promotion and encouragement of respect for an observance of human rights and fundamental freedoms is one of the purposes of the United Nations. The Charter of United Nations mentions the term human rights seven times, but makes no reference to "protection" of "human rights." A question arises how this purpose is achieved by the United Nations? It is to be noted that the role and scope of U.N. action in promoting and protecting human rights have tremendously increased in the last fifty-five years. It has been able to promote and protect human rights by a number of ways which are as follows.

1. Human Rights Consciousness

The First and the most important role which the United Nations has played is that it has made the people and the States conscious about the human rights and fundamental freedoms. It has set a pace in establishing minimum standards of acceptable behaviour by states. The proclamation of the Universal Declaration of Human Rights containing the universal code of human rights may be regarded as the first step towards the promotion and protection of human rights.

2. Codification of the Law of Human Rights

The United Nations has codified the different rights and freedoms by making treaties for all sections of the people such as women, child, migrant workers, refugees and stateless persons. In addition to the above the prohibition on the commission of in-human acts such as genocide, apartheid, racial discrimination and torture have been brought within the international rule of law.

3. Monitoring of Human Rights

Treaty bodies, Special Rapporteurs and Working Groups of the Commission on Human Rights have procedure and mechanism to monitor compliance with conventions and investigate allegations of human rights abuses. Their resolutions on specific cases carry a moral weight that few Governments are willing to defy. In the past, U.N. Human Rights Monitors have been sent to many countries including El Slavdor and Cambodia Human Rights Monitors have also worked as part of peace-keeping operations in Haiti, Rwanda, Guatemala and the former Yugoslavia.

4. Procedure for Individual's Complaints

A number of human rights treaties permit individuals to make petition before the appropriate bodies. For instance, the First Optional Protocol to the International Covenant on Civil and Political Rights, the International Convention on the Elimination of All Forms of Racial Discrimination and Conventions. Against Torture, have permitted individuals to make petitions against their states that have accepted relevant international legal procedures. Also, under procedures established by the commission on Human Rights, the Commission, its sub-commission on Prevention of Discrimination and Protection of Minorites and their Working Groups, hear numerous complaints annually submitted by individuals as well as by non-governmental organisations (NGOs). Further, the Commission on Human Rights is authorised to discuss human rights situations anywhere in the world and examine information from individuals, NGOs and other sources.

5. Compilation of Information on the Violation of Human Rights

The original mandate of Commission on Human Rights to examine situations where massive violation of rights appeaı to be taking place has been complemented by a new function, i.e., compiling information on the incidence of certain kinds of violations, or violation in a specific country. This task is performed by Special Rapporteurs/Representative or Working Groups. They gather facts, keep contacts with local groups and government authorities, conduct on-site visits when Governments permit, and make recommendations on how human rights institutions might be strengthened.

6. Examination of Human Rights Situations

The Commission on Human Rights may ask the Secretary-General to intervene or send an expert to examine a human rights situation with a view to prevent flagrant violations. Such tasks may be performed by the Secretary-General himself in the exercise of his good offices and may establish the U.Ns legitimate concern and curb abuses. The Secretary-General, or his special representative and the High Commissioner for Human Rights, confidentially raise human rights concerns with member States, including items such as the release of prisoners, communication of death sentences and other issues.

7. Coordination of Human Rights Activities

The post of High Commissioner for Human Rights was created in 1993 with the intention of strengthening the co-ordination and impact of UN Human Rights activities. He is charged with promoting and protecting the effective enjoyment by all of all human rights and maintains a permanent dialogue with the Member States.

8. By Providing Advisory Services

The Centre for Human Rights provided advisory services to Governments seeking to improve their human rights performance. Assistance may be given to draft a constitution, to improve electoral laws, establish or upgrade human rights institutions, prepare new criminal codes, or overhaul the judiciary.

The above points go to prove that the United Nations has been performing a variety of functions successfully to promote and protect human rights and it has promoted global culture of human rights through education and awareness. However, Human Rights continue to be widely violated around the globe. Fundamental rights continue to be widely violated around the globe. Fundamental rights of individual's life, liberty, and physical security, right to health, housing and work as well as cultural rights, continue to be threatened by forces of repression, ethnic hatred and exploitation. Torture, cruel and inhuman punishment for discruption of societies and ethnic, religious and other conflicts. In the face of these challenges, the United Nations has to be more active. It has to intervene in cases of massive human rights violations. It has to work with the cooperation of the member States to strengthen the commitments of promoting and protecting human rights.

Course Design for Human Rights Education

General Objectives: The Teacher Trainee

1. Acquires an awareness of human rights and their significance

to every individual.

2. Understands the need to include instruction for human rights and how to impart these in the secondary and higher secondary curriculum.
3. Acquires the ability to organise co-curricular activities centering round human rights and democratic functioning.
4. Develops active interest in extending guidance for human rights to the community at large.
5. Gets acquainted with the techniques of evaluation to assess the students practice of human rights.

Specific Objectives

1. The teacher trainee traces briefly the events leading to the universal declaration of human rights.
2. Identifies the commonality in human rights and fundamental rights cited in India's Constitution.
3. Explains the need for asserting human rights to members of culturally diverse nations and minority groups within the nations.
4. Lists out points to oppose bonded labour, abuse and exploitation of children, women, tribals and deprived sections of society.
5. Identifies the connection between the concepts of national integration and international understanding.
6. Analyses the circumstances that lead to social unrest, drug addiction, terrorism.
7. Enlists points in support of social responsibility of the government.
8. Takes active part in organising class debates, seminars, discussions on human rights issues.
9. Plans for and participates in role play, dramatization, composing poetry, songs depicting human rights.
10. Plans for and participates in meetings to observe Human Rights Day, UN Day, International Day of the Disabled, the Aged, Girl-child, etc.
11. Collects news items from massmedia reporting about violation of human rights and presents them for discussion.
12. Contacts members of the working class, rural people to familiarize them with fundamental rights.
13. Interacts with the peer group, teachers, students, neighbours

and family members on the rights of the consumer.

14. Identifies situations, ways and means to pass information about human rights to school students.
15. Participates as a member of N.S.S. Community Service in service activities.
16. Gets familiar with the tools and techniques to collect data regarding practice of human rights.
17. Analyses, infers, draws conclusions and reports the observed.
18. Conducts a case study on a child labour or a school drop out or female infanticide or unemployed individual.

Course Content

Unit 1—Historical Perspectives

Preamble of the UN-Universal Declaration of Human Rights, 1948, Need and Significance. The Constitution of India Fundamental Rights—Special reference to the right of the minorities: culturally diverse groups; children; women. Ethnic issues-racial segregation the apartheid-restriction in religions practices leading to the denial of fundamental human rights (Classroom work in the form of lecture, group activity, discussion and preparation of group report and presentation of the same: 5 hours of teacher educator-peer group feedback).

Unit 2—Human Rights Education

UNESCO 1974 Recommendations concerning education for International cooperation and peace—Education for human rights and fundamental freedom. Essential features of democracy. Law-related education-the Legal Competence Models—Compliance Models—Education for Economic responsibility—The Committee of Minister's Recommendation R (85) 7 on the teaching and learning about human rights. (Classroom work as lectures, seminar and discussion amounting to 6 hours of teacher educations trainee participation. Extra classroom work as library reference and preparation of papers for seminar for 9 hours. Evaluation in the form of assignment, class test rating, paper presentation and participation in discussion).

Unit 3—Education for Citizenship

Duties and responsibilities of a citizen—right for education—right to vote need to educate the voters. Right for access to information—rights of the consumer-need for consumer education-role of the consumer courts. (Classroom work for 4 hours consisting of lecture, group discussion and presentation of conclusions to the class. Extra class work as reference of material from books, periodicals attending speeches by consumer activists, observance of demonstration about adulteration and low quality of goods etc. 6 hrs. Evaluation through oral test, assignment, rating the participation).

Unit 4—Massmedia and Agencies for Human Rights Education

Role of massmedia in creating awareness about human rights—reporting of exploitation—citizens' Forums, Clubs and non-government organisations spreading human rights education. Analysis of reports and programmes depicting significance of human rights (Classroom work of 4 hours covering lecture, group discussion, reading of note prepared by trainees and feedback. Extra classroom work for 6 hours for collection of material, analysis and preparation of report by trainees. Evaluation through test, rating of participation in group discussion, rating of reports).

Unit 5—Extension Programme in Human Rights Education

Contacting members of working community to understand their problems in exercising fundamental rights—meeting out-of-school children and youth who are denied the right to education, participation in NSS activities or role play debate, dramatization creating awareness of fundamental rights—awareness of rights of consumer. (Classroom activity of introductory lecture discussion and planning for community activities covering 5 hours. Extra classroom work of trainees to know the tools and techniques like interview observation filling schedules and questionnaires to collect data totaling to 5 hours. Evaluation through rating and grading trainees abilities, skills and involvement in planning, executing community activities, use of data collecting techniques, individual and group work assignments). The entire course work amounts to a total of 60 hours which is split into 50 hours of content coverage (as per details given above unit-wise) and 10 hours of case study compulsory for each traineee (which may be on a child labour, a girl drop out an unemployed person as to study in depth the deprivation of rights and the circumstances or forces responsible to them and finally to suggest rectification in the proposed course is designed for 2 credits, each requiring 30 hours of work from trainees.

The course being a new one, there is need to collect and compile relevant material to be used by the teacher educators. Collective effort by participants in a workshop would serve this purpose.

HUMAN RIGHTS

Curriculum Plan

Unit—I (Theory)

1. Human Rights:
   Meaning/Concept/Definition
   Kinds of Human Rights

2. Human Rights and Responsibilities

Unit—II (Practicals)

(At College Level)

1. Rally on Human Rights Day, i.e., 10th December.
2. Visit to Court and Interview of Lawyer.
3. Drama and Cultural Programme for Legal awareness.
4. Seminars/Conferences on "Human Rights" and "Legal Awareness."
5. Quiz Competition, Eassy writing, Debates etc. on "Human Rights" and "Legal Literacy."
6. Poster making, cartoon making, slogan writing, card making etc. on "Human Rights" and "Legal Literacy."
7. Bulletin Board Competition cum Exhibition.
   Competition of the products made, then exhibition cum sale of the same products like posters, cards etc.
8. Starting a Magazine or a Journal at Departmental Level or College level.
9. Panel Discussion.
10. Field Study/experience:
    Survey of the area
    Find problems or cases related to "Human Rights"
    Design a strategy to approach community or target.

Perform or implement the strategy

Take feedback and follow up after a month or so.

Practicals (At School Level)

1. Celebrating Human Rights, Day i.e., 10th December
2. Expert talk on "Human Rights" and "Legal Literacy"

3. Puppet show on "Human Rights" and "Legal Literacy"
4. Song/Poem Writing competition
   — Essay writing competition
   — Quiz competition
   — Cartoon making, slogan writing
5. Starting a School Magazine on "Human rights" and "Legal Literacy."

SUGGESTIONS FOR EFFECTIVE IMPLEMENTATION

The stipulation of the rights in the Covenants alone is not enough. They themselves cannot serve any useful purpose. At present, there is a wide gap between the 'promise and performance' because of the absence of an effective international implementation machinery. Amnesty Reports have very often laid down that human rights are violated in a number of States. Further, assault on human dignity sometimes on a massive scale is a cause for deep anxiety. The international protection of individuals against the States is very much required because States should no longer be entrusted as their guardian in life. In the law of human rights, the individuals and the State constitute the two opposing subjects of rights and duties. While the former has rights, the latter has a duty to protect them. International law has a function to see that duties are performed by the States against the individuals. The effectiveness of the measures in matters of human rights is inextricably linked with the attitude of the States. It is the responsibility of each State to ensure respect for human rights within its jurisdiction.

In some countries, especially in those which are referred to as developing countries or the least developed countries the problem for the protection of human rights is quite different. They are fighting for providing basic necessities of life to their people because of their poor economic conditions. How can a State think of providing civil and political rights to its people unless food, shelter and clothings are made available? No doubt, it is the responsibility of the States themselves to make every possible effort to make available the basic necessities of life. But to speak of human rights without speaking of developmental issues or the new international economic order was to take precisely one-sided approach. It would not serve the cause of promoting the full enjoyment of human rights. The Cooperation of other States especially those of developed States is much needed to meet the challenge in view of its close relationship with the maintenance of international peace and security. Although developing countries gave a call to establish a New International Economic Order, it has not been suitably responded by the developed countries. The U.N. system has also failed considerably to put the solution envisaged in the New International Economic Order into effect. It has posed a threat to the idea of economic betterment and also of greater human dignity, secuity, justice and equality. The forces of confrontation and tension amongst the States have prevented to arrive at a conclusion agreeable to all. It again shows that the developed countries have different approach towards the term human rights. While they might be serious as to the respect of human dignity and honour for the people of their own States, they are not concerned for those human beings who are living across the border.

The future of the promotion of human rights on International level is therefore grim. It is likely to remain so, as long as the attitude of the States of developed countries towards the developing countries is not changed. The paper progress has, of course, been made. Various meetings, conferences, and seminars have been organised where speakers have at length advocated the need for the protection of global human rights, but in reality things are quite different. Millions of people are still deprived of the basic necessities of life due to extremely bad economic and social conditions. What the affluent States and their people who are advocating for the cause of human rights outside as well as inside the United Nations is doing for them is totally insignificant. What is needed on their part is the realization of the conditions of those who are deprived of these basic necessities. They are required to realize that mankind is one and human beings are equal and must enjoy at least the minimum of rights and freedoms.

Suggestions for the Consideration

1. Open Human Rights Education Cell in Schools and Colleges to associate the younger generation with this campaign.
2. Nominate District Project Directors and help them to find resources for implementing their projects.
3. Obtain from UN and other agencies materials on Human

Rights and publish it in Regional Languages for the benefit of grass-root workers.

4. Feeds Massmedia, TV, Radio, Print Media with progress of the campaign and make it a mass movement.
5. Universities should organise Training courses and seminars for all workers to develop their competence.
6. Associate with National Commission on Human Rights and State Commissions for promoting human rights awareness and render help in cases of violations of human rights.
7. Help rural youth to establish new NGOs for launching new projects in the rural sector.
8. Prajapita Brahmkumari Ishwariya Vishwa Vidyalaya can help by establishing a new Department of Human Rights Education to provide trained personnel to Universities, Colleges and Schools.

Conclusion

All people have rights. They include the right of life, dignity, in fact all political, civil, social, cultural and other rights. These rights are in alienable birth rights, which are enjoyed by all without discrimination of gender, age, sex, race, language, creed, class, colour or any other status. In the recent past, concern for human right has emerged as the single most important issue for mankind due to activities of the United Nations, focus of the media and increased awarness of human rights as well as magnitude of violations of human rights all over the world.

Human Rights Education is a necessary pre-condition for a healthy democratic society. It helps in developing global perspectives and awareness in protecting us from discrimination, in preparing to raise our voices against abuses of human rights in the world and in accepting our responsibilities vis-a-vis our rights.

Teaching of Human Rights is meant to arouse awareness; impart education and ultimately achieve the liberty of Human mind and spirit. It is a continuing process. The Teaching of Human Rights is, therefore an essential means of bringing about change in human behaviour.

Ideally, such an education starts at home. The family provides the surest foundation for fostering respect for human rights, for acquiring habits of tolerance, partnership, sharing and developing reflexes of gender equality and a spirit of dialogue. Next to family, comes the school which unfortunately is not available to about a quarter of the young learners at the primary and secondary school level in developing countries. Formal instruction, apart, the entire school system should constitute an initiation to democratic living to the assumption of responsibilities, to the challenges of participation, to learning about the linkage between rights and duties and respecting the worth and dignity of each individual. The school today has a powerful role to play when it comes to shaping values and behaviour of children. The television, in particular, weighs heavy in the balance of young people's choices in the contemporary world, consequently the need for partnership between education and the media has never been greater than what it is today.

Teacher eductors should always take initiative and take suitable steps to equip both the novices and practitioners of the teaching profession in meeting the challenges of education for a better future. It will be appropriate to recall the preamble of WCCI Constitution which states:

As members of the world community, educators have a responsibility to ensure that education contributes to the promotion of equity peace and the universal realization of human rights. To this end curricular and instructional programmes of all educational enterprises for children, youth or adults should aim to develop in every person self-respect, social awareness and the capacity to participate at all levels of world society from local to global.

References

1. Agarwal, H.O. *Human Rights*, Central Law Publications, Delhi.

2. Amnesty International, British Section, *Teaching and Learning about Human Rights*, Amnesty International, London, 1983.

3. Banerji, N.P. Human Rights and Education of the Socially disadvantaged. *Journal of All India Association for Educational Research* 8, 3-4, 29-32, Sep-Dec. 1996.

4. Best, F. Education, Culture, Human Rights and International Understanding. UNESCO, Paris, 1990.

5. Council of Europe. Recommendation : R 85 Teaching and

Learning About Human Rights in school. The Author, Starbourg, 985.

6. Gurepdesh Singh, Human Rights Education Agenda for Educational Institutions, *University News* 36 (3) Jan 19, pp. 5-7, 1998.

7. Gosh, A.K. Human Rights Education. *University News* 36 (15) April 13, pp. 4-7, 1998.

8. The Rights to the Human, *India International Centre Quarterly* Vol. 13, No. 3 and 4, Dec. 1986.

9. Human Rights in the Family-Issues and Recommendations for implementation. April (IWRAW) 1993.

10. Henry Shue, *Basic Rights, subsistence Affluence* and *U.S. Foreign Policy*, Princeton University Press.

11. Jagamath Mohanty. *Human Rights Education,* Deep and Deep Publication, New Delhi.

12. Kunja Kusum Kakati, Adult Education and Human Rights for Women. *Indian Journal of Adult Education*, pp. 5-13. July-Sep. 1999.

13. NCTE. Human Rights and National Values : Self Learning Packages. NCTE, New Delhi, 1996.

14. Sharma, R.S. and Sinha R.K. *Perspectives in Human Rights.* Commonwealth Publishers.

15. Sunil Behari Mohanty. Education for Human Rights. *University News* 37 (49) pp. 14-19, Dec. 6, 1999.

16. Valchev, R. The Civic Education Experiment. Council of Europe. Strasbourg. 1992.

17. Winin Perara. *Human Rights,* India Press, Goa.

18. Zgaga, P. Human Rights : Principles and theoretical starting point of education. In UNESCO, Education for Human Rights and Citizenship in Central and Eastern Europe. Charles University 77-80, 1995.

32

Violation of Women Rights in Industries : A Need for Value Education

Reema Chaurasia, Maneesha Shukul

The position of the women in society is an important indicator of social progress (Devi. 1998). Moreover, it is well known that the education that a society provides for its women and their social position in society are closely inter-related. Improvement in the social status of women is generally accompanied by their educational advancement and a corresponding change in the character of their education. Improvement in their education enhances their status in society.

The National Committee on Women's Education (1959) recommended Government to regard the education of women as a major and special problem in education to close the existing gap between the education of men and women in as short time as possible. Accordingly special efforts, were made from 1960 onwards as a result of which female enrolment improved substantially in the subsequent years.

Education not only adapts an individual to the existing or emerging social situation but it also has a creative role that it has the potential for liberating the mind from shackles of the established culture. It is, therefore, inevitable that the liberal ideas of freedom, equality and dignity of the individual should in course of time produce educated women but like the progress of education, the change in the social position of women is also very uneven. It differs from region to region and from one social segment or community to another. Clearly changes in the social position of women, their role and status have to be gauged both at the *ideational* level and at the level of actual social practice.

According to Lakshmi C.S. (1976), "In the progressive society of tomorrow, life should be a joint venture for men and women. Men should share the responsibility of parenthood and home-making with women and women in their turn should share the social and economic responsibilities of men" Gender-role differentiation produces sexual division of labour in the family as well as in the formal labour market. Evidences show that women are exploited at their work place not only in India but all over the world. This is the result of technological change, the emergence of new products and production processes as well as industrialisation. In the process of development the safety and health at work place are a matter of discussion.

Women are deprived of their rights at their work place. In Bangladesh, young women are forced to work from 7:30 am to 8.00 pm 7 days a week, sewing clothing for Wal-Mart, earning just 9-20 cents an hour. In El-Salvador they are paid just 3 cents for every $14.99/-yale Univ T-shirts they sew. Women are fired, if they become pregnant, refused to work overtime or even suspected of trying to organise. Women are paid 8 (4 cents an hour) for a month to sew London Fog, Karl Kani, Porodless. Sport Authority clothing in Burma and if they dare question or challenge factory condition, they are arrested or tortured. Tele-tubbies—the best selling toy in US are made in China by young women forced to work 18 hour/day from 7:00 am to 1:00 am, 7 days a week. They are allowed 4 hours. sleep a night and receive a half day off each month. They are paid 13 cents an hour, earning $14.42 for the entire 112 hours work week. Women in El Salvador are paid 20 cents for every 75 Nike shirt they sew. In another factory, the workers earn 74 cents to sew 198 Liz Claiborne Jackets. Women are fired if they try to learn or defend their rights. In the US territory of Saipan, migrant workers from China toiling under condition of indentured servitude sew clothing 12-14 hours a day earning 3.00 an hour for Wal-Mart. In case, she falls in love, becomes pregnant, fail to reach their high daily production quota, complain about the harsh working or living condition or become involved in political activities or organising, they are immediately fired and deported back to China. 21,000 workers in Northern China assemble Nike Sneakers for 23 cents an hour working 10-15 hours shift.

The studies conducted in India show the same condition of the women workers that of other countries. According to the study conducted by Sharma (1970) about the physical conditions of the workplace, the unit was housed in old shanties or old dilaphidated buildings with only one door and no window. The workplace had no provisions for either electricity or ventilation. Drinking water tap was situated in the stinking toilet.

Another study on construction workers (Ministry of Human Resource Development, 1988) reveals that women were susceptible to occupational stress due to constant shifting of mortar apart from various other physical problems like fatigue, cramps and postural defects. Rao and Hussain's study (1994) reveals the facts regrading the women workers, machine operators and others doing stitching, folding and automatic pressing. These workers complained of extreme tiredness, headaches, spells of nausea and at times fainted.

A study conducted by Nihila (1993) on the health problems of women workers in tanning industry, the findings revealed that during the different stages of the tanning process workers are exposed to numerous toxic substances which resulted in diseases like anthrax, dermatitis, several skin diseases, chronic bronchitis, poor vision, giddiness, poor appetite, etc.

A study on the health status of tribal women (Chatterjee, 1993) show that women carrying heavy load suffer from cervical, spinal and lower limb joints and osteoarthritis. Women working mining quarrying and stone crushing suffer from respiratory disorders like asthma, silicosis, tuberculosis, bronchitis, dermatitis and chronic conjunctivitis. Women in agriculture mostly had contacted dermatitis, chronic chemical poisoning and fungal infection.

A document released by Women Links (1999) showed that there was an increase in incidence of breast cancer, ovarian cancer, reproductive and gynecological disorders, early onset of puberty, postponement of menopause, etc. due to a class of chemicals, called persistent organic pollutants (PoPs). Those were highly toxic and potential to injure human and other organisms even at low concentration. Those were silent killers and had long term chronic effects.

The fundamental rights in India constitution at country level and human rights at large are there to help women to overcome their problem because every human being is entitled to enjoy her/his rights and to have them protected by the laws and practice of her/ his country of residence.

They play an increasingly important role in relationship between states and international policies particularly as calls for democracy intensify throughout the world. In different contexts advocates perceive the human rights framework as having a great potential to further aspirations for social justice including the elimination of discrimination against women and greater protection of children, prisoners, indigenous peoples and other socially and economically disadvantaged groups.

It is within this tradition of social justice that in recent years thousands of activists from around the world began to coalesce as a movement for the recognition and protection of women's human rights. Many had been advocates of women's rights at local and national levels using national laws. Others were involved in movements for economic empowerment, women's health and education and other women specific issues. Those joining this growing movement, all came to believe that human rights could provide a powerful additional tool for advancing women's interests.

There are three main reasons for calling attention to women's human rights.

1. To inform women that they have human rights and are entitled to enjoy them; woman should know their rights to use them. It is through awareness and knowledge that women can exercise their rights and use national, regional and international human rights system for their protection. Information of woman's human rights also helps woman recognize cultural practices and national laws that violate their human rights.
2. To expose and combat rights violations that are based on sex or gender. These violations are justified on the basis of biological differences (e.g., A women's capacity to be pregnant). Others are based on gender on the socially constructed roles and values ascribed to women (e.g., Home making). In either case, abusive laws or practices motivated or justified by sex or gender have not yet gained full international recognition as human rights violations.

3. To shape a new human practices that fully addresses the human rights of woman. The understanding of how human rights could or should protect women remains underdeveloped. Secondly, human rights mechanism has not adequately developed procedures that facilitate woman's access to them.

The World Trade Organisation (WTO) opposes any link between global trade and human rights. Today, there is not one single multinational corporation, i.e., willing to even sit down to discuss conditioning trade upon respect for human and worker rights and environmental protections. On the other hand, they are growing fast and gaining an unfair competitive advantage through exploiting woman, firing, pregnant woman, paying starvation charger, forming 12-14 hours shifts or firing and blacklisting workers struggling to defend their basic rights.

Therefore, there is need to create awareness among women. Education plays a crucial role in developing consciousness regarding the use of rights and at the same time preventing the exploitation. Education becomes significant in bringing social change by producing readiness on the part of people but it has to be borne in mind that the task of establishing social equality could not be attained alone by the government. The cooperation and participation of the people as a whole in this great task of social change leading to equality is paramount.

Education must be planned in a manner which is in keeping with the aspiration and needs of the people as a whole. The data shows that today women need to know much about their changing circumstances. These changed circumstances equip women with such rights that strengthen the position of women. Education must reach to the grass-root level. Though the Government, NGOs, private institutions and people themselves are trying to inculcate the value of education among women to use their rights but woman herself has to come forward and has to look for the opportunities to utilize their rights and to make the best use of the education they have.

References

1. Chatterjee, K.K. (Dec. 1993). Health Status of Tribal Women. *Social Change*. Vol. 23 No. 4 pp. 53-56.

2. C.S. Lakshmi (1976). Tradition and Modernity of Tamil Women Writers. *Social Scientist*. No. 45, p. 39.

3. Ministry of Human Resource Development (1988). Occupational health Issues of Women in the unorganized sector. Report of the Task Force on Health prepared for the National Commission on Self-Employment.

4. Nihila, Millie (1993). Development, process and status of women: Training Industry in Tamil Nadu. *Economic and Political Weekly*. Vol. 28, No. 41. Bombay: Sameeksha Trust Publications pp. 2220-2227.

5. Rao, R. and Hussain, S. (1984). *One step Forward, Two step Backward*. Women's work and struggle in the Garment Export, Industry, Second. National Conference on Women's Studies, Trivandrum. pp. 7-21.

6. Report of the National Committee on Women's Education, Ministry of Education (1959), New Delhi, pp. 32, 192.

7. Sharma, G.R. (1970). Living conditions of workers in Jharia Coal Field.

8. Unpublished Doctoral Dissertation of Ranchi University, Ranchi.

9. http://www. derechos. org/nizkor/doc/articulos/ chossadovskye. html.

Part V
Values for Saving the Environment

33

Impact of Environmental Degradation on Human Health

Shivani Bala, Neeti Sharma, Amiteshwar Ratra & Savita Singal

Health status of an individual, a community or a nation is determined by the interplay and integration of two ecological universes the internal environment of man himself and external environment which surrounds him. The disturbance in the delicate balance between man and his environment causes severe problems. Environmental pollution is one of the most formidable danger that confronts mankind today, because where we are living, it is almost fully polluted, whatever we drink, we breath, we eat contains pollutants. It has, at present attained unequal proportions as a result of man's abuse of environment and natural resources. The pollution of environment is almost wholly manmade. The demographic growth and fast urbanisation are bringing profound social and environmental changes.

It is an established fact that environment has a direct impact on physical, mental, social and economic well being of those living in it. No nation, rich or poor, can ever afford to neglect environment. The price that has to be paid for the negligence is virtually immeasurable. The problems of environmental health are many and varied. So, it is of utmost importance to save our planet, for the present as well as future generations.

Now the question arises what is environment' and after that what is pollution.

The air, water, minerals, organisms and all other external factors surrounding and affecting a given organism at any given time, is environment. The social and cultural forces that make the life of a person or a population.

Pollution is an undesiarble change in the physical, chemical or biological characteristics for air, water and land that may or will affect human life adversely, has a direct impact on the quality of life and environmental degradation. The main causes of degradation are:

Population
Industrialisation
Deforestation
Urbanisation

Population explosion is affecting our planet. Large population demands more resources. But scarcity of the resources leads man to exploit the nature for more and more resources which further hampers the quality of living (Model 1 and Model 2 enclosed).

To meet the needs of people, we cut down our forests, thereby resulting in deforestation. Deforestation has resulted in floods, green house effect, drought, polluted air, etc. Temperatue change may further cause various health problems such as cardiovascular, respiratory, yellow fever, dangu etc.

Way to Protect our Health by Reducing Environmental Degradation

It is our moral responsibility to protect our environment at different levels.

At individual level

- Be vegetarian
- Don't eat junk food
- Use cycle in the place of scooter,
- Save petrol
- Grow more trees at family and community level
- Quit smoking
- Don't blow horn continuously
- Use tube lights
- Use public transport
- Before leaving the room, switch off all the switches

At family level

- Grow more trees in your backyard
- Use ecofriendly refrigerator
- Use unleaded petrol

- Check your vehicle regularly
- Avoid use of own car, use public transport
- Use solar cooker
- Pool you work like dropping the children in the school
- Don't use AC, refrigerator
- Grow indoor plants
- Use lower *cinestor* and small water tank in your toilet
- Don't use more flush
- Say no to the polythene bags
- Don't use non-biodegradable items
- Use paper, cloth or jute bag.
- Always 'On' your T.V. or Radio at low volume
- Restrict the use of loudspeaker and crackers at the time of festival and marriage.
- Regular tuning of your vehicle, use silencer in your vehicles
- Don't start vehicles within the house
- Dispose your garbage at proper place
- Re-use the water of the bathroom in the garden or kitchen garden
- Reduce the use of detergent.

At community level

- Pool your vehicle if you are living or going to be same place. Use your vehicle in rotation-wise manner.
- Grow more trees
- Use unleaded petrol
- Restrict the use of loudspeaker at the time of marriage, jagran, etc.
- Minimum use of crackers at the time of festival
- Start campaign for community interest and to check the pollution
- Organise play, drama, exhibition and "Nukkad Natak"
- Raise your voice against the wrong work done by any one
- Minimum use of pesticides and insecticides

At last, always remember four R's

- Reuse
- Recycle
- Reduce
- Repair
- Repairing is also an important factor to protect the

environment. Don't buy too many things. Repairs your old ones.

The Ministry of Environment and Forest, Govt. of India has instituted a scheme of labeling environment friendly products (Ref. Gazetted Notification No. 71-21-2-91). This scheme is known as eco-mark scheme. Under this scheme the products which are less harmful to environment (including human health) or have benign impact on the environment through the various stages of development, manufacture, use, packaging, distribution, consumption and disposal or recycling, may be awarded ECO-mark. ECO-mark is given to Ecofriendly products.

Any product which is made, packed, used or disposed-off in a way that significantly reduce the harm it would otherwise cause to the environment is considered as environment friendly product. Products which are biodegradable or photodegradable are more environment friendly than those which are not degradable.

Conclusion

The development and growth of civilization results in rapid industrialisation and urbanisation. This has polluted the natural environment to such as extent that it has been brought to its brink of destruction and disaster. The environmental degradation has resulted in ill health among the individuals. Several diseases affect the mankind because of environmental pollution increasing everyday. Therefore, there is dire need to re-evaluate our values of present age. Values provide the basis to all our motivational needs. Home scientis, extension health workers, social workers and environmentalists should make an effort to inculcate right values in our young generation to become more environment conscious.

References

1. Dhaliwal, G.S. and Dilawari, V.K. (Eds) 1990. *Environmental management*, PAU, Ludhiana.

2. (1996). How green is your world. *The Tribune*, June 1, Saturday Plus: 6.

3. (1996). Ecological alarm call ! *The Tribune*, June 1, Saturday Plus: 6.

4. (1996). Polythene problems. *The Tribune*, June 1, Saturday Plus: 5.

5. (1999). Women in Calcutta plan Chipko-Type stir to protect trees. *The Hindustan Times*, November 15, Monday: 11.

6. Sahya, K.B. (1998). Population and Environment. *The Hindustan Times*, January 14.

7. Hansra, B.S., Dhaliwal, G.A., NS Jerath, N. (1992). *Changing senario of our environment*. Punjab Agricultural University, Ludhiana.

8. Gazetted Notification 1991. No. 71-21-2-91. The Directorate of Environment. SCO 1-2-3 Sector, 17-D, Chandigarh.

9. Approach Paper on Nine Five Year Plan, Government of India, Planning Commission, New Delhi, 1997.

10. Biswal, A. Value orientation in Teacher Education in Venkataiah, N. (ed) Value Education. APH Publishing Corporation, New Delhi, 1998.

11. Commonwealth Secretariat Better Schools : Resource Materials for Schools, Heads, London, 1993.

12. Dhar, S. Human Development Index in some states of India. *Journal of Rural Reconstruction* 26 (1) ; 71-79, 1990.

13. Menon, N.V.C. Role of NGO's in Disaster Management. *Indian Journal of Adult Education*. Vol. 59, No. 3, July-Sept. 1998.

14. Srinivasan, V. *Health Update : Multiple Perspectives on Health Empowerment*, 3 (12) Aug. 1999.

15. T. Gopal Das and S. Seshadri, *Nutrition Monitoring and Assessments* Oxford University Press, Delhi, 1987.

34
Awareness in Haryana Regarding Air Pollution

Shivani Bala and Savita Singal

Man has recently become conscious of the threat to environment by scientific and technological developments. For the last few decades, environmental deterioration has been attributed to a number of factors, such as, over population, over production, over wastage, the exploitation of natural resources, industrialisation, urbanisation, depletion of traditional natural ecological balance and denudation of forests.

Environment is, in fact, the mythological 'Kamdhenu' which gives everything we ask for. Frederic Engles (1974) warned, "let us not, however, flatter ourselves much on account of our human victories over nature." For each such victory takes its revenge. Each victory, it is true, in the first place brings about the results we expected, but in the second and third place it has quite different unforeseen effect which only too often cancel the first.

No nation, rich or poor, can ever afford to neglect its environment. Rural areas constitute a major backbone of our country. The health status in rural areas is effected because the means to have a healthy life are depleting. There is increase of pollutants in our rural environment, once considered to have clean and healthy air.

Air is precious natural resource without which life cannot be sustained for more than a few minutes. This increase in air pollution to some extent is a result of changing human values. Man's greed of acquisition of more and more wealth and material goods is degrading the environment.

The present study was conducted with following specific objectives:

1. To assess awareness among rural homemakers regarding sources of air pollution.
2. To assess perceived ill effects of air pollution on human health by rural homemakers.

Methodology

This study was conducted in Devan village of Hissar district in Haryana state, which was purposively selected, as this village was easily assessable. A sample of fifty female respondents was randomly selected, restricting one respondent from one household.

To achieve the objectives of the present study, a questionnaire was prepared, which was duly pre-tested to increase its credibility and validity. Data so collected was suitably analysed, using frequencies, percentages and scores.

Analysis

Fifty per cent of the respondents were in the middle age group of 31-45 years, followed by 40 per cent belonging to younger age group of upto 30 years.

Respondents were aware that burning of garbage (76%) and smoke produced at the time of cooking (62%) are internal sources of air pollution (Table 1). Only 26 per cent of respondents knew that smoking cigarette also added to air pollution.

Most of the respondents were unaware of most of the other internal sources of air pollution such as dust particles produced through house cleaning (82%); CFC gas emitted from refrigerator/AC (92%); fumes from LPG stove (86%); gas emitted from sprays, perfumes, etc (90%); gas emitted from starting of vehicles (74%); fumes emitted from household pesticides (84%) and from pillows, mattresses, paints, etc (88%).

Rural homemakers awareness regarding external sources of air pollution was much better than that of internal sources. Respondents (60-70%) were aware of major external air pollutants such as, improper disposal of garbage, smoke from vehicles, exhaust emitted from industries, fumes from use of insecticides/pesticides, dust particles from agricultural operation and smell from industrial effluents.

Rural homemakers were also aware of the occasional sources of air pollution. Respondents were aware of burning of crackers (92%) and smoke and dust from construction of roads (64%) as air pollutants. Half of the respondents were aware of nuclear explosions, fire in oil wells and forest fires leading to air pollution.

All the respondents felt that the irritation of eyes, nose, throat, etc were the major physiological effects of air pollution (Table 2). By a large majority of respondents, headache (98%), chest pain (80%), coughing (09%), dizziness (66%), suffocation (58%) and nausea (56%) were also perceived as ill effects on physiological health of human beings.

Almost all the respondents reported reduced work ability, fatigue and dullness as psychological effects of air pollution.

Majority of the respondents, perceived that air pollutants adversely effected their day to day life, such as, soiling of clothes and household goods, sore throat, breathing problem, destruction of whitewash or exterior paints, breathing problem, stickiness of hair, and, feeling of sand in mouth and some occasional sources like burning of crackers, explosion, fire in well, etc.

Conclusions and Implications

From the present study, it can be concluded, that, rural homemakers were aware that smoke from vehicles, exhaust emitted from industries, smoke and dust from construction of roads, burning of crackers, etc. were the sources of air pollution. They were also able to perceive the ill effects of air pollution on human health, but they were not able to identify most of the internal sources of air pollution. Such as, fumes from kerosene stove, fumes from LPG, gas emitted from starting of vehicles, etc.

With the change in the demands and needs to today's fast moving life the human values are also changing. There is need to bring awareness among the inhabitants of this planet and especially among the rural homemakers regarding the control measures which could be incorporated at family level to curtail air pollution. Some of the control measures that can be adopted at different levels, are discussed below:

1. At individual level

(i) Lower down consumption and reduce waste, so that one's life style reflects the conservation of natural resources.
(ii) Stay informed on environmental topics.
(iii) Share knowledge with others.
(iv) Get involved in environmental issues.

(v) Reduce cigarette smoking.
(vi) By adopting vegetarian diet.
(vii) First check yourself, so that, you can be an example to others.

2. At family levels

(i) Use of solar devices in homes also saves energy and reduces air pollution.
(ii) Use of indoor plants.
(iii) Use of organic pesticides in home.
(iv) Use of eco-friendly goods.
(v) Use of exhaust fan in kitchen.
(vi) No starting of vehicle within house.
(vii) Grow more trees.

3. At community level

(i) Trees should be grown along roadsides, as they absorb polluted air and give fresh air.
(ii) Industrial smoke should be filtered before releasing it in air.
(iii) Use of unleaded petrol and regular tuning of vehicles.
(iv) Banning polluting units around residential areas.
(v) Minimum use of vehicles.

4. At government level

By making some important rules and regulation at both state and central level and also check from time to time their implementation.

Creating awareness on such important issues can help in building a positive value system and can go a long way in checking air pollution. Home Science extension specialists, field functionaries and massmedia, especially Doordarshan can play a very effective role in developing environment conscious values among the rural families

Table 1: Awareness Regarding Sources of Air Pollution

S.No.	*Sources*	*Awareness* F	(%)
Internal sources			
1.	Dust and particles produced through house cleaning	9	18
2.	Smoke at time of cooking	31	62
3.	Smoke of cigarette	13	26
4.	CFC Gas emitted from refrigerator/AC	4	18
5.	Fumes from kerosene stove	20	40
6.	Fires from LPG Stove	7	14
7.	Smoke from burning of garbage	38	76
8.	Gas emitted from sprays, perfumes, etc.	5	10
9.	Gas emitted from starting of vehicles	13	26
10.	Fumes emitted from household pesticides	8	16
11.	Smell from pillows, mattresses, paints, etc.	6	12
External Sources			
1.	Improper disposal of garbage	32	64
2.	Smoke from vehicles	36	72
3.	Exhaust emitted from industries	35	70
4.	Fumes from use of insecticides/pesticides	32	64
5.	Dust particles from agricultural operation	36	72
6.	Gas from thermal power plants generating electricity by burning	17	34
7.	Dust released from crushers, bricks kilns	15	30
8.	Gases emitted from dead bodies	36	72
9.	Smell from industrial effluents	37	74
10.	Gases emitted from incinerators	15	30
11.	Foul smell from slaughter houses	24	48
Occasional sources			
1.	Smoke and dust from construction of roads	32	64
2.	Burning of crackers	46	92
3.	Nuclear explosions	24	48
4.	Fire in oil wells	26	52
5.	Forest fires	24	48

Table 2: Perceived Ill-Effects of Air Pollution on Human Health

S.No.	Effects	Perceived ill-effects F	(%)
Physiological effects			
1.	Irritation in eyes, nose, throat, etc.	50	100
2.	Headache	49	98
3.	Nausea	28	56
4.	Suffocation	29	58
5.	Chest pain	40	80
6.	Coughing	45	90
7.	Dizziness	35	66
Psychological effects			
1.	Reduce work ability	46	92
2.	.Fatigue	46	92
3.	Dullness	42	84
Daily life effects			
1.	Feeling of sand in mouth	41	82
2.	Stickiness of hair	35	70
3.	Increase in susceptibility of infection	24	48
4.	Breathing problems	40	80
5.	Sore throat	36	72
6.	Soiling of clothes and household goods	49	98
7.	Destruction of white wash or exterior paints	31	62

References

1. Dhaliwal, G.S., and Dilawari, V.K. 1990. Man and Environment. Environment Management (Edf.) PAU, Ludhiana.

2. Basu, B. 1988. Twin threat to your atmosphere. *Yojna* 32 (7): 5-6.

3. (1999). Air emission norms to be effective from June, 1. *The Hindustan Times*. November 18: 5.

4. Contingency Action Plan for National Calamities. Ministry of Agriculture, Govt. of India, 1990.

5. Agarwal, V. Sanjay Raj and S. Kumar. Noise Pollution-A case study. Proceedings MIN-ENV-95, Udaipur, pp. 67-72, 1995.

6. Alvin Toffler, *Power Shift*. New York Bantain, 1991.

7. Dewey, John, *Theory of Valuation*. Chicago Publication, 1939.

8. WRI, IUCN, UNEP. Global Biodiversity Strategy Policy Maker's Guide. Washington D.C., 1997.

35

Environmental Values in the Curriculum of Home Science

Debolina Talapatra, Renu Kumari, Piyali Roy

Introduction

According to Frobel Education is a process by which child makes its internal-external development. According to Dr. Dewy education is the development of all those capacities in the individual which will enable him to control his environment and feeling his potentialities.

Ultimate aim of education is self-realisation, the fulfillment of man's instincts potentialities for many in addition to the realisation of eternal life. Thus, education system becomes effective if it fulfils the needs and demands of society. At present environmental problems have become one of the burning issues in society. People are not aware of environmental degradation. Thus, there is need for internalisation of values to save environment.

Hence, educational system is required to impart proper education for environmental protection. But in reality educational system is unable to fulfil this demand of society and proper emphasis is not given on it.

Role of UGC

Environmental problems have reached a level where almost everyone is conscious of it. This rising consciousness has also given rise to a widespread responsiveness of the idea for the need to do something about it. Education is obviously a powerful vehicle for bringing about change and there has been a growing interest in Environmental Education (EE) to serve this function. In fact, EE at all levels of formal education was mandated by

Supreme Court in 1991 in response to a public interest law suit on the need for action to create environmental awareness among the citizens of India.

As the approach to environment education challenges many of the existing deeply entrenched structure, systems and method in education, perhaps the most important support must come from the management. Such support will be forthcoming only if the management and the academic decision makers are sensitive to the need for EE and the need for change. A member of the Board of Studies of a prestigious university responded to the UGC recommendation to introduce EE in the arts, science and commerce streams at the GC level by demanding?

As education and teachers as people concerned with shaping the lives of future citizens, as people anxious about a better tomorrow which includes a better environment, UGC had planned to bring changes in the education system and incorporate environment education.

Definition of Environment

According to P. Gislert, "Environment is anything immediately surrounding an object and exerting a direct influence on it."

"Environment is an external force which influences us" said E.J. Ross.

Definition of Environment Education

According to the International Union for the Conservation of Nature and Natural Resources (1970).

"Environment education is the process of recognising values, and clarifying concepts in order to develop skills and attitudes necessary to understand and appreciate the inter-relatedness among man, his culture and his biophysical surroundings. Environmental education also entails practice in decision making and self-formulating of a code of behaviour about issues concerning environmental quality."

Environmental education is an action process related to the work of almost all subject areas. It is concerned with the dynamic relationships between man and nature. It aims at improving the environmental quality.

Environmental education may also be described as "Environmental education is a way of understanding environments, and here humans are part of it and influence, environments arena."

Importance of Environment Education

Environmental problem exists in all countries and at all stages of development, but they vary in nature, magnitude and complexity. Environmental problems of developing countries are mostly related to improper modes of development and underdevelopment such as poverty, hunger, malnutrition and diseases. In developed countries, on the other hand, environmental problems rise due to fast development, which results in depletion of resources, wastage of resources and pollution, India was an underdeveloped country and now being a developing country both these problems exists in India.

The present environment is being degraded as a result of unsustainable exploitation of natural resources and environmentally bound practices of human being. This is done in the form of mismanagement of natural environment, faulty practices, negative attitudes and deteriorating value structure in society. The agricultural and industrial revolution and subsequent modernisation process have been responsible for the pollution and degradation of air, water and soil with consequent adverse effect on human health and well being (Young 1992).

Environmental degradation occurs because the highly educated specialists who created many of the modern technologies, and society which used them, did not understand two fundamental environmental principles (1) that everything in nature is connected and consequently, (2) anything we do has numerous effect, often unpredictable and unwanted. So, sophistical technological solutions to one problem often create several other problems. Today we realize that solutions which addressed very pressing problem at one time, used as the need for greater food productivity, have unintentionally contributed to adding poisons to our water, and soil, and causing of certain plant and animal species and also of some essential microbes and soil nutrients.

Thus, there is urgent need for environmental protection from disaster. The National Policy of Education of India, announced in 1986, and modified in 1992 reports that protection of environment is a value that should be promoted in the common cause of education in the country. People need to be aware of total environment and its problems. They need to gain knowledge about how it functions, how humans and the environment interact, how problems arise, and how they can be solved. They need to acquire and internalize values to feel concerned about the environment and feel motivated and committed to repair, maintain and improve it.

We know that youth are the future of nation so, if proper values regarding environmental protection are inculcated in them, then they would become environmentally conscious citizens and would be able to work for environment sustainability.

These values can be inculcated through various learning experience. As school, college or universities are the places where youth gather maximum learning experiences, thus to achieve the objective of educating youth to be environmentally aware and responsible, the overall educational curriculum needs to be infused with environmental concerns.

Need for Incorporation of Environmental Education in the Curriculum

In a way, all education is basically environmental education. All disciplines try to understand and explain in the world we live. In physical and biological sciences focus on different aspects of the natural environment. The social sciences and humanities deal with cultural environment and even the internal environments of the human mind. If that is so then why do we need environmental education.

Environmental educators believe that any good education in fact is environmental education. It is the weakness of our conventional education due to its rigid disciplinary boundaries, which obscures the *interconnectedness* of things. It is this that makes *it 'not environmental* education.

A survey of any curriculum would reveal atleast some environmental content in every subject. But it is usually not, related to the students cognitive universe. It does not draw upon examples from the students environment, it does not have any relevance to their dual lives. Nor is the content of one subject connected to the content of the other.

Because we are trained to rote learning, many of us may be

able to spout the two laws faultlessly. Because the emphasis is on memorizing the facts but not understanding the concepts on being able to apply them, we are not able to extend our knowledge any further to explaining the above quote. Our mainstream conventional education emphasizes the learning of answers rather than exploring question memorization rather than critical thought and fragmented learning as opposed to understanding in context the examination system and other established reward structures in schools and universities and in society encourage this kind of learning.

Environment education seeks to do what conventional education is not doing. It seeks to equip students to integrate learning from different disciplines, to demolish the wall which divides, them, the become aware and to act to become responsibly functioning citizens. Essentially environment education is education in environmentally responsible decision-making and problem solving. To be able to make such decision and solve such problems students need to become aware of the total environment and its problems. Environment education cannot provide solution to environmental problems. It can provide knowledge, skills, attitudes and values needed to seek solution and act upon them.

Experience and research have both shown that the most successful kinds of environment education is outdoor education where students learn 'about' the environment 'in' the environment, 'for' learning how to solve problems related with the environment. There is a popular but fundamental maxim of education which is the guiding principle for environmental education.

What I learn, I forget
What I see, I remember
What I do, I understand

Successful environmental education therefore has to be handson, activity based and investigative, some useful techniques for environmental learning are field studies, investigation of issues, stimulation, case discussion, and action projects.

Formal Environmental Education

The chief objective of environmental education is that

individual and social groups should acquire awareness and knowledge, develop attitudes, skills and abilities and participate in solving real-life environmental problems. The lay public in rural, tribal, slum and urban areas, women and students and teachers in schools, colleges and universities as well as planners and decision policy makes, programme implementers and R& D workers need to be educated about environment.

There is need for a new approach to education which cuts across various subjects at schools and higher levels. Environmental concerns are to be brought in all subject at schools and higher levels. Environmental concerns are to be brought in all subject areas, rather than to introduce one more new subject.

(1) ***Primary school stage.*** Here the emphasis should be mostly (75%) on building up awareness, followed by real-life situations (20%) and conservation (5%). Thus, attempt should be to only sensitise the child about environment. The content to be used are surroundings from home to school to outdoor situations. Teaching strategy includes audio -visual and field visits.

(2) ***Lower secondary stage.*** From the lower secondary stage onwards, the quantvm of awareness must decrease and there should be increased knowledge of real-life situations, conservation and sustainable development. At lower secondary level, objective must be real life experience, awareness and problem identification. The contents to be used are those used at Primary School level supplemented with general science. Teaching, practicals and field visits are to be done.

(3) ***Higher Secondary school stage.*** Here the emphasis must be conservation, assimilation of knowledge, problem identification and action skills. The content used may be science-based and action oriented work. There should be proper teaching, practicals and field work.

(4) ***Territory (College) stage.*** At this level, the picture would be almost reverse of the Primary level, as maximum emphasis would be here on knowledge regarding sustainable development based on experience with conservation followed in a descending order, by conservation, real-life situations and awareness. The content must be College/ University based on Science and Technology. Teaching,

practical and action oriented field work is to be done.

In the school education NCERT has been playing vital role in designing syllabi, text books help books, guide books, charts, kits, teaching materials and aids both for students and teachers.

(5) ***University education***. Environmental education at this level is being looked after the University Grants Commission. There is high-powered committee to suggest areas of EE at postgraduate level. There are about 10 universities teaching courses in environmental areas. Besides these, there are also research institutes and professional institutions as Indian Institutes of Technology, Engineering Colleges, Schools of Planning and Architecture, which offer courses in environmental engineering. The University education has three major components: teaching, research and extension. At postgraduate level, four major areas are recognized:

(a) ***Environmental Engineering***. It includes the subjects like architecture, civil engineering, town and country planning, including human settlement, slum improvement, landscape architecture, industrial design, regional science and urban ecosystem studies.

(b) ***Conservation and Management***. It includes fields like land use, forestry, agriculture, energy, waste management, wildlife management, national parks, biosphere reserves, biological diversity, water management, national parks, mining management, non-polluting renewable energy development, etc.

(c) ***Environmental health***. This deals with public health and hygiene, sanitary and chemical engineering, occupational health, toxicology, nutrition and drug use etc.

(d) ***Social ecology***. It includes subjects like ecology, sociology, social planning, cost-benefit, community organisation and services, psychology and counseling, environmental ethics and related areas of humanities.

There are some institutes, centres assisted by Department of Environment which provide formal education/training in environmental areas. For instance, Centre for Environment Education (CEE), Ahmedabad, Indian Institute of Forest Management, Bhopal and Indira Gandhi National Forest Academy, Dehradun.

Importance of Environment Education in Home Science Curriculum

Home Science Extension conducts various extension activities like childcare, family planning, health education through its non-formal education. Though they are involved in various community work but still there is a gap in Home Science Curriculum, students are not properly sensitized regarding environment issues. Thus, there is need for *interalization* or inculcation of values for environmental concern among students. Hence, Environment education is required to be incorporated in the Home Science curriculum. This will help the students to become aware of different environmental degradations, sensitize them and they will be motivated to work for environmental sustainability they will be able to extend knowledge as well as develop skills and attitudes spread Environment Education among people.

Curriculum For Environment Education

Objectives:

(a) To develop environmental awareness
(b) To develop understanding regarding environment
(c) To develop the skill of working for the environment awareness.

Unit I

Concept of Environment

1.1 Definition of environment
1.2 Types of environment
  (a) Natural environment
  (b) Cultural environment
  (c) Social environment.

Unit II

Different Problems of Environment

2.1 Problems arising out of poverty or inadequacy of development itself reflected in the poor social and economic conditions that prevail both in Urban and Rural Areas.
2.2 Problems that arise out of the very process of development: Includes pollution (Air, Water, Noise).

Unit III

Different Environmental Issues:

3.1 Global warming
3.2 Depletion of Ozone Layer
3.3 Acid rains
3.4 Pollution of world's ocean
3.5 Desertification
3.6 Biological Diversity Loss
3.7 Deforestation.

Unit IV

Values of Environmental Sustainability:

4.1 Concept of Environmental sustainability
4.2 Different values
  (a) Personal
  (b) Neighbourly
  (c) Community.

Unit V

Measures for Environmental Education:

5.1
  (a) Different policies and programmes
  (b) Acts
  (c) Role of Government
  (d) Role of NGO

1.2 Role of media in environmental awareness
1.3 Role of Home Science Department

There are basically three types of environmental values which can be inculcated among Home Science Students through various learning experience:

— Personal values
— Neighbourly values
— Community values.

Personal Values

Personal values refer to those which are practiced by the individual alone, irrespective of his social relationship. e.g., Excellence

The personal values like:

- Cleanliness
- Nature's appreciation

- Courage
- Punctuality/regularity
- Self-confidence
- Honesty
- Evaluation

Objective

To inculcate personal values required in home science student.

Learning experience

- Interfaculty cleanliness competition
- Watering the plants
- Planting of trees
- Keeping the garden clean
- Exhibition on ecofriendly products like preparation of jutebags, paper bags.
- Slide presentation and preparation on environmental issues
- Drama
- Street play
- Puppet play
- Campaigning
- Card making
- Faculty Quiz Competition
- Poster making
- Chart making
- Seminar
- Debate
- Discussion
- Expert talk
- Visit to environmental institution as well as NGO's
- Celebration of various days

  Wildlife week—22 July
  Earth day—22nd April
  Green Consumer day—28th September
  World Environment day—5th June
  Environment month—19th November to 18th December
  World water day—22nd March
  Van Mahotsav-1st July
  Energy Conservation day-14th December

Neighbourly values

The interaction of two or more persons, e.g. patience

Neighbourly values like:

- Patience
- Tolerance
- Courtesy

Learning expereince

- Debate
- Field work
- Looking after disposal of waste materials Dustbin
- Discussion
- Expert talk

Community values

Community values entail the competition of wider interaction between group of people, e.g., brotherhood

- Love
- Brotherhood
- Sharing
- Services
- Team Spirit
- Responsibility

Learning experience

Field visit (visit to a village and giving informal talk on environmental issues)

- Survey on water purification
- Street play
- Puppet show
- Drama
- Plantation of trees
- Visit to Government and NGOs
- Expert talk
- Debate
- Extempore speech

Parent's role

(1) Watering garden
(2) Keeping rooms clean
(3) Plantation of trees
(4) Proper caring of trees
(5) Use of Eco-friendly materials

For example jute bags, paper bags, folders, files photo stands, etc.

(6) Playing water conservation games and energy conservation games, e.g., snakes and ladders
(7) Making cards related to environment
(8) Playing crossword puzzels, related to environmental issues
(9) Taking children to zoo, botanical garden
(10) Arrangement of Programmes on environment day
- Fancy dress competition
- Drama/Plays
- Writing slogans (prize)
- Speech on Environmental issues
- Cleanliness competition
- Making chart, posters
- Environmental Quize competition
- Poem competition
- Essay competition

(11) Utilization of leisure time
- Making paper bags, files etc.
- Making cartoons on environmental issues
- Making models from waste materials. Collection of articles on environmental issues, from various sources like newspapers, maganzines, etc.

(12) Showing movies related to environment
(13) Watching Discovery and National Geographic channels
(14) Sensitize children regarding the importance of natural medicine, e.g. Ayurvedic Medicine.
(15) Parent should buy books related to environment
(16) Parents should make children aware regarding noise pollution
- Talk softly
- Listening to radio, tapes and watching television in low volume

(17) Keeping aquarium in home.

Environmental Organisation and Agencies

1. Earth scan
2. Convention on International Trade in Endangered Species (CITES)
3. Environmental Protection Agency (EPA)
4. European Economic Community (EEC)

5. Human Exposure Assessment Location (HEAL)
6. International Council of Scientific Unions (ICSU)
7. International Union for Conservation of Nature and Natural Resources (IUCNNR)
8. International Marine Consultative Organisation (IMCO)
9. South Asia Cooperative Environment Programme (SACEP)
10. United Nations Educational, Scientific and Cultural Organisation (UNESCO)
11. United Nations Environment Programme (UNEP)
12. World Commission on Environment and Development (WCED)
13. Earth Watch Programme
14. Project Earth
15. Earth Walks
16. Man and Biosphere Programme (MAB).

References

1. De, N.K. and Raha, S. *Women and Environment in Rural India : Social and Economic Development in India* (edited), Ashish Publishing House, New Delhi, 1996.

2. Field John. Environmental education and training : Reflections on a survey. *Adult Education and Development* 40, 105-15, 1999.

3. Home Science Association of India. Proceedings of the Biennial Conference from the first Biennial Conference of 1953 to the 21st Biennial of 1994. Baroda. HSAI office Indumati Mahal.

4. Human Environmental Conservation and development. Analysis of administrative structure and policy issue adopted by the Himachal Pradesh University, Shimla, 1990.

5. Kreis, Bensheimer. Resolution on environment and development. *Adult Education Dev.* 40, 147-62, 1993.

6. Lal Pritam. Ecological education for children. Social Welfare, 39 (3) July 1992, pp. 12-13.

7. Regunathan, Sudhamahi, Environmental Law; Fresh Pastures (Centre for Environmental Law, Orissa) *The Hindustan Times,* 29.11.94.

8. Shukla, A. and Rajalaxmi. Hisotry and Development of Home Science in India. *Indian Journal of Home Science*, pp. 38-41, 1980.

36

Importance of Energy Conservation in Residential Sector

H.R. Karandikar, B.N. Raval

Introduction

The availability of reliable and economic forms of energy is an important prerequisite for the economic and social development of a nation. The energy needs to cover various human activities in the agricultural, industrial and domestic fields have been on the rise since the advent of the industrial revolution. The fossil fuels provide bulk of energy resources and these are non-renewable in nature.

India has 16 per cent of world population, but less than 1% of the world's energy resources. We import 60 per cent of our oil and with large foreign debt, the Indian rupee will always be weak and import of any form of energy like coal, oil or gas will be difficult. The continuously widening gap between the availability of energy and its requirement, as witnessed during the past few years, has today become a matter of national concern. This situation has arisen despite the emphasis that has been given to the development of the energy sector which is evident from the progress in its share in plans outlays.

India has, no doubt, made great strides in developing its energy resources. However, the fact to be noted is that we are still faced with energy shortages. The urgent need for conservation of energy resources is recognized world-wide. However, initiatives by India in this area leave much to be desired. This is especially so when we compare India's performance in this field to those of the industrialized nations and the levels of success they have achieved. Energy costs can be reduced by improvement of efficiency of industrial operation and equipment. USA, Japan and Western Europe have improved their overall energy efficiency by 30 per cent to 40 per cent in last 20 years.

When energey is conserved, the rewards are two-fold. There's an immediate reward, a saving of money and a long-term reward, the saving of our earth's resources for future generations. Undoubtedly energy availability must keep pace with growing demands. To meet these demands all possible sources of energy must be taken into account. And yet, at the same time, energy efficiency cannot be ignored. If only efforts are made in right earnest to reduce waste and efficient use, the level of consumption can be brought down by as much as 25 per cent. Thus in our country, where resources are limited, energy conservation cannot but be given the highest priority. It is established through small scale scientific experiments and field trial in different sectors of energy consumption that energy conservation is be the best, the cheapest and the most convenient remedy to ease the energy crisis. The challenge, ofcourse, lies in motivating ourselves to adopt efficient energy practices and improved technologies.

The scope for conservation of commercial energy in India is vast. Demand Side Management (DSM) is an alternative approach which has gained favour in recent years. This approach looks at augmenting capacity by way of saving on energy use by existing consumers.

Every MW that is saved from the existing load is free to be delivered to new customers. DSM and load management are aimed at reducing the consumption of energy without affecting the level of services.

The first step for implementing energy conservation measures requires energy audit.

Financial auditing is regularly carried out to keep the track of profitability trend. Similarly energy auditing should be carried out to keep a track of system efficiency and finding out areas of weakness. Regular Energy auditing involves the monitoring and reviews periodically energy conserving targets and it's achievements. The management initiative for setting goals and translating them into achievable target is essential for motivation.

Group incentives at department level for achieving energy targets, rewards to personnel making significant contribution in energy conservation, suggestion schemes, performance awards, and recognition for motivation personnel and achieving wider participation.

Energy Conservation implies suppression of wastages in the use of energy. It is one of the easier solutions for bridging the gap between demand and supply at least cost. Gujarat Electricity Board have realized the importance of energy conservation and have put on the efforts in promoting energy conservation measures by various types of consumers. The publicity campaign for awareness and information on all aspects of energy conservation on a wide scale is being carried out. Seminars and exhibition of energy saving equipments are arranged at different locations in Gujarat State. The merit awards are also given to HT industries who have actually implemented the energy conservation work.

Energy Conservation in Industrial Sector

"War against Waste" slogan for the industrial unit has been framed and the survey has been arranged to carry out preliminary energy audit for the benefit of the industries on the voluntary basis has been successfully carried out. In Gujarat almost 45 per cent of total energy consumption is utilized by the various sectors of industries both at high and low tension consumers. The cost of electricity to many industries (which are not power intensive) is hardly around 5 to 10% of the production cost. Any marginal hike in tariff is passed on the end cost of product. This tendency on the part of the manufacturers as well as the low percentage cost of energy in overall cost is one of the greatest disincentives in adopting the corrective measures for reducing energy consumption.

In order to focus the attention on energy conservation GEB has already setup the energy conservation cell who have successfully taken up the energy audit of 225 HT consumers. During energy audit a critical analysis and review of consumption and installation is done which helps in identifying the areas of excessive consumption which can be controlled. It has been observed that some small industries do not engage the full time electrical engineers or care to study the energy bills. The tariff structures many times offer incentives for proper load management. Plant operations also can be rescheduled to take advantage of the tariff.

The measures suggested to conserve energy are such as:

1. Load factor improvement
2. Power factor improvement
3. Demand control
4. Proper motor applications
5. Proper furnace operation cycles
6. Electrolysis process
7. Waste heat recovery
8. Providing proper size of transformers and capacitors
9. Use of proper compressors
10. Improvement in lighting and illumination

During the energy audit we have been pursuing the various industries to adopt the better power utilization methods which will help in reducing the contract demand. The consumers are also given guidance not to inflate the contract demand. It is observed that substantial contract demand has been reduced by adopting the proper energy conservation measures. This helps in reducing the peak demand on the GEB system.

During the energy audit, feasibility study of co-generation has also been undertaken as there exists ample possibility of providing co-generation by improving the utilization of waste fuel heat in various industries. During the energy audit the industrial consumers are also educated for the standard norms of consumption in advanced countries and some efforts have been made to achieve this specific consumption of electricity in various industries such as cement, sugar, paper, steel, rolling mills etc. The results of the efforts have been quite impressive. The energy audit can thus be viewed as a positive orientation to the energy cost reduction, preventive maintenarce and quality control programmes which are vital for energy conservation.

It may be remembered that use of more efficient motors, power factor improvement/capacitors, more efficient illumination scheme energy saving campaign have a very short pay back period, i.e., the additional investment due to them is returned in a short period in the form of saving in energy bill.

Energy Conservation in Agricultural Sector

In view of the alarming increase of use of power by agricultural sector due to extremely low HP based tariff, the Government of India has given directive to the state electricity boards to have minimum tariff of atleast 50 paise per kwh for the agricultural consumers. Many states have yet to implement these guidelines given by the Central Government. Under this circumstance it is very essential that we should implement the conservation measures in the agricultural sector so as to reduce the irrigation power demand on the grid system.

Several field studies have been conducted to evaluate the operating efficiency of the existing electrical as well as diesel pumps. The centrifugal pumps can operate at 70 per cent efficiency in field conditions, but they are actually found to be working only between 45 to 55 per cent. The overall system efficiency for the pump, motor and the associated piping and foot valves which can be as high as 60 per cent efficiency level, is observed to be in the field condition around 25 to 30 per cent only. The low level of operating efficiency means excessive consumption of electricity. To assess the scope for energy conservation several field experiments have been carried out by the Gujarat Electricity Board as well as many other agencies involving various types of rectification works. The results are very encouraging from the conservation point of view. The farmers are ignorant about low operating efficiency of their pumps. GEB has therefore made a special drive. It has arranged demonstrations at various farms to inculcate in the farmers the need and method for adopting the energy conservation.

In practice of following observations are noted and improvements suggested after affecting energy conservation in the agricultural pump sets.

1. Replacement of conventional foot valve of pump by efficient low friction foot valve. This can give an average energy saving of 10 per cent to 12 per cent.
2. Replacement of rusted G.I. pipe sections of suction pipe by RPVE Pipe alongwith the foot valves. This can give an average energy saving of 20 per cent to 22 per cent.
3. Replacement of rusted G.I. pipe sections of suction as well as delivery pipes by RPVC pipes alongwith the foot valve.

This can give an average energy savings of 25 per cent to 30 per cent.

4. Replacement of complete pumping system, i.e.
   - Pump set of required working range
   - Conventional foot valve by efficient low friction foot valve
   - Suction and delivery pipes through efficient low friction rigid PVC piping system.

Such rectification can give energy saving of 40 per cent to 50 per cent and also result in reduction of connected load by about 40 per cent. The cost of rectification of the replacement of foot valves and G.I. Pipes by energy efficient foot valves and PVC pipes is around Rs. 4500/- (at present) per agricultural pump installation. With the help of funds of Government of India, REC, GEB has carried out rectification of almost 40,000 agricultural pump sets and further programme has been chalked out for the coming years.

Energy Conservation in Lighting and in Domestic Appliances

About 8 to 12 per cent of electricity is used by domestic, lighting, commercial and street light consumers. Illumination is one of the important areas in which the electricity consumption could be easily brought down through simple good housekeeping measures. Replacement of incandescent lamps dimmer control in combination with best use of day light and provision of appropriate control to glow the lamps only when and where lighting is required. 'Consumers Guidance Bureau' should be set up to educate consumers regarding proper utilization of electrical energy with correct power factor and efficient luminaries. In the developing countries like India consumers awareness is the prime conditions to achieve the goal. Good housekeeping should be regular practice. This comprises of cleaning of luminaries-fixtures and inner room surface. It is found that by periodical cleaning of luminaries illumination is increased by 15 per cent to 20 per cent.

Tests have proved that through cleaning of luminaries, reflectors of glassware should be done to increase the lighting efficiency.

In a large commercial complex or in industrial plants, cleaning of luminaries should be planned on the basis of an annual programme. This method needs one trained crew to do all the cleaning as they progress from one section of the plant to another. The annual schedule can be worked by considering the following points:

1. Inventory of all lighting equipments in the plant.
2. Determination of time required to clean luminaries in each department.
3. Determination of approximate frequency of cleaning.

The essential requirements of ideal illumination such as uniform and glare-free, high efficacy, acceptable colour rendering. Correct choice of the luminaries will lead to energy effective solutions.

The use of refrigerators and coolers should be done in an economical manner. Frequent opening of refrigerator door should be avoided. The setting of thermostat and cleaning of condenser coil and proper location of the refrigerator also helps in reducing the energy consumption. Many domestic appliances such as air conditioners, electric irons, water heater, toaster, washing machines, electric cookers, ovens, etc. can be used in more efficient manner. This can reduce the power consumption. We should follow the guidelines given with the electrical appliances for its efficient and economic use.

Tariff as Tool for Energy Conservation

When consumers use electricity the consumption is measured in kilowatt hours (kwh), so from their point of view it is not convenient to be invoiced continually by the same kwh price. The producer however has other considerations, sufficient capacity must be reserved for each consumer without knowing exactly when and how much electricity will be needed. Yet, due to the nature of electricity, it is practically impossible to store-production must follow consumption. To transfer cost of production and transmission to consumers, utilities have created tariff systems. Consumption of electricity depends on many different factors:

- Climatic heating/cooling
- Industry cycle day/night, week rhythm
- Sunlight
- People's habit
- Standards of living

In order to suppress the peak demand GEB has adopted the time of day tariff since 1984 with higher energy charges for energy consumption during peak hours, i.e, 7.00 am to 11.00 am and 5.00 pm to 9.00 pm. This was done so as to impress upon the HT consumers to minimize the use of power during the peak hours. Besides the peak hour tariff, GEB is having it's HT tariff based on kva demand. The consumers having power factor less than 9 are levied penal rate so as to impress upon the consumers the use of capacitors for improving power factor. All the agriculture and industrial consumers in Gujarat State are required to provide sufficient capacitor banks in the contract demand is 5 HP and above. There are special checking squads to see that the capacitors at the consumer end are installed or are in working condition.

37
A Study of Effectiveness of Value Clarifying Analysis Model in Developing Values in Students of Standard IX

Daksha Kamal Shah

Introduction

Human being is known as a social animal. She/He constantly interacts with each other in a society. The society in which he/she lives provide a framework for his/her harmonious living. Each society has its own rules, traditions and values and transmit them to its inhabitant. Practice of values varies from one stage of development of a particular society to another.

The growing child has certain in born instincts and traits. He learns or acquires knowledge by experience. He observes, imbibes and reacts to values practiced by his parents. As he grows he becomes inquisitive about peoples behaviour and environments around him. Gradually he develops his individual personality.

The 21st century is passing through explosion of technology and knowledge, which has brought about tremendous change in individual value system and society at large.

Value Education

There is a vast difference between urban and rural society. Urban society has changed its values as per the present need of the society. It is trying to abolish caste system and socio-religious values, which are also changing. The national policy on education lays great stress on the need of ridicule reconstruction of the education system to improve its quality at all stages, and pays greater attention to the cultivation of moral values and to develop a closer relation between education and the life of the people.

Role of Education

In a society, education essentially plays a vital role in development on achievement of goals. Mahatma Gandhi had rightly said, "Education is preparation to complete living adjustment, perfection for ones nature, character building and harmonious development of personality."[1]

1. Gandhi M.K. (1977) Sampuran Gandhi Varnmay, New Delhi, Government of India p. 123.

Statement of the problem

It is necessary to study the effectiveness of different approaches developing values of adolescents. Keeping in view the need, the following topic was selected. A study of effectiveness of value clarifying analysis model in developing values in students of STD IX.

General Objective of the Study

1. To study the effectiveness of intervention program in developing value clarifying competencies among students of STD IX.

Specific Objectives

1. To study the moral developments of students of standard IX.
2. To study the relationship between the father's education and moral development of students of STD IX.
3. To study the relationship between father's occupation and moral development of students of STD. IX.
4. To study the relationship between academic achievements and moral development of students of STD. IX.
5. To study the effect of value analysis model on and moral development of students of STD IX.

Assumptions

1. All students included in the sample are mentally normal.
2. There is no intervention program affecting moral development during the program time.

Hypotheses

1. There is no significant gender difference in the pretest scores on DIT of boys and girls.
2. There is no significant association between the moral development of the students and their father's level of education.
3. There is no significant association between the father's occupation and student's moral development.
4. There is no significant relationship between the academic achievement of boys and their level of moral development.
5. There is no significant relationship between the academic achievement of girls and their level of moral development.
6. There is no significant relationship between the academic achievement of the total sample of boys and girls and their level of moral development.
7. There is no significant gender difference in the post-test scores on the DIT of boys and girls.
8. There is no significant difference in the pre-test and post-test scores of boys on DIT.
9. There is no significant difference in the pre-test and post-test scores on DIT of girls.
10. There is no significant difference in the pre and post test sample of the students of STD. IX.

Scope and Limitation

— The study is restricted to the students of STD. IX of Kendriya Vidyalaya No. 2.

— The school is situated in South Bombay. Medium of instruction is English or Hindi.

— The students involved in the experiment come from different strata of the society.

Design of the study

Quasi experimental Design

Sample

One class of STD IX from Kendriya Vidyalaya No. 2 was selected as sample. The group was selected by purposive sampling. There were 30 students. 19 boys and 12 girls were present in the class. Out of them only 12 boys and 8 girls were present for all the sections of the programme as well as for pre and post-test. Hence, the final sample consisted of 12 boys and 8 girls.

Tools

1. Personal information Proforma
2. Defining issue test
3. Test to measure moral development No. 1
4. Test to measure moral development No. 2

Findings

The students selected for the sample came neither from a very low nor from a very high socio-economic stratum of the society.

The following are the findings of the present study:

1. There was no significant gender difference found in the pre-test scores on DIT.
2. There was no significant association found between the father's education and the student's moral development.
3. There was no significant association found between the student's moral development and their father's occupation.
4. There was no significant relationship found between boy's academic achievement and their level of moral development.
5. There was no significant relationship found between girls academic achievement and their level of moral development.
6. There was no significant relationship found between student's academic achievement and their level of moral development.
7. The significant gender difference was not found in the post-test scores of DIT of the boys and the girls.
8. The significant difference was found in the pre-test and post-test scores on DIT of boys. This shows that the intervention programme had positive effect on the level of moral development of the boys.
9. The significant difference was found in the pre-test and post-test scores on DIT of the girls which indicates that the intervention programme had positive effect on the level of moral development of girls.
10. The significant difference was found in the pre-test and post-test scores of DIT of the total sample. This reveals that the intervention programme had positive effect on the level of moral development on the total sample.

Initially when the intervention programme was started students rational and realistic from analysis of the investigator's observations. It can be stated that the programme was considerably stimulating and encouraging in developing cognitive and analytical capacity of students both girls as well as boys.

Suggestions

The process of clarifying value helps to develop an analytical thinking in one's mind. The following are the suggestions:

1. There has to be a provision in the school timetable to discuss situations posing moral problems.
2. The person or group who is going to lead the discussion should be humane, open minded, ready to listen to others, encourages divergent and shocking view points.
3. The students should be given freedom to discuss openly, which might help then to discuss and develop creative thinking.
4. The situation selected for this process should be according to the student's age, social background and their ability.

Conclusion

Various studies with improved method; techniques and various model of teaching vlaues have been carried out in value oriented education programme. In the present study, the investigator has used value clarifying analysis model, especially in the secondary school children, it was found that the student of std IX had shown improvement in their level of moral development, power of reasoning, judgement and analytical thinking after administering the intervention programme. Thus, it was found to be quite effective in achieving some success in developing rational thinking rather than going by blind faith, traditional approach or customs.

References

1. Allport Vermon. Lindzey. *Status of Values,* Boston Houghton. Miffilin 1980.

2. Durrant Story of Philosophy refered in values are permeated A.P. Sharma, *University News* 11 Dec. 1995.

3. B.K. Passi. Need of valuing not values in education. *University News* 11 Sep. 1995.

4. Seema Rani. Approaches to value education and the Role of the School and curriculum, *University News* 18 March 1996.

5. Shukla, R.P. Towards developing Values among children. An Analytical Approach. *University News* 35 (39) Sep. 29, 1997.

6. Shukla, R.P. Curriculum and value based education. Paper presented in the seminar on value Based education. Comprehensive Rural Development Services. Dimapur. Nagaland. 8 May 1997.

7. Sinha, D. Basic Indian Values and behaviour disposition in the context of national development. In D. Sinha & H.S.R. Rao (eds) Social values and development : Asian Perspective, Sage Publication, New Delhi, 1988.

8. Tripathi, R.C. Interplay of value in the functioning of Indian organizations. *International Journal of Psychology*. Vol. 25, pp. 715-734, 1990.

9. Venkataiah, N. *Value Education–An overview in Value Education*. New Delhi, APH Publishing Corporation, 1998.

10. Values and the Schools. Sixty years ago and now Phi Delta. Kappa. *Research Newsletter*, Council for Teacher Education, Vol. 7. No. 2, April 1997.

Index

W

Y

Z